W9-API-492

Cathy H. C. Hsu, PhD
Editor

Legalized Casino Gaming
in the United States
The Economic and Social Impact

Pre-publication
REVIEW

Legalized Casino Gaming in the United States

The Economic and Social Impact

HAWORTH HOSPITALITY PRESS
Hospitality, Travel, and Tourism
K. S. Chon, PhD
Executive Editor

Marketing Your City, U.S.A.: A Guide to Developing a Strategic Tourism Marketing Plan by Ronald A. Nykiel and Elizabeth Jascolt

Hospitality Management Education by Clayton W. Barrows and Robert H. Bosselman

Legalized Casino Gaming in the United States: The Economic and Social Impact edited by Cathy H. C. Hsu

Consumer Behavior in Travel and Tourism by Abraham Pizam and Yoel Mansfeld

The International Hospitality Business: Management and Operations by Larry Yu

Practice of Graduate Research in Hospitality and Tourism by K. S. Chon

Legalized Casino Gaming in the United States
The Economic and Social Impact

Cathy H. C. Hsu, PhD
Editor

The Haworth Hospitality Press
An Imprint of The Haworth Press, Inc.
New York • London • Oxford

Published by

The Haworth Hospitality Press, an imprint of The Haworth Press, Inc., 10 Alice Street, Binghamton, NY 13904-1580

Cover design by Jennifer M. Gaska.

Library of Congress Cataloging-in-Publication Data

Legalized casino gaming in the United States : the economic and social impact / Cathy H. C. Hsu, editor.
    p. cm.
  Includes bibliographical references (p.) and index.
  ISBN 0-7809-0640-5 (alk. paper)
  1. Casinos—Economic aspects—United States. 2. Casinos—Social aspects—United States. 3. Gambling—Economic aspects—United States. 4. Gambling—Social aspects—United States. I. Hsu, Cathy H. C.
HV6711.L44 1999
338.4'3795'0973—dc21
                                                          98-37326
                                                              CIP

CONTENTS

About the Editor   ix

Contributors   xi

Preface   xiii

**SECTION I: HISTORY, DEVELOPMENT,
   AND LEGISLATION**

**Chapter 1. History, Development, and Legislation
   of Las Vegas Casino Gaming**   3
   Shannon Bybee

   Historical Development   3
   Las Vegas Gaming Today   15
   Nevada's Gaming Regulatory System   17
   Summary   22

**Chapter 2. Personal Recollections of the New Jersey
   Gambling "Experiment" in Atlantic City**   25
   James F. Wortman

   Background   25
   Let the Games Begin!   29
   My Odyssey   31
   Events/Agencies   33
   The Future   38
   Summary   39

**Chapter 3. History, Development, and Legislation
   of Native American Casino Gaming**   41
   William N. Thompson

   Native Populations: Some Unhappy Perspectives   41
   Promoting Tribal Self-Sufficiency: The Promise   44
   Gaming: Beginning to Realize the Promise   46

Efforts to Regulate Native American Gaming   47
The Indian Gaming Regulatory Act of 1988   48
The Future of Native American Gaming   54
The Bottom Line: Does Gaming Help or Not?   55

**Chapter 4. History, Development, and Legislation
of Riverboat and Land-Based Non-Native
American Casino Gaming**   **63**
    Cathy H. C. Hsu

Riverboats   64
Land-Based Non-Native American Casinos   81
Other States   88

SECTION II: ECONOMIC IMPACTS

**Chapter 5. Casinos in Las Vegas:
Where Impacts Are Not the Issue**   **93**
    William N. Thompson

Introduction   93
The Success Story That Is Las Vegas   94
Why Las Vegas Is Successful and Growing   100
The Future Economic Health of Las Vegas   104
A Casino Development Model   107
Some Downsides for the Las Vegas Economy   109
The Bottom-Line Upside   111

**Chapter 6. Economic Impacts of Casino Gaming
in Atlantic City**   **113**
    Dan Heneghan

The Queen of Resorts   113
The Decline of Atlantic City   115
Atlantic City Turns to Casinos   117
Promises Made   119
An Explosion of Growth   120
More Jobs Than Ever Imagined   121
Tax Revenues Soar   123
Billions Invested   125
Casino Benefits for All of New Jersey   127

Some Social Problems Addressed, Not Cured 128
Gaming Helps Seniors 129
Reinvestment in Nongaming Sectors 130
A City Rebuilt 131

**Chapter 7. Economic Impacts of Native American
Casino Gaming** **135**
Carl A. Boger Jr.
Daniel Spears
Kara Wolfe
Li-Chun Lin

Background 135
History of Their Economic Development 136
Economic and Community Impact 138
Tax Benefits 139
Economic Impact Studies 140
Current Issues and Challenges 150

**Chapter 8. Economic Impacts of Riverboat
and Land-Based Non-Native American
Casino Gaming** **155**
Patricia A. Stokowski

Evaluating Economic Impacts 157
Gaming Industry Growth 158
Public Economic Impacts 161
Trends and Projections 169

SECTION III: SOCIAL IMPACTS

**Chapter 9. Social Impacts of Casino Gaming:
The Case of Las Vegas** **177**
Haemoon Oh

Introduction 177
Assessing Social Impacts of Gaming in Las Vegas 178
Social Impacts of Gaming in Las Vegas:
    A Comparative Approach 180
City-Specific Social Impacts of Gaming 194
Summary 197

Chapter 10. Social Impacts of Atlantic City Casino Gaming   **201**
Denis P. Rudd

Introduction   201
Demographics   201
Casinos   203
Pathological Gambling   205
Crime   208
Antigaming   212
New Jersey Casino Control Act   213
Politics   214
Urban Redevelopment   215
Conclusion   216

Chapter 11. Social Impacts of Native American Casino Gaming   **221**
Cathy H. C. Hsu

Tribal Division and Residents' Attitudes   222
Initial Struggle and Exploitation   223
Gaming Contribution   224
Not All Rosy   226
Continued Debate   229

Chapter 12. Social Impacts of Riverboat and Land-Based Non-Native American Casino Gaming   **233**
Patricia A. Stokowski

Assessing Social Impacts   234
Social Impacts of Gambling and Gaming Development   235
Conclusions   247

Index   **253**

ABOUT THE EDITOR

Cathy H. C. Hsu, PhD, is Associate Professor of Hotel, Restaurant, Institution Management, and Dietetics at Kansas State University. She has researched the impacts of riverboat, race track, and Native American casinos since 1991, when the first riverboat casinos started operation in Iowa. Her articles have been published in several professional journals, such as *Gaming Research and Review Journal, Journal of Travel Research,* and the *Journal of Hospitality and Tourism Research.* A member of the International Society of Travel and Tourism Educators, Asia Pacific Tourism Association, and the Council on Hotel, Restaurant, and Institutional Education, Dr. Hsu also serves on the editorial boards of *Pacific Tourism Review* and the *Journal of Hospitality and Tourism Research,* among others. She is currently researching residents' perceptions of riverboat gaming and its impact on community quality and casino customers' attitudes and behaviors toward gaming.

Contributors

Carl A. Boger Jr., PhD, is Assistant Professor in Hotel, Restaurant, Institution Management, and Dietetics at Kansas State University, Manhattan, Kansas. Co-authors of the chapter, Daniel Spears, Kara Wolfe, and Li-Chun Lin, are graduate students in the same department. Their research interest is in the impact of gambling in midwestern states.

Shannon Bybee, JD, is Executive Director of the International Gaming Institute and is Associate Professor of casino management and gaming law and regulation at the William F. Harrah College of Hotel Administration, University of Nevada, Las Vegas. He has extensive experience as a gaming regulator, gaming consultant, gaming attorney, and casino executive, and is active in both local and national organizations concerned with problem and compulsive gambling.

Dan Heneghan is the public Information Officer for the New Jersey Casino Control Commission and a former journalist who covered the gaming industry for seventeen years. In addition to writing for the *Press of Atlantic City,* his work has been published in *International Gaming and Wagering Business, Casino Executive, Casino Gaming,* and other trade publications. He has also contributed to *The Wall Street Journal, Business Week,* several large newspapers, and all of the country's major wire services. He has received more than a dozen awards for his writing.

Haemoon Oh, PhD, is Assistant Professor of marketing in the Department of Hotel, Restaurant, and Institution Management at Iowa State University, Ames, Iowa.

Denis P. Rudd, EdD, CHA, FMP, is Director and Professor of the Hospitality and Tourism Management Program at Robert Morris college in Moon Township, Pennsylvania. He is the co-author of the first textbook on Casino and Gaming Operations, and has presented numerous papers and articles on gaming, hotel, restaurant, tourism, and convention operations. He has done extensive research on bed-and-breakfasts and the senior market.

Patricia A. Stokowski is Associate Professor with the Recreation Management Program, School of Natural Resources, University of Vermont, Burlington, Vermont. Her research and teaching interests center on social aspects of rural community tourism development and natural resources management. She is the author of *Riches and Regrets* (1996), which analyzed the social, economic, and political impacts of contemporary gaming developments in Colorado. Stokowski formerly held faculty positions at Texas A&M University and the University of Colorado at Boulder.

William N. Thompson, PhD, is Chair of Public Administration at the University of Nevada, Las Vegas. His books include: *Legalized Gambling: A Reference Handbook*; *Native American Issues*; *The Last Resort: Success and Failure in Campaigns for Casinos* (with John Dombrink); *Casino Customer Service* (with Michele Comeau); and *International Casino Law* (with Carl Braunlich, Tony Cabot, and Andrew Tottenham). Often quoted in the media, he has been a consultant with the President's Commission on Organized Crime, and the National Gambling Impact Study Commission.

James F. Wortman, MEd, is the Director of the Office of Gaming Education and Research, Conrad N. Hilton College of Hotel and Restaurant Management, University of Houston, Houston, Texas.

Preface

Modern-age casino gaming in the United States began in 1931 when Nevada legalized gaming. Nevada, and Las Vegas in particular, enjoyed a monopoly in the United States until 1976 when Atlantic City began its casino industry on the other side of the country. Due to recessionary economic conditions, federal and state budget deficits, and Americans' changing attitudes toward gaming, the casino gaming industry took off in the late 1980s, which started the latest wave of casino gaming fever. First, the Indian Gaming Regulatory Act (IGRA) was passed by Congress. Then, mining towns in South Dakota and Colorado legalized limited-stakes gaming. The riverboat casino industry in various states was not far behind in joining the competition, and a few more land-based casinos were allowed in Iowa, Louisiana, and Michigan (see Figure A).

More than half the states have introduced legislation related to gaming since the late 1980s. Whenever and wherever gaming legislation was introduced and discussed, heated debates arose between proponents and opponents of gaming because it is a political, economic, moral, religious, and social issue. Everybody has an opinion and something to say about it. At the beginning of the current casino gaming fever, proponents of gaming legislation were usually sponsored by major gaming corporations who wished to expand their markets into areas other than Nevada and New Jersey. However, in the past few years, these corporations have sponsored opponents of gaming legislation in some areas to protect their market shares in the nearly saturated marketplace.

The recurring underlying reason for casino legalization from 1931 to the present is economic and tourism development. The casino industry has definitely helped some areas, such as Las Vegas, in building their economy and tourism industry. However, for other areas, casinos have not been the magical solution to severe economic problems the government and people had hoped. The pace of

FIGURE A. Casino Locations in the United States

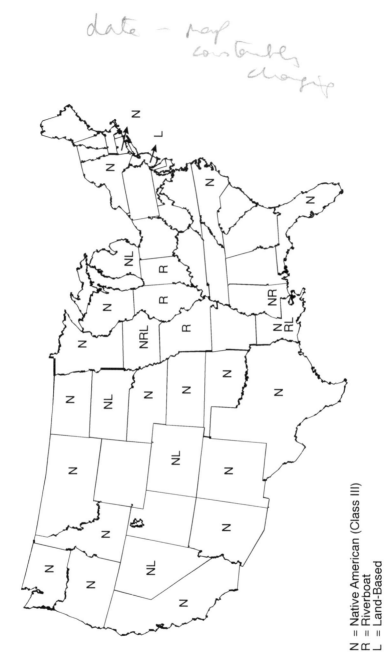

N = Native American (Class III)
R = Riverboat
L = Land-Based

gaming legislation passage has slowed down. Since 1994, Michigan is the only state to have legalized casino gaming. Market saturation may be one reason for the slowdown. Gaming interest groups have not been as active in lobbying as they were in the late 1980s and early 1990s. Another reason for the slowdown may be that residents in some communities with casino operations have not seen the significant economic contributions projected by the gaming industry. Therefore, voters are more suspicious of the benefits of having casino operations in their community. In addition, it is only natural that bad news travels faster than good news. It is possible that reports of negative social impacts in communities that legalized gaming in the past few years, with or without scientific evidence, have a more significant influence on voters' opinions of gaming.

The product life cycle of casino gaming in the United States seems to be at the end of the rapid expansion stage and moving toward the maturity stage. The capital market theory of supply and demand will stabilize the market by eliminating weaker competitors in oversupplied areas and allowing new operations to join the undersupplied areas. Of course, not all casinos in the United States serve and compete for the same market, as chapters in this book will detail. Some casinos are locally oriented, others are regional minded, while others have the whole world as their market. A few battles will be waged over territory and customer base among casinos, but eventually, each casino will find its own market niche. Any competitive activities after that will only make the casino industry, as a whole, stronger and healthier.

Numerous good studies of gaming have been conducted across the country; however, most studies had a regional focus, and rightly so. A comprehensive source of information is needed for all gaming research projects completed across the country in the recent past. The intent of this book is to incorporate all research studies conducted in the field of casino gaming and to serve as a reference or overview of the industry's development and regulations, as well as its economic and social impacts. The book is also intended to provide a review of the gaming industry from various perspectives, and therefore authors of all chapters remain neutral on the gaming issue and simply report facts related to casinos in the United States. As reflected in the title, the focus of this book is casinos. Therefore, when the generic term gaming or gambling is used, it implies the casino form.

Upper-level undergraduate students and graduate students will find this book useful as an introduction to the modern casino industry in the United States. Gaming researchers will find this book helpful as an extensive review of current literature, as well as for the included status report on gaming research. Policymakers will find this book particularly valuable because all the scientific "evidence" of advantages and disadvantages of having a casino in their jurisdiction is summarized by authors of various chapters.

The book is organized into three sections: *History, Development, and Legislation*; *Economic Impacts*; and *Social Impacts*. Within each section are four chapters that focus on four particular areas: Las Vegas gaming, Atlantic City gaming, Native American gaming, and riverboat and land-based non–Native American gaming. In the first section, each chapter includes a comprehensive review of the history and development of gaming for a particular location or segment of the industry. Laws and regulations of each location and segment are discussed to report changes and document current legislation. For the riverboat and land-based non–Native American gaming, a state-by-state review is conducted. In the second section, each chapter examines the economic consequences of legalized gaming in a particular area. A comprehensive review and discussion of existing studies is included. Statistical indexes on economic indicators are collected and compared. As for the third section, social impacts examined include crime; quality of life; community services; social amenities, such as availability of entertainment, recreation, and cultural activities; community image, such as reputation, appearance, cleanliness, and traffic; local residents' attitudes; and pathological gambling.

Chapter 1 reviews the historical development of Las Vegas gaming, as well as that of the community, starting from 1861. Amendments to the Nevada Gaming Control Act and the development of the Las Vegas "Strip" over the years are chronicled in the first part of the chapter. The chapter also explains Nevada's gaming regulatory system, including the makeup and roles of the Nevada Gaming Commission and Gaming Control Board, and issues related to currency transactions, exclusion lists, work permits, customer disputes, and underage gambling.

Chapter 2 takes a personal approach to chronicle the development of gaming in Atlantic City. The tourism industry in early Atlantic City is briefly reviewed. Background information on legislation campaigns and preparation for the first casino opening is provided. Personal experience in the casino industry is used to illustrate the regulation and development. Major events and agencies that help define and shape the gaming industry in Atlantic City also are discussed.

Chapter 3 starts with a survey of casino operations on reservation lands in the United States, followed by a brief Native American history and related federal programs since the 1960s. Also included is the chronological evolution of the IGRA, as well as a detailed explanation of the act. Issues related to the act discussed include the three classes of gaming; management contracts; enforcement, taxation, and revenues; and regulation implementation difficulties. This chapter ends by listing the positive impacts of gaming on reservations and potential problems that gaming could cause.

Chapter 4 takes a state-by-state approach, detailing the development of riverboat and land-based casino operations and legislation. For each state, a brief background is provided, followed by a description of the gaming legalization process, governing body, and major components of the gaming law. Locations and number of casino operations in each state are shown on a map. Tables of gaming taxes and fees collection and distribution, as well as gaming regulations, are included for easy comparison among states.

Chapter 5 begins with economic indexes of Las Vegas, demonstrating the success of its gaming industry. Reasons why Las Vegas is successful and growing, including the changing demographics, growth of gaming nationwide, and product packaging, are explored. Despite competition from other gaming locations across the country, the good health of Las Vegas's future economy is projected, with tourism data as support. A few downsides of the Las Vegas economy also are discussed.

Chapter 6 illustrates the economic impacts of casino gaming in Atlantic City, with a brief description of the ups and downs of the resort community; promises made by a consulting firm hired by the city during the campaigning stage; and the explosion of growth in tourism and hotel revenues, payrolls, and taxes after the legalization of casino gaming. The author also quantifies the enhancement of some social services and the decline of recipients of some social programs to demonstrate the far-reaching economic benefits of casino gaming. The chapter concludes with current rebuilding efforts to illustrate casinos' contributions to the economy of Atlantic City and the region.

Chapter 7 addresses the economic benefits of Native American gaming. The authors provide an overview of the economic history of Native American reservations, followed by a summary of casinos' economic impacts on reservations and nearby communities. Tax benefits are specifically discussed. Casinos and their impacts in Connecticut, Wisconsin, Minnesota, and Oregon are analyzed individually. Current issues and challenges are also identified.

Chapter 8 discusses the reasons for different perspectives regarding the magnitude of economic impacts of gaming. The author documents the public economic impacts of gaming by examining government revenues, employment, business diversity, redevelopment issues, and economic costs. Positive and negative impacts are discussed for each category. The chapter ends with a look into future trends and projections of the gaming industry and its economic consequences.

Chapter 9 takes a comparative approach in analyzing the social impacts of gaming due to Las Vegas' unique situation, for which a "before and after" analysis is not appropriate and most residents are drawn to the city because of the gaming industry. The author compares several social indexes, including demographics, traffic and transportation, crime, cost of living, health care environment, and government expenditure, of Las Vegas with those of four other comparable cities. The limited number of studies conducted in social impacts of gaming on Las Vegas also are reviewed.

Chapter 10 discusses the social impacts of casino gaming on Atlantic City. The chapter begins with a brief demographic overview of Atlantic City before and after the legalization of gaming. Casinos' impacts on pathological gambling and crime are the focus of discussion. The author also visits the political issue related to gaming, as well as the execution of the New Jersey Casino Control

Act. Urban redevelopment activities using gaming revenues also are reviewed.

Chapter 11 reviews the positive and negative social impacts of gaming on Native American reservations and nearby non–Native American communities. The chapter reports tribal divisions caused by gaming, non–Native American neighbors' attitudes toward gaming on reservations, and the initial struggles and exploitation Indian gaming operations experienced. This chapter also documents the contributions gaming revenues have made to improving the quality of life for Native Americans. Problems, such as traffic, crime, and pathological gambling also are addressed.

Chapter 12 provides a very comprehensive review of current literature on social impacts of gaming in Colorado, South Dakota, and states with riverboat casinos. The author raises concerns about the difficulty of assessing social impacts. The literature reviewed is organized as follows: residents' attitudes toward community and gambling, traffic, residential population, community services, community amenities, crime, and public and private social services. The author calls for better public information and comprehensive longitudinal research on the real costs and benefits of gaming development.

References listed at the end of each chapter are impressive; however, it is evident that more research is needed in the gaming area. In terms of economic impact studies, systematic comparisons and analyses of economic indexes, such as unemployment rates, total retail sales, retail sales by merchandise categories, hotel/motel sales, per capita income, and local and state government tax bases, are needed. Analyzing the economic condition of adjacent communities is equally important as analyzing that of the host communities because it is necessary to understand the spatial distribution of casinos' economic impact. In addition to evaluating the financial returns of casinos to the local economy, initial and continuing investments should also be taken into consideration, as with any other business. Initial investments may include infrastructure improvement, establishment of regulatory agencies, and any other up-front costs. Continuing investments may be needed to enhance public safety measures, maintain public facilities due to increased wear and tear, and fund gaming addiction treatment programs.

Limited information is available on the economic or social impacts of Native American casinos on reservations. Part of the reason is that casino revenues are not reported and there is no gaming, sales, or income tax revenue information to statistically measure the real economic impacts of Native American casinos. Native American casinos usually employ a large number of non–Native Americans who live in nearby communities and have residents in those communities as their major customer base. Therefore, the economic and social changes of nearby communities should also be examined to document the impact or lack of impact from casinos on reservation land. It is to Native Americans' benefit to document the economic and social benefits and costs of gaming. When their compacts with the states expire, objective hard data on economic and social impacts of gaming on reservation land, as well as on nonreservation communities, will be crucial to the renewal of their contracts.

Another important area of research is residents' attitudes toward gaming and toward using gaming as an economic development tool and tourism attraction. The whole philosophy behind economic and tourism development is to improve the quality of life for residents. If residents dislike the idea of using gaming as a means to an end, their apprehension defeats the purpose and makes the community an unpleasant place to live and to visit. The legalization of a casino in a locale usually requires voter approval. However, residents may not be fully aware of the magnitude of change and impact on personal life that could be brought about by casinos. Residents' attitudes need to be assessed regularly, and their opinions considered, when casino development and expansion plans are made.

Research on casino-related issues is often complex and requires viewpoints and expertise from more than one discipline. Scholars in the areas of tourism, hospitality management, business, economics, environmental science, philosophy, political science, psychology, public policy, and sociology should work collaboratively to provide a holistic view and analysis of the modern casino gaming phenomenon. Opportunities to make a contribution to the casino gaming industry are abundant for practitioners, academia, and public policymakers.

Cathy H. C. Hsu

SECTION I:
HISTORY, DEVELOPMENT, AND LEGISLATION

Chapter 1

History, Development, and Legislation of Las Vegas Casino Gaming

Shannon Bybee

HISTORICAL DEVELOPMENT

People have been gambling in Clark County, where Las Vegas is located, for at least 2,000 years, according to archaeologists (Nevada Gaming Commission and State Gaming Control Board [NGC and SGCB], 1985, p. 7). However, the gambling history of Las Vegas is generally marked from the time territorial and state government first took legislative action to determine gambling's legal status.

The Commission on the Review of the National Policy Toward Gambling (1976) concluded that the history of gambling policy in the United States has been a conflict between two philosophies:

- Gambling is morally and socially destructive and should be suppressed.
- The popularity of gambling makes it a suitable activity to achieve useful and productive ends through licensing and taxation (p. 49).

Nevada's history of casino-style gambling illustrates well this conflict of philosophies.

The First Period of Legalization in Nevada: 1869-1910

The first meeting of the Territorial Legislature of Nevada in 1861 produced a law banning all forms of gambling, making the operation of a gambling game a felony and providing for a bounty of $100 for every conviction by a district attorney, though no bounty was ever paid. The first legislative session of the new state legislature in 1864 replaced the territorial law banning gambling with a state law banning gambling, but without the bounty provision. Violations were reduced from a felony to a misdemeanor (State Gaming Control Board [SGCB], 1970, pp. 6-7). In 1869, four years after statehood was achieved, Nevada became a legal casino gaming jurisdiction when the legislature managed to override Governor Blaisdel's vote (SGCB, 1970, p. 7).

In 1909, the Nevada Legislature outlawed casino gambling effective October 1, 1910. This resulted from the efforts of a reform movement that swept the country (Rosecrance, 1988). Reno was the center of the opposition in Nevada, and opponents of gaming included such influential Nevada public officials as the acting governor, a U.S. senator, a state supreme court justice, and the president of the University of Nevada (SGCB, 1970, p. 8).

Between 1910 and 1931, gambling, although illegal, remained widely available because there was little or no enforcement of the laws against gambling. Limited gaming activities were authorized by the legislature in 1915 on the recommendation of Governor Oddie. Social games and slot machines were permitted so long as the play was for drinks, cigars, or other prizes not exceeding $2.00. Also allowed were games in which the deal changed to a new player with each hand. These efforts apparently did little to deter illegal gambling (SGCB, 1970).

Gaming Is Legalized Again—The Early Years: 1931-1949

By 1931, a national recession and widespread illegal gambling led to legalization of casinos in Nevada. The nation was in a serious economic depression in 1931, and Nevada legislators were looking for ways to stimulate the economy of the state. It was believed that legalizing gambling would have a beneficial effect on the state's economy. In addition, many people recognized that illegal and uncontrolled gaming was a reality and believed it was having a corruptive effect on the community. Noting that government was either unable or unwilling to suppress illegal gambling, they concluded that the state should legalize gaming, obtain the tax and economic benefits that gaming could produce, and reduce the corruptive effect of illegal and uncontrolled gambling (SGCB, 1970; NGC and SGCB, 1985).

Nevada would be the only legal casino gaming jurisdiction until 1976 when New Jersey voters approved casinos in Atlantic City. As Cabot observes, Nevada is not only legal gaming's first frontier but also "an American success story" (1997, p. 5). The Nevada experience can best be examined through the lens of Las Vegas, where everything about gaming, both good and bad, seems accentuated.

Las Vegas, first settled by Mormon pioneers in 1857, was not much more than a way station on the Spanish Trail until the railroad platted the town site and sold lots in 1905 (Spanier, 1992, pp. 61-63; Castleman, 1993, pp. 28-41). After gambling was approved in 1931, Las Vegas became the beneficiary of substantial federal government expenditures that attracted people and dollars to the city and its newly legalized casinos. Moehring reviews the various federal programs that helped build Las Vegas (1989, pp. 13-40). From 1931 to 1935, it was the construction of Boulder (Hoover) Dam. This was followed by New Deal programs that produced a fish hatchery, a golf course, and paved the Los Angeles Highway. With the commencement of World War II, federal funding financed the building and operation of what is known today as the Nellis Air Force Base north of the city and the Basic Magnesium plant in Henderson at the southeast end of the Las Vegas valley. The latter projects were part of our country's World War II mobilization effort. They continue to contribute to the southern Nevada economy today.

The first license issued in the City of Las Vegas following legalization in 1931 was to the Northern Club on Fremont Street. Tony Cornero's Meadows Club on the Los Angeles Highway beyond the city limits was the first license issued in Clark County (Moehring, 1989, pp. 20-22). The city initially limited casinos to three blocks on Fremont Street. This was to keep casinos out of residential neighborhoods. As Las Vegas grew, a continuing conflict arose between developers wanting to put "local" casinos closer to the residents and those residents who do not want a casino in their backyard.

NIMBY (Not in My Backyard) in Las Vegas

The 1997 session of the Nevada Legislature adopted an amendment to the Gaming Control Act, Senate Bill 208, 1997 Nev. Stats.

chap. 452, approved July 16, 1997, amending Nev. Rev. Stats. § 463.0129 (1995). Senate Bill 208 declares the public policy of the state to be "that establishments where gaming is conducted and where gambling devices are operated do not unduly impact the quality of life enjoyed by residents of the surrounding neighborhoods. . . ." Senate Bill 208 further amends the Gaming Control Act to limit casinos to specified gaming zones and prohibit new casinos near homes, schools, and churches. New casino projects require notice to residents when a project would be within 2,500 feet of their homes, schools, or churches, and the casino must be approved by at least three-fourths of the county commission or city council. If residents are unhappy with an affirmative decision for such a casino project, they may have the decision reviewed by the Gaming Policy Committee. Current efforts by local taverns in Las Vegas to expand their operations were blocked by a provision in Senate Bill 208 that limits existing taverns in Las Vegas to no more than thirty-five slot machines. This prevents the expansion of existing gaming locations into large casinos.

The Gaming Policy Committee, which is chaired by the governor and meets on his call, has not been convened for years. Its action is limited to conducting public hearings on issues and making recommendations that are not binding on the Gaming Commission. This legislation may give the Gaming Policy Committee new life and require state gaming authorities to become involved in local political issues that go beyond integrity and statewide policy issues. These changes will certainly make it difficult to expand gaming into areas where casinos are not already approved.

Boulder Dam: Las Vegas's First Major Tourist Attraction

Coincident with the legalization of gambling in Nevada was the construction of Boulder (Hoover) Dam about thirty miles from Las Vegas. This project pumped money and jobs into the Las Vegas economy from 1930 to 1939 (Moehring, 1989, pp. 14-15). Five thousand construction workers were working on the Dam. The federal government built Boulder City to house the workers, and they did not allow gambling in this government-owned city. Though the federal government privatized the town in 1960, the townspeople have maintained the gambling ban.

Dam construction attracted visitors, just as the dam does today. By 1934, the annual number of visitors had increased to 265,000 at the dam and 300,000 for Las Vegas. The Las Vegas tourist economy was underway! In 1932, the first luxury hotel in Las Vegas was completed: the Apache Hotel on Fremont Street, featuring the first elevator in Las Vegas (Moehring, 1989, pp. 20-21).

In these depression years, it was not only the dam construction that fueled the Las Vegas economy. Divorces were another economic boon. The same legislature that legalized gambling shortened the residency period to obtain a divorce from three months to six weeks. Moehring (1989, pp. 29-30) notes the publicity value of the Clark Gable-Ria Langham divorce in 1939 that attracted many others seeking divorces in the months and years that followed.

In 1938, Los Angeles elected a reform mayor who mounted a campaign to close illegal brothels and casinos in Los Angeles. Guy McAfee, a Los Angeles vice squad commander and gambling operator, and others moved to Las Vegas where their expertise was welcomed. McAfee opened a casino on the Los Angeles Highway and gave the "Las Vegas Strip" its name, taken from Sunset Strip between Beverly Hills and Hollywood.

Start of the Strip

Fremont Street was the center of development in these early years, until Thomas Hull, a California hotelier, was convinced by local businessmen to build a hotel in Las Vegas. Instead of joining the other operators on Fremont Street, Hull built his El Rancho Vegas at Sahara and the Las Vegas Strip, just outside the city limits. The El Rancho opened in April 1941. With its Spanish mission styling, its casino, restaurant, showroom, large pool, and lush landscaping, the El Rancho became the first "resort hotel" in Las Vegas. Its success demonstrated the viability of the resort hotel concept in Las Vegas and the practicality of building large resort hotels on large plats of ground along the Strip instead of on small downtown lots on Fremont Street (Moehring, 1989, pp. 43-45).

During World War II, the development of Nellis Army Air Corps Base as a training center and the construction and operation of the Basic Magnesium Plant in Henderson boosted the southern Nevada economy. By 1946, several present-day casinos were operating downtown: the Golden Nugget, El Cortez, and Las Vegas Club, along with others that are now only memories. Along the Strip, the Last Frontier (1942), the Flamingo (1946), and the Thunderbird (1948) followed Hull's El Rancho (Moehring, 1989, pp. 45-50).

The Saga of Bugsy Siegel and the Flamingo

Benjamin "Bugsy" Siegel's Flamingo is noteworthy on several accounts. It was the first real "luxury" resort hotel in Las Vegas. Its historical importance is well described by Moehring (1989):

> The crucial event which transformed Las Vegas from a recreational to a full-fledged resort city was Bugsy Siegel's Flamingo Hotel. . . . [I]t combined the sophisticated ambience of a Monte Carlo casino with the exotic luxury of a Miami Beach–Caribbean resort. The Flamingo liberated Las Vegas from the confines of its western heritage . . . (p. 49)

Siegel was not your average developer or resort operator. He and his associates were some of the most notorious mobsters in the country. Author Robert Lacey describes Siegel as a childhood friend and sometimes business associate of Meyer Lansky (1991, pp. 150-159). According to Lacey, Siegel moved to the West Coast from New York after prohibition ended to pursue gambling and starlets. Other writers assert that Lansky dispatched Siegel to the West Coast to consolidate mob activities and oversee the race-wire business that provided race results for illegal bookmakers in California and casinos in Las Vegas (Castleman, 1993, pp. 54-57; Moehring, 1989, pp. 47-49). These authors are in agreement, however, that the race-wire business brought Siegel to Las Vegas in 1941 and that he invested in a number of casinos before pursuing his dream of building a luxurious resort casino.

Siegel, after raising money from his mob associates, bought a two-thirds interest in a casino resort project already underway by California nightclub owner Billy Wilkerson. Siegel took control of the project, eventually buying the balance of Wilkerson's interest and pursued his dream of a luxury resort unlike anything then existing in Las Vegas. To build the Flamingo, Bugsy hired the Del Webb corporation, a prominent Arizona construction firm that later became one of the first publicly traded casino operators. When completed, the cost totaled somewhere between $4 million and $6 million, far exceeding the original budget of $1 million (Castleman, 1993, pp. 54-55; Lacey, 1991, pp. 154-159; Moehring, 1989, p. 47; and Spanier, 1992, p. 65).

This 300 to 500 percent cost overrun under Bugsy's management established a record never since equaled, or even approached, by Las Vegas casino builders. Bugsy's associates in the mob who invested in the project were reportedly unhappy with the construction cost. And when the Flamingo lost money after opening, they were even less happy with Bugsy's management. This may have led to Bugsy Siegel's termination—Mafia style. A gunman killed him while at his girlfriend's home in Beverly Hills a few months after the Flamingo was completed. His murder was never solved.

Bugsy Siegel was the first "mob" investor and operator in Las Vegas gaming, but, unfortunately, not the last. During the 1940s and 1950s, many of the people coming to Nevada to open casinos or invest in casinos could be characterized as "mob" members or associates. Deke Castleman cites Siegel's activities as the beginning of "forty years of the Italian-Jewish crime syndicate's presence in Las Vegas" (1993, p. 57).

The Birth of Gaming Regulation

In 1947, after Bugsy's killing and the attendant publicity, the Nevada Tax Commission sought a legal opinion from then Attorney General Allen Bible (father of Gaming Control Board and National Gambling Impact Study Commission member Bill Bible). They asked whether they could require license applicants to furnish personal and financial information and whether they could deny a license to a person who was deemed to be unsuitable. The Attorney General replied in the affirmative to both questions and the first regulation of gaming licensees was initiated (Attorney General's Opinion, 1947).

The 1950s: Nevada and Gaming Draw National Attention

Development on the Strip expanded rapidly in the 1950s, commencing with the opening of the Desert Inn in 1950, followed by the Sahara and the Sands in 1952; in 1955, in a short period of time, the Riviera, Dunes, New Frontier, and Royal Nevada; the Hacienda in 1956; Tropicana in 1957; and Stardust in 1958. Downtown also added properties in the 1950s with the opening of the Mint and the Fremont in 1956. The Showboat opened in 1954 on Fremont Street, but some distance from downtown (Castleman, 1993, pp. 72-110; Moehring, 1989, pp. 73-94).

The Kefauver Hearings

The 1950s were a significant period in Nevada's gaming history, and the casino openings previously described may not have been the most significant events. Senator Estes Kefauver, and the Senate Crime Investigating Committee, which he chaired, conducted televised hearings in many cities throughout the United States between May 1950 and May 1951. These hearings exposed the extent of organized crime throughout the country, particularly in gaming— illegal everywhere except Nevada. One of those televised hearings was held in Las Vegas and focused attention on many of the owners or operators of Las Vegas casinos and their connection with organized crime.

In his book on the work of the committee, Senator Kefauver (1951) quoted from the committee's report:

> It seems clear to the committee that too many of the men running gambling operations in Nevada are either members of existing out-of-state gambling syndicates or have had histories of close association with the underworld characters who operate those syndicates. The licensing system which is in effect in this state has not resulted in excluding the undesirables from the state but has merely served to give their activities a seeming cloak of respectability. (p. 236)

Gaming Control Board Established

Some Nevada legislators agreed with Senator Kefauver that the Tax Commission was not an effective regulatory body (Cahill, 1977), and in 1955, the Nevada legislature established the Nevada Gaming

Control Board to conduct background investigations of license applicants and determine suitability (Gaming Control Act, Nev. Stat.
§ 883 [1955]). The development of an effective regulatory system,
after this "colorful" beginning, is a major reason for the growth and
prosperity of the gaming industry today (Bybee, 1997, p. 43).

The 1960s: Commencement of the Corporate Era

After an eight-year period with no new hotels, the 1960s finished
strong, beginning with the Aladdin (opened in 1966); followed by
Caesars (1966); Circus Circus (1968); Landmark (1969); and International (1969). The Las Vegas Hilton was opened in 1973 (Castleman, 1993, pp. 111-121).

The 1960s are important to the history of gaming in Las Vegas for
more than the opening of casino hotels. In 1960, the Nevada Gaming
Control Board issued its "Black Book," listing eleven mobsters
whose presence in a casino was deemed by gaming authorities to
constitute an unsuitable manner of operation. John Marshall, who
had his name legally changed from Marchello Caifano, was one of
the Chicago mob's top representatives and reported to be their
enforcer in Las Vegas. When evicted from the Desert Inn because he
was in the "Black Book," Marshall sued in federal court, and two
levels of the federal court both upheld Nevada's authority to exclude
notorious and unsavory individuals from casinos (*Marshall v. Sawyer*, 1962/1966). This ratification by a federal court of the power of a
state to regulate gaming was a significant step in the development of
strong gaming regulation.

The Corporate Era Begins

Another important event of the 1960s was the arrival of Howard
Hughes and his subsequent acquisition of six casinos in Las Vegas
and one in Reno. Author and former Federal Bureau of Investigation agent William F. Roemer Jr., an expert on organized crime, has
written that Howard Hughes's acquisition of Nevada casinos was
"the beginning of the end for the mobs" (Roemer, 1994, p. 69). By
the time he moved from Las Vegas in 1970, Howard Hughes had
acquired the Desert Inn, the Sands, the Castaways, the Frontier, the

Silver Slipper, and the Landmark in Las Vegas and Harold's Club in Reno. Mob ownership was suspected or established in the Las Vegas sites, but not Harold's Club. Thus, one way the mob was eliminated in Nevada was through acquisition by legitimate operators.

Accounting and Accountability

In 1967, the Nevada legislature directed the Gaming Commission to adopt regulations requiring casinos to submit annual financial statements audited by an independent public accountant (Nev. Rev. Stat., 1995, § 463.159; Regulations of the Nevada Gaming Commission [NGC] and State Gaming Control Board [SGCB], 1995, 6.080). This gave a strong hand to accountants in casinos where the casino manager had previously ruled with little opposition. The same legislature made legislative changes that permitted publicly traded companies to acquire casinos without having to license each shareholder (Nev. Rev. Stat., 1995, § 463.625-643). Licensing of publicly traded companies focused on the controlling shareholders, directors, and officers. These two changes facilitated the eventual domination of Las Vegas by publicly traded companies. Their ability to raise large sums of money on Wall Street has enabled them to build the megaresorts that define Las Vegas today.

The 1970s: A Decade of Pluses and Minuses

Some Pluses

The biggest opening in the decade of the 1970s was the 2,000-room MGM Grand (1973), now Bally's Grand. But it was not the only opening, only the largest. Other openings in the 1970s were the Royal Las Vegas (1970), the Union Plaza (1971), Holiday Hotel (1972) (now Harrah's), Continental Hotel (1975), California Hotel (1975), Marina Hotel (1975) (now part of MGM Grand), and the Maxim (1977). The decade ended with a rush as Sam's Town, Barbary Coast, and Vegas World all opened in 1979 (Castleman, 1993, pp. 121-127).

Some Minuses

As in other eras, the 1970s are remembered most for events other than the building of casinos. The 1970s were memorialized by author Nicholas Pileggi (1995) in his reportorial description of the activities of Tony Spilotro and Frank "Lefty" Rosenthal, who became major players in Las Vegas at the beginning of the decade as representatives of the Chicago mob. This was also a period of continued strengthening and refining of the regulatory process.

Internal Control Systems—A Plus

In 1974, the Nevada Gaming Control Board and Nevada Gaming Commission adopted new accounting regulations that had been in development since 1971. The new regulations required each casino to develop detailed internal control procedures for the handling of cash and other assets. Each casino's system is required to be reviewed by an independent certified public accountant who must ensure that it provides adequate internal controls and meets the guidelines developed and published by the Gaming Control Board's Audit Division (Regulations of the NGC and SGCB, 1995, 6.090). Over the years, these internal controls have been refined and improved. The efficacy of such controls in casinos has enabled investors and lenders to have confidence in the financial statements of casinos. This, in turn, has allowed the gaming industry to raise money from suitable financial sources. Wall Street has replaced the Central and Southwest Teamsters Pension Fund as the primary source of casino financing.

Turning a Minus into a Plus

In a landmark decision, *State v. Rosenthal* (1977)—the "Lefty" Rosenthal from the movie "Casino"—the Nevada Supreme Court strengthened the hand of regulators when it held that a decision to deny a gaming license may not be appealed to, or reviewed by, the courts. The court's opinion also made clear that convictions and indictments for bribing athletes to fix the outcome of events on which wagering occurs, bribing government officials, and being barred from a racetrack are adequate grounds for denying a license.

Until this decision was rendered, gaming regulators were always concerned that some of the powers they wielded would be reduced or eliminated if challenged in court. The Nevada Supreme Court made clear in *State v. Rosenthal* that Nevada gaming authorities have been given very broad powers by the legislature and that many limitations on government action enjoyed by other businesses do not apply to regulation of the gaming industry.

The 1980s: End of the Mob's Influence in Las Vegas

During the 1980s, new hotels were smaller, mostly off-Strip properties before 1989 when the Mirage opened. The Sundance, now Fitzgerald's, opened in 1980, the Gold Coast in 1986, and Arizona Charlie's in 1988.

Construction gives visual evidence of progress and change. Other changes are more subtle, less evident to the public eye, but no less important to the growth and change of an industry or a community. Philip R. Manuel, Chief Investigator for the U.S. Senate Permanent Subcommittee on Investigations in the 1970s, and a member of the President's Commission on Organized Crime in the 1980's, speaking to the International Association of Gaming Attorneys (IAGA) in Monaco in October 1996, said that the Nevada gaming regulators' forced sale of the Stardust Casino Hotel in 1982 broke the chain of influence and skimming by the Chicago mob.

This was followed by the Tropicana case, in which federal prosecutors convicted eleven casino executives and mobsters from Kansas City, St. Louis, and Chicago of having a hidden interest in and skimming from the Tropicana (Roemer, 1994, pp. 227-233). In the Stardust case, which followed, fifteen underworld figures from five cities were convicted of having a hidden interest in and skimming from the Stardust (Roemer, 1994, pp. 244-257). The executive director of the Chicago Crime Commission exclaimed that this case "pretty well gutted the top hierarchy of the mob, not only in Chicago, but in Milwaukee and Kansas City" (Roemer, 1994, p. 245).

The association of mobsters with casinos in Nevada, particularly Las Vegas, has, over the years, resulted in much negative publicity for Las Vegas. This association lasted from the 1940s until the 1980s in some casinos, and one unfortunate result is that many people associate all casinos with organized crime, though the "mob" was never involved in all casinos, even in Las Vegas. William F. Roemer Jr., in his book on mobster Tony Spilotro (1994, p. 82), states that the major hotels—Golden Nugget, Mirage, Treasure Island, MGM Grand, Luxor, and Excalibur—have never been thought to be under any organized crime influence. The casinos Roemer describes as having been "mobbed-up" at one time are, in his words:

> now owned by legitimate concerns. Organized crime no longer has a hold on them. These include the Tropicana, the Stardust, Desert Inn, Circus-Circus, Caesars Palace, the Fremont, the Aladdin, the Sands, the Riviera, and the Sundance. The Dunes and the Marina have been torn down. (Roemer, 1994, pp. 276-277)

The elimination of organized crime from casinos in Nevada is the result of efforts on the part of many people over many years on a variety of levels. Legitimate operators such as Howard Hughes, Kirk Kirkorian, Hilton Hotels, Del Webb Corporation, Boyd Gaming, and Ramada (now Aztar) acquired gaming operations that were once mob influenced or mob controlled. The authority and power of regulators have been clarified and confirmed by the courts (Bybee, 1995). Regulators have been given additional powers, have developed additional tools for regulation, and have gained valuable experience through the years, making them more effective. Federal prosecution of organized criminal elements sent many to prison and decimated mob leadership in several states, a feat that would have been impossible for state law enforcement or gaming regulators to accomplish. The efforts continue.

LAS VEGAS GAMING TODAY

One Era Ends; Another Begins

With the opening of the Mirage in 1989, a new era dawned: the age of the entertainment megaresort. A resort could offer at least 2,000, and as many as 5,000, rooms; a decorative theme; interior and exterior design features that attract and entertain visitors; lots of shopping; a variety of types and venues for entertainment; and activities for the whole family, if desired (Eade, 1997). The mob had been excised from the Las Vegas gaming industry. A new image as a "family resort" could be believable. This reinventing or re-defining of Las Vegas has probably enabled it to not only survive the expansion of gaming since 1988 but to enjoy the greatest period of prosperity in its history.

Las Vegas: A Family Resort

Much has been made of the family resort concept for Las Vegas, both good and bad. In reality, it is still an adult resort. Only 11 percent of visitors had a person under age twenty-one in their party. This figure has not changed in the two years since it was added to the Las Vegas Convention and Visitors Authority's (LVCVA) visitor survey instrument (1996, p. 41). The biggest benefit to Las Vegas of this change in image from "Sin City" to "family resort" has been that if it is all right for families to go to Las Vegas, it is certainly suitable for all adults. This image adjustment may have helped Las Vegas appeal to a much broader market at a time when its visitor capacity was rapidly increasing.

Although considerable expansion of existing hotels occurred in the 1970s and 1980s, along with the construction of some twenty smaller hotel casinos, the Mirage was the first resort hotel constructed on the Strip since the MGM Grand opened in 1973 (Castleman, 1993, p. 129). Its initial cost of a reported $750 million (Arthur Andersen, 1996) totaled more than all of the hotel construction in the history of Las Vegas (without adjusting those dollars for inflation). Since the Mirage opened, more than $5 billion of new casino hotel construction has been completed (Arthur Andersen, 1996).

Las Vegas Growth Statistics

Las Vegas has continued to grow and prosper beyond the most optimistic expectations. A few statistics paint a picture of a large and dynamic gaming industry in Las Vegas. Nine of the ten largest hotels in the world are in Las Vegas. On the four corners of Tropicana and

Las Vegas Boulevard, there are over 13,000 rooms; more than in Atlantic City, New Jersey (Ader and Lumpkins, 1997). The U.S. Travel Industry Association reports that 38 percent of all U.S. residents have been to Las Vegas at least once (LVCVA, 1997). In 1996, 29.6 million people visited Las Vegas, arriving by air (47.4 percent), by car (46.2 percent), by bus (6.2 percent), and by train (0.2 percent). Approximately 87 percent of the 1996 visitors said they gambled, although only 5 percent say their main reason for coming was for gambling. Most say they come for recreation and entertainment (LVCVA, 1996). Three days into 1997, the largest room base in the world had increased to 101,106 with the opening of New York New York. The next largest room base in the United States, Orlando, has 85,635 rooms. Hotel occupancy rates were 93.4 percent in 1996. Motels lowered the combined average to 90.4 percent, still impressive compared to the national average of 65.2 percent. The average number of nights stayed was 3.7 nights in 1996 (LVCVA, 1997).

Revenues and employment figures provide a picture of how the largest casinos on the Las Vegas Strip dominate the gaming industry in Nevada and how much the industry has grown in the last twenty years. Total revenue for casinos with over $1 million in gaming revenue increased from $1.9 billion in 1976 (SGCB, 1976), to $12.8 billion in 1996 (SGCB, 1996). Statewide, there were 101 such casinos in 1976 with 79,328 employees and 229 such casinos in 1996 employing 186,103. The nineteen largest casinos on the Las Vegas Strip employed 34.5 percent of the state's gaming employees in 1996 and generated 47.4 percent of the statewide revenue. In 1976, the eleven largest casinos on the Strip produced 43.6 percent of the statewide revenue, with 31.2 percent of the statewide gaming workforce. Although the dominance of the largest casinos has increased over the past twenty years, it has not been a dramatic increase.

NEVADA'S GAMING REGULATORY SYSTEM

Gaming is a "privileged" business. There is no "right" to conduct a gaming business. In contrast, most businesses operate by right, not by privilege, and cannot be legislated or regulated out of existence. Gaming can be legislated out of existence (Bybee, 1995).

The U.S. Supreme Court, in *Posados de Puerto Rico Assoc. v. Tourism Co.* (1986), has ruled that gaming can be prohibited by the state, and the power to ban casino gaming includes the power to prohibit advertising of casino gaming. In effect, the Supreme Court said that the power to eliminate gaming includes the power to regulate it up to that point.

Nevada Gaming Commission

The Nevada Gaming Commission consists of five commissioners, each appointed by the governor for a four-year term. It is a lay body that meets at least once a month in a public meeting to conduct business. The commission is empowered to adopt gaming regulations that have the force of law, to grant or deny licenses, and to take disciplinary action against licensees, including revocation of a license (Nev. Rev. Stat., 1995, § 463.022-029). Other than the executive secretary shared with the State Gaming Control Board, the Gaming Commission has no staff. Any needed staff services must be requested from the Gaming Control Board.

After an applicant for a gaming license files an application and all supporting documents with the Gaming Control Board, the Board's Investigation Division conducts a thorough investigation and submits a report to the board and commission (Nev. Rev. Stat., 1995, § 463.210-220; Regulations of the NGC and SGCB, 1995, 3-4) (Sayre, 1994). The historical connection between organized crime and gambling makes any link between an applicant and organized crime a serious licensing issue. Regulators do not have to prove an applicant is unsuitable. Applicants must prove their suitability by clear and convincing evidence. The board conducts a public hearing on the application and makes a recommendation to the commission.

The commission then conducts a public hearing on the application and grants or denies the license. If the board recommends denial, a unanimous vote by the commission is required to grant the license. Nevada statutes prohibit the granting of a gaming license unless the commission is satisfied that the applicant is "a person of good character, honesty, and integrity" and "a person whose prior activities, criminal record, if any, reputation, habits, and associations do not pose a threat to the public interest" (Nev. Rev. Stat., 1995, § 463.170). If the commission approves the license, it may impose such conditions or limitations as deemed appropriate. The denial of a gaming license is not subject to review by the courts.

When the Gaming Control Board files a complaint against a licensee, the commission hears the disciplinary actions in a proceeding similar to a court trial. After hearing the charges and the respondent licensee's defense, if any, the commission may impose a fine, or it may limit, condition, suspend, or revoke the gaming license (Nev. Rev. Stat., 1995, § 463.310-3145; Regulations of the NGC and SGCB, 1995, 7) (Friedman, 1994). Most complaints are settled without a hearing upon a stipulation between the licensee and the board, in which the licensee admits the violation and agrees to a fine. The commission may accept the stipulation or reject it and proceed with a disciplinary hearing. The commission's action is subject to review by the courts (Nev. Rev. Stat., 1995, § 463.315).

Gaming Control Board

Nevada's Gaming Control Board consists of three members appointed by the governor for four-year terms. No legislator or holder of any elective office or official of any political party may be a board member. The chairman must have at least five years of administrative experience. One member must have law or law enforcement experience, and one member must have accounting, finance, economics, or gaming knowledge or experience (Nev. Rev. Stat., 1995, § 463.040-110). Approximately 400 employees and agents are assigned to seven divisions: administrative services, audit, corporate securities, electronic services, enforcement, investigation, and tax collection.

The Gaming Control Board monitors a licensee's compliance with all regulations, performs audits (Gale, 1994), and conducts investigations of possible violations of law or regulations. New games are tested in the board's electronic laboratory and undergo a trial period in a casino; then the board makes its recommendations to the Gaming Commission, which must approve any new gambling games or gaming devices (Nev. Rev. Stat., 1995, § 463.150 (h) (j); Regulations of the NGC and SGCB, 1995, 14).

Miscellaneous Regulatory Issues

Currency Transactions

In 1970, Congress enacted the Bank Secrecy Act to prevent money laundering by drug dealers through banks and other financial institutions. In 1985, the U.S. Treasury Department adopted 31 CFR 103 pursuant to the Bank Secrecy Act, requiring casinos to file a Currency Transaction Report (CTR) for currency transactions over $10,000. States adopting similar provisions could obtain a waiver from the federal regulations. Nevada adopted Reg. 6A, as authorized by Nev. Rev. Stat. § 463.125 (1995). Reg. 6A was substantially revised in 1997 after negotiations between Treasury and the Gaming Control Board.

The Gaming Control Board periodically conducts "stings," testing compliance with Reg. 6A. Violations almost always result in a fine. Fines for violation of Reg. 6A range from $25,000 to $250,000 for each separate violation (Nev. Rev. Stat., 1995, § 463.310). The largest fine imposed to date for multiple violations is $1 million (Friedman, 1994).

Exclusion List

In 1960, the Gaming Control Board, without authority of a statute or a specific regulation, sent to casino operators a list of eleven individuals who were not to be permitted on the casino premises. The list had a black cover and became known as the "Black Book." For a contrast in perspectives on this subject compare Sawyer (1993, pp. 153-163); Skolnick (1978); Olsen (1973); Lionel Sawyer and Collins (1995, pp. 285-297); and Farrell and Case (1995).

Following the decision in *Marshall v. Sawyer* (1962/1966), the legislature adopted statutes providing for an exclusion list and making it a crime for persons on the list to enter a casino (Nev. Rev. Stat., 1995, § 463.151-155). The Gaming Commission subsequently adopted Reg. 28 containing procedures for adding and removing names and responsibilities of casinos when they discover listed individuals on their premises. Courts have continued to uphold the authority of regulators to exclude from casinos people whose presence is contrary to the best interests of the state. Currently, over twenty individuals are on the exclusion list.

Work Permits

All gaming employees are required to have a work permit. If local government does not issue work permits, one must be obtained from the Gaming Control Board (Nev. Rev. Stat., 1995, § 463.335-3403; Regulations of the NGC and SGCB, 1995, 4). The investigation is normally limited to a criminal record check with local and statewide law enforcement agencies and the FBI. Criminal convictions, especially for gaming crimes, drug-related crimes, theft, or fraud, are cause for objection or denial (Tatro, 1994a). If the board objects to the issuance of a work permit by local agencies or refuses to issue one, applicants may appeal to the commission.

Customer Disputes

In Nevada, gaming debts generally cannot be enforced in the courts. In 1983, legislation was enacted that allowed courts to enforce payment of gaming debts owed to licensed casinos (Nev. Rev. Stat., 1995, § 463.368) (Cabot, 1989). Companion legislation provided that casino/patron disputes over payment of wagers are to be handled by the Gaming Control Board. This provides prompt, fair, independent, and knowledgeable review of disputed patron claims. Casinos are required to notify the Gaming Control Board if the amount is $500 or more and to inform customers of their right to call the board if the amount in dispute is under $500 (Nev. Rev. Stat., 1995, § 463.361-3668; Regulations of the NGC and SGCB, 1995, 7A) (Tatro, 1994b).

Underage Gambling

Since 1994, the Gaming Control Board has emphasized enforcement of the laws and regulations prohibiting gambling by minors. In Nevada, as in most states, the legal gambling age is twenty-one (Nev. Rev. Stat., 1995, § 463.350). Underage gambling and violation of Reg. 6A, currency transactions, are the most frequent subjects of disciplinary action against casinos.

SUMMARY

Las Vegas is the premier gaming market in the world. Its sheer size and variety of gaming locations will not likely be matched in any jurisdiction in the world. Certainly none are likely to duplicate its sixty-five-plus years of experience with every problem associated with gambling. Las Vegas has provided exemplar lessons in both what to do and what to avoid. This accumulation of experience and ultimate success has made it the object of attention as other jurisdictions have contemplated legalizing casino gambling (Bybee, 1997, pp. 25, 42). Las Vegas contains people with years of experience in all aspects of gaming and government of a gaming economy, together with visual models of every size and description of gaming operations (Eade, 1997, pp. 207). This combination makes it a rare laboratory for anyone with a need or desire to better understand the design, construction, and operation of a casino or the workings of a gaming economy and its impact on, and interaction with, a community.

REFERENCES

Ader, J.N. and Lumpkins, C.J. (1997). *Bear Stearns global gaming almanac.* New York: Bear Stearns and Company, Inc.

Arthur Andersen (1996). *Economic impact of casino gaming in the United States: Volume 1. Macro study.* Washington, DC: American Gaming Association.

Attorney General's Opinion (1947). No. 528, October 14.

Bybee, S. (1995). The legal status of gaming and its impact on licensing. *Gaming Research and Review Journal, 2*(1), 61-71.

Bybee, S. (1997). Gaming regulation. In V. Eade (Ed.), *Overview of the gaming industry* (pp. 23-46). Las Vegas, NV: UNLV International Gaming Institute.

Cabot, A.N. (Ed.) (1989). *Casino credit and collection law.* Las Vegas, NV: International Association of Gaming Attorneys.

Cabot, A. (1997). What history tells of the growth of the American gaming industry. In V. Eade (Ed.), *Overview of the gaming industry* (pp. 1-21). Las Vegas, NV: UNLV International Gaming Institute.

Cahill, R.E. (1977). *Recollections of work in state politics, government, taxation, gaming control, Clark County Administration and the Nevada Resort Association.* Reno, NV: University of Nevada, Reno.

Castleman, D. (1993). *Las Vegas* (Third edition). Oakland, CA: Compass American Guides.

Commission on the Review of the National Policy Toward Gambling (1976). *Gambling in America.* Washington, DC: U.S. Government Printing Office.

Eade, V. (1997). Las Vegas gaming trends and analysis. In V. Eade (Ed.). *Overview of the gaming industry* (pp. 207-223). Las Vegas, NV: UNLV International Gaming Institute.

Farrell, R.A. and Case, C. (1995). *The black book and the mob.* Madison, WI: The University of Wisconsin Press.

Friedman, N.H. (1994). An overview of the disciplinary proceedings before the Nevada Gaming Commission. *Gaming Research and Review Journal, 1*(1), 55-61.

Gale, G. (1994). The audit division of the State Gaming Control Board: Overview of organization and current tax issues. *Gaming Research and Review Journal, 1*(1), 69-75.

Kefauver, E. (1951). *Crime in America.* Garden City, NY: Doubleday and Company.

Lacey, R. (1991). *Little man: Meyer Lansky and the gangster life.* Boston: Little, Brown and Company, Inc.

Las Vegas Convention and Visitors Authority (LVCVA) (1996). *1996 Las Vegas visitor profile study.* Las Vegas, NV: Author.

Las Vegas Convention and Visitors Authority (LVCVA) (1997). *Las Vegas Marketing Bulletin, Fourth Quarter 1996 Summary, 24*(100), 1-28.

Lionel Sawyer and Collins. (1995). *Nevada gaming law* (Second Edition). Las Vegas, NV: Author.

Marshall v. Sawyer (1962/1966). 301 F.2d 639 (Ninth Cir. Nev. 1962); *aff'd.* 365 F.2d 105 (1966).

Moehring, E.P. (1989). *Resort city in the sunbelt.* Reno, NV: University of Nevada Press, Reno and Las Vegas.

Nevada Gaming Commission and State Gaming Control Board (NGC and SGCB) (1985). *Gaming Nevada style.* Carson City, NV: Author.

Olsen, E.A. (1973). The black book episode: An exercise in muscle. In E. Bushnell (Ed.), *Sagebrush and neon: Studies in Nevada politics* (pp. 1-21). Reno, NV: Bureau of Government Research, University of Nevada, Reno.

Pileggi, N. (1995). *Casino: Love and honor in Las Vegas.* New York: Simon and Schuster.

Posados de Puerto Rico Assoc. v. Tourism Co. (1986). 478 U.S. 328.

Roemer, W.F., Jr. (1994). *The enforcer—Spilotro: The Chicago mob's man over Las Vegas.* New York: Ivy Books.

Rosecrance, J. (1988). *Gambling without guilt.* Belmont, CA: Brooks Cole.

Sawyer, G. (1993). *Hang tough.* Reno, NV: University of Nevada Oral History Program.

Sayre, R.E. (1994). The investigations division of the State Gaming Control Board: An introduction to the investigative process. *Gaming Research and Review Journal, 1*(1), 89-93.

Skolnick, J.H. (1978). *House of cards.* Boston: Little, Brown and Company, Inc.

Spanier, D. (1992). *Welcome to the pleasuredome inside Las Vegas.* Reno, NV: University of Nevada Press.

State Gaming Control Board (SGCB) (Ed.) (1970). *Legalized gambling in Nevada: Its history, economics and control* (Second edition). Carson City, NV: Nevada Gaming Commission and State Gaming Control Board.

State Gaming Control Board (SGCB) (1976). *Nevada gaming abstract.* Carson City, NV: Author.

State Gaming Control Board (SGCB) (1996). *Nevada gaming abstract.* Carson City, NV: Author.

State v. Rosenthal (1977). 559 P.2d 830. Appeal dismissed by *Rosenthal v. Nevada,* 434 U.S. 803 (1977).

Tatro, J. (1994a). Work permit hearings. *Gaming Research and Review Journal, 1*(1), 55-67.

Tatro, J. (1994b). Casino/patron disputes. *Gaming Research and Review Journal, 1*(1), 99-101.

Chapter 2

Personal Recollections of the New Jersey Gambling "Experiment" in Atlantic City

James F. Wortman

BACKGROUND

Atlantic and Cape May counties were economically the two poorest counties in the state of New Jersey in the early 1970s. The major sources of income in these counties were agriculture, commercial fishing, and tourism. The main attractions for tourists were the Atlantic City Boardwalk of Monopoly fame and, to a slightly lesser degree, the city's hosting of the annual Miss America Pageant. Cape May, in the meantime, was noted for the Victorian architecture of Cape May City and the boardwalk and beaches of Wildwood.

Since the turn of the century, tourism had been, by far, the most significant industry in both counties. While achieving worldwide recognition as a resort, Atlantic City and, to a lesser extent, Cape May could count on the populations of New York City and, especially, Philadelphia coming to the "Jersey Shore" to find respite from the summer heat of their respective cities. This form of recreation attracted people from all levels of social strata, and for generations, going to the shore during the summer was what was done.

After World War II, a combination of circumstances conspired to lead the Atlantic City resort industry into a decline. Travel by automobile and airplane became much less expensive. Society, as a rule, started to view vacation travel as an exciting alternative to the traditional short-term stay at the locations they had been visiting for the past ten or twenty years. Many of the grand hotels were getting old and beginning to look their age. Little reinvestment was made into the properties to modernize or upgrade the amenities that were becoming the standard throughout the rest of the industry. Much of the entertainment that had been exclusively booked to perform at the resorts was now readily available on television. Declining seasonal bookings and smaller weekend crowds indicated that the "Home of Salt Water Taffy and the Steel Pier" was indeed in economic trouble.

In an attempt to stem the tide and prolong the tourist season, that most traditional of summer attractions, the Miss America Pageant, which had been, since its inception in the 1920s, a fixture on Labor Day weekend, moved the festivities to the following weekend. This strategy proved to be effective only for the short term. A local state senator, Frank Farley, who, through long and distinguished service, had risen to the rank of speaker of the New Jersey Senate, did his best politically to serve his constituents. Using all of his political savvy, he almost single-handedly pushed the Garden State Parkway Bill through the legislature. This bill established a highway that ran the length of the state, from the northernmost counties to Cape May. The unique feature of this highway is that it is a multilane toll road which runs through all of the "seashore" counties. He followed this up with the Atlantic City Expressway Bill, which provided a multilane toll road that ran the breadth of the state, from Philadelphia across the Delaware River directly into Atlantic City.

These two bills should have improved tourism in Atlantic and Cape May counties. Tourism was improved, but not to any significant extent. Although these highways reduced transportation problems, the tourism industry in southern New Jersey was unable to provide additional attractions that would entice tourists to stay longer. If anything, the tourist industry became a "day-tripper" business, due in part to the ease of travel. This concept of the day-tripper is significant in light of the bussing programs that Atlantic City casinos are noted for, but I am getting ahead of myself.

Those individuals and families who were still desirous of extended stays or season-long accommodations used this ease of travel to visit places such as Ocean City, Avalon, and Stone Harbor in the south or Brigantine and Barnegat in the north. In any event, movement away from stays in expensive hotels to rentals of cottages or condominiums outside of Atlantic City was becoming the norm. One no longer had to stay in Atlantic City to partake of the 500 Club or Steel Pier. Trips could be planned from anywhere on the shore to take advantage of "headliners" appearing in Atlantic City.

Concerned civic leaders, businesspersons, educators, and other citizens came together and formed the Committee to Rebuild Atlantic City (CRAC), an unfortunate acronym in today's parlance. Recalling the success of "casinos" in Atlantic City's Golden Era, a petition was put forth to place casino gaming on a statewide referendum. The first referendum was soundly defeated. Not easily discouraged, CRAC decided to hire an advertising agency to educate the public statewide and influence them to "Vote Yes" for casino gambling. Southern New Jersey had long been a drain on the resources of the state government, and the northern counties were growing weary of having to constantly provide aid for the major manufacturing–poor seashore counties. The possibility of the casino gaming industry providing an economic impetus and relieving economic pressure in the northern counties was viewed as favorable. Most experts were skeptical that it would have a great impact, but at this point, it was something. It has been rumored that even with this tacit acceptance, the referendum was headed for a second defeat, when some last-minute compromising enabled the caveat ". . . in Atlantic City only" to be added. This quieted the homeowners in the northern counties, who were afraid that having casinos nearby would lower property values. In fact, they rather liked the idea of having the ability to play in a casino "at the Shore," so long as they were sure it would never expand to their neighborhood. In November 1976, the referendum passed, by the slimmest of margins.

Passage of the bill produced some very interesting responses from the business community, which have been played over and over again as new jurisdictions have opened up. The owners of real estate, which was already for sale in a dreadful market, called their sales agents and doubled the asking price of the property. Gift shops on the Boardwalk started selling souvenirs proclaiming Atlantic City as "the Gaming Capital of the World." Convenience stores started selling "Casino Dogs" at double the price. The problem was that they did this *two full years* before the first casino opened up. They expected people to travel from Philadelphia and New York to visit future casino sites. One year before the first casino opened, businesses were closing and citizens were bitterly complaining that casinos had not lived up to their billing. Everyone in Atlantic City was not wealthy, and the crowds had not returned to transform the city back to its halcyon days of glory.

The passage of the referendum had an interesting effect on the state government. Reality was swift and scary. No one in the government knew enough about gaming to draw up enabling legislation, never mind promulgate any kind of regulation and oversight strategy. The governor and state legislature assembled a Blue Ribbon Panel, comprised primarily of attorneys general, auditors, law enforcement personnel, and educators. This panel traveled to all of those states and countries that had legalized casino gaming. They were interested in what worked, what did not work, what should be considered, and answers to the "if you had to do it over again" question. There were time constraints, so the panel agreed to become as eclectic as possible. Keep the best, reject the parts that did not work well in other jurisdictions, and incorporate what was left into what was to become the format for New Jersey's gambling statutes.

Some issues were unique to New Jersey. Certain mandates were placed upon the legislators. First, the public was to perceive that the regulations were to be sufficiently strict to make it virtually impossible for organized crime to gain any type of foothold in the overall casino operation of any casino in New Jersey. Second, the Equal Employment Opportunity (EEO) guidelines would be based upon the U.S. Census figures for the State of New Jersey. These EEO guidelines would be tied to the casino's licensing process to ensure compliance. Basically, the Jobs Compendium of the casino was to be filled reflecting the census figures. This was to be accomplished department by department. Third, licensing of casinos and their employees was to be a "privilege and not a right," thereby placing the burden of proof for licensing qualification on the casino or the individual. Fourth, a residency requirement would be added. This was inserted to ensure casinos hired local people and did not just import workers from Nevada and other legal jurisdictions. Fifth, an experiential requirement was added to ensure that prospective local employees were adequately trained to compete for licenses and jobs. In-house upward mobility programs were required so local employees who attained positions at entry levels were given the opportunity to prepare themselves for promotion. The experiential requirements also provided longevity guidelines as to when licensure would be granted for promotion to the next supervisory level.

One of the civic leaders associated with CRAC went to the New Jersey Board of Higher Education and requested that the community college in Atlantic County be given the mandate to develop programs and curricula. These programs would be developed to train primarily Atlantic and Cape May County residents, but open to all who applied, to compete for the jobs this new industry would provide. That civic leader was Steven Perskie, who became the chairman of the New Jersey Casino Control Commission at a later date. In 1977, the Casino Career Institute of Atlantic Community College became the first public institution in the country with a curriculum approved by the state to provide noncredit dealer, surveillance, and slot mechanic training. Additional not-required-for-licensure programs were developed for the positions of cage cashier, pit clerk, security, slot attendant, and slot booth cashier. The Casino Career Institute (CCI) still operates today despite the experiential requirements being removed in 1995. As of 1996, CCI had 32,000 graduates working in virtually every gaming jurisdiction in the United States, in addition to those employed in Atlantic City.

LET THE GAMES BEGIN!

The Mary Carter Paint Company, dba Resorts International (Resorts), purchased the Chalfonte-Haddon Hall Hotel on the historic Atlantic City Boardwalk. Resorts started a $77-million renovation of the hotel to prepare it for casino gaming. While construction was taking place, the New Jersey Casino Control Commission was selected by the governor and approved by the state legislature, with a former Essex County prosecutor, Joseph Lordi, as chairman. The commission and its staff immediately wrote regulations that would govern operation of casinos, vendors, training schools, and ancillary casino support functions. The New Jersey Division of Gaming Enforcement was created to ensure due diligence in investigations and to be the law enforcement body monitoring regulatory compliance. The bulk of this group was the New Jersey State Police, with support from retired law enforcement officers hired as civilian agents. All that was being promulgated and performed ultimately had to be approved by the state legislature.

The time from mid-1977 through the opening of the casino on Memorial Day in 1978 was among the most frenetic Atlantic City and its environs had experienced in decades. Rumors were running rampant. Entrepreneurship was the norm, as it seemed that everyone had a scheme or an idea on how to cash in on the arrival of casinos. The *Atlantic City Press* published an article in which thirty-five prospective casino sites were mapped out. Thousands of people enrolled in noncredit classes at the local community college to learn whatever they could about this new industry. People were moving into the county from all over the East Coast to satisfy the residency requirements established by the Casino Control Commission.

The state of New Jersey and Atlantic City viewed all of this activity benignly. They did not believe that the opening of this new industry would be very dramatic, either in customer volume or in financial rewards. They also believed that the prognostications made by CRAC were generous, to say the least. No one, even the most experienced of casino personnel, was prepared for the numbers that were produced on opening day. The staff of the Casino Control Commission delivered the finalized copy of the regulations and the certificate of operation the night before the casino was scheduled to open—10:00 a.m. the following day. Between 500 and 1,000 people were expected during the entire day, most of whom would likely be "sightseers." When the doors opened, they found a line three abreast, three city blocks long. These lines continued for weeks.

Once inside the casino, the patrons proved that most of them were not sightseers. Tables filled, and every slot machine, regardless of denomination, had someone pulling a handle. Due to enormous crowds, most gaming spaces had players two deep, and in some instances, three deep, waiting to try their hand. The casino, by regulation, was open for eighteen hours a day during the week and for twenty hours a day on the weekend. The lines stayed formed on the Boardwalk regardless of the weather or the hour. Everyone was caught unprepared for the sheer volume of humanity and money involved. Resorts did not reconcile the first days' accounts until months later because an insufficient number of licensed personnel was available to count the huge volumes of money. Every licensed employee was pressed into "extra duty." This included corporate management, clerical staff, and anyone capable of holding a valid license. They were asked to sell change, empty overflowing drop boxes, work either in hard or soft count, and refill or replenish table games or slot booths with chips or coins during the time that the casino was closed. It has been rumored that Resorts was successful enough to pay the principal of the $77-million refurbishing debt after only ten months of operation.

The success Resorts exhibited spurred the construction for those casino companies which were soon to follow, many with familiar Las Vegas names, such as Caesar's, Bally's, Sands, and Harrah's, some with a local flair, such as the Brighton, or recognizable in noncasino venues, such as Playboy. Ultimately, thirteen casinos were built; however, Hugh Hefner, at Playboy, lost his casino license, and Playboy became the Atlantis, which went into receivership and was purchased by Donald Trump. Mr. Trump closed the Atlantis Casino, renovated the building, and reopened it as Trump Regency. This left Atlantic City with twelve casinos. Much later, Mr. Trump petitioned the New Jersey Casino Control Commission to allow Trump Regency to become part of the Trump Plaza, even though the two buildings were separated by the famous old Atlantic City Convention Hall. His petition was successful.

MY ODYSSEY

The heady potential success of the casinos reached throughout South Jersey. I was an associate professor and a department chairman at Atlantic Community College at the time. One of my friends and colleagues was Frank Creveling, founder and initial resident director of the Casino Career Institute, mentioned previously. I had been asked to be part of the first class that Resorts was training, but having a family and being conservative about my future and the casino industry, I declined. Three years later, armed with the knowledge that many of my poorer students were making twice my salary and the advice of a favorite uncle, who had not been corrupted by working in the casino industry in Las Vegas, I enrolled in a craps class at CCI. While in school, I was interviewed and hired as a dealer by Playboy.

My family, friends, and parents were convinced that this forty-one-year-old was going through the throes of midlife crisis. Their son, the associate professor, dealing craps at Playboy—where had they gone wrong? I dealt and floored craps and blackjack and eventually moved upstairs to help design and implement an employee evaluation program. An interesting aside is that the day I started dealing I was making more money than I made as an associate professor and department chairman with a master's degree and forty-five-plus graduate credits. As is the norm in the casino industry, I followed the vice president of casino operations to another property. This is the individual who had given me the opportunity to move into the management side of the industry. I became the casino administrator at the Tropicana Hotel and Casino. After two eventful years, we moved on to "open" what we believed would be Atlantic City's premier property, the Atlantic City Hilton. My responsibilities were to coordinate the hiring of casino personnel, design and implement the training program for the entire casino, and coordinate the training with programs for all noncasino departments. Much of the entry-level training was to be accomplished off site, and as the opening approached, the hiring of casino personnel and operation of a "mock casino" facility was to be accomplished. Interdepartmental scenarios were daily exercises in the mock casino. No one was prepared for what came next. Hilton was denied a license! At the last minute, what was to be the Atlantic City Hilton became Trump Castle. We made the transition and still had the most successful "opening" the town had ever seen. Near the end of my time at the Castle, I voluntarily returned to the casino floor to complete my experiential requirements for pit boss licensure.

One day, Frank Creveling, the aforementioned resident director of CCI, visited the casino and asked me for the "last time" if I would come back to Atlantic Community College. It had been a running joke between us for about ten years. My response had always been that I was having too much fun and was making too much money to come back. This time I accepted. I had children who were approaching college age, and with free tuition and an opportunity to succeed as the resident director of CCI, the decision was an easy one. I had to work part-time at Showboat as a floorman because of the salary differential, but that was only for a short time. I was the resident director of CCI for five years.

EVENTS/AGENCIES

Mentioned in my discussions with the people I interviewed* and prevalent in my own recollections are a number of events/agencies in Atlantic City gaming history that helped to define and shape, both positively and negatively, the "experiment."

The New Jersey Casino Control Commission

The New Jersey Casino Control Commission is a body appointed by the governor and the state legislature with regulatory oversight responsibility and broad powers to accomplish that task. In the beginning, with an acknowledged lack of casino expertise and difficult mandates to achieve, the commission relied upon the Blue Ribbon Panel findings to establish a framework of regulations. To the casino operators and prospective employees, the regulations were, and often still are, perceived as oppressive, inane, unnecessary, and stifling. While working in the casino industry, I subscribed to those terms and could have added a few more. I also came to understand that the regulations are a work in progress. The regulations of today are vastly different from the initial set. I am not an apologist for the commission, but history has shown that the adversarial relationship which originally characterized dealings between casino operators and the commission has become more of a cooper-

---

*In addition to my own recollections, I performed personal interviews with the following individuals: Steven Perskie, founder of the Committee to Rebuild Atlantic City and Chairman of the New Jersey Casino Control Commission; Deno Marino, Chief of Casino Control Commission staff; Fred Gushin, Deputy Attorney General, Division of Gaming Enforcement; John McLaughlin, Civilian Agent, Division of Gaming Enforcement; Dan Heneghan, Director of Public Relations, New Jersey Casino Control Commission and reporter for *Atlantic City Press* and *Casino Beat.*

ative venture partnership. Both sides have yielded a little while continuing to work to ensure that the integrity of the gaming operation and the public's perception thereof have not been affected. This has led to the regulations derived being used in a modified form by many emerging gaming jurisdictions. In 1995, the regulations were modified to include an elimination of the experiential requirement for licensure. In addition, modifications were made to relinquish control of what were considered to be business decisions by the casino operators. Operators with a history of dealing with strict New Jersey regulations included some of the procedures in their non-New Jersey operations. They found that they could better handle their operations and that the procedures and reports made good business sense.

The Division of Gaming Enforcement

The Division of Gaming Enforcement (DGE) is a body appointed to ensure that the regulations are followed. It is staffed primarily by members of the New Jersey State Police and aided by civilian agents. Primary responsibilities include due diligence investigations for licensure, establishment and maintenance of an exclusion list of undesirable patrons, arrest and prosecution of criminals in the casino (the State Police prosecute, not the hotel or the local police), and working conjointly with all federal law enforcement agencies. The DGE's relationship with the Casino Control Commission is an advisory one. It makes due diligence recommendations regarding licensure, both for issuance and suspension. The Casino Control Commission is not bound by these recommendations. The fact that the DGE prosecutes the offenders is a relief to the operators, who may be accused of wrongful or malicious prosecution. The DGE will not prosecute until it is satisfied that a crime has taken place. This is usually substantiated by surveillance videotape.

The Atlantic City Casino Association

The Atlantic City Casino Association was a body whose membership included most of the existing casino hotels of the time. It no longer is in operation. It was formed to represent the casinos in most political matters. The reason it is mentioned here is that, although appearing to be inept at controlling the negative publicity concerning Atlantic City gaming, in this author's opinion, it kept competition from starting in other states for at least ten years. Indeed, the executive director once described Atlantic City as an "aging prostitute." Needless to say, the quote was carried nationwide. During the first fifteen years, representatives from jurisdictions considering gaming as an economic development tool came to Atlantic City to see the "experiment" firsthand. Rather than showing the casinos, tours started in the inlet section (abandoned houses and overgrown lots) through the demilitarized zone (city blocks devoid of any hope of attracting casino development) to the city offices for a review of the increase in crime statistics and infrastructure problems. Most of the representatives left town muttering, "Not in my city or state." This was especially effective in those states which could provide stiff competition for Atlantic City, namely Pennsylvania, New York, Connecticut, Maryland, as well as the District of Columbia. Infighting among the casinos themselves led to the dissolution of the association.

ABSCAM

This was the most serious of the scandals Atlantic City had to endure. The federal government set up an influence-peddling "sting operation." Their targets were elected officials on all levels and anyone else they could involve. Posing as Arab sheikhs, they offered bribes to obtain influence in smoothing the way for their corporations during the licensure process. They were successful in their bribery attempts. When the smoke cleared, U.S. Senator Harrison Williams from New Jersey and Mayor Michael Matthews of Atlantic City were among those indicted. The New Jersey Legislature responded by appointing a new by-the-book Casino Control Commission. Their inflexibility, although understandable, probably set back ten years commission–casino operator relations.

Atlantic City Government

The city government of Atlantic City was totally unprepared for the advent of gaming. I will reiterate that *no one* expected gaming in

Atlantic City to be as successful as it has become. A succession of inept, and sometimes corrupt, politicians kept Atlantic City from realizing its growth potential. One needs to look no further than the Casino Redevelopment Authority as the classic example. Part of the enabling legislation established a fund to which all of the casinos would contribute. This fund was to be controlled by the Casino Redevelopment Authority. For the first six years of the fund's existence, 100 percent of the fund was to be earmarked for urban redevelopment in Atlantic City. Other cities in New Jersey were eligible for funding during the seventh year. Projects were to be submitted to the authority for approval, and money for the project would come from the fund. To make a long story short, only one project was submitted and funded during this six-year exclusivity. Infighting in the city council and lack of leadership from the mayor's office were largely responsible for this wasted opportunity. Only in the past few years has Atlantic City started to realize the promises made by the Committee to Rebuild Atlantic City in the 1970s.

Playboy

The Playboy casino started with such bright prospects, only to suffer an ignominious end: receivership. Playboy was elegant yet naughty, an evoker of hedonistic fantasies, a catalyst of the sexual revolution, and an extremely successful casino in England. A "natural" for the Atlantic City Boardwalk, Playboy planned to bring their very successful British formula to the United States. Their executives modeled their property after the typical English casinos, gaming on three levels. The plan was to introduce European-style gaming to Atlantic City while inviting their best customers to experience gaming in the United States. All the training, facilities, and amenities were directed toward European gaming, with the Playboy touch. When a number of executives, key to the success of the plan, were not licensed by the Casino Control Commission just prior to opening, the plan began to fall apart. American customers were attracted to Playboy but were turned off by the three levels and the condescending manner of the European casino personnel. When Playboy CEO and founder Hugh Hefner admitted to bribing an official in New York State to obtain a liquor license for his Playboy

Club in New York City, the Casino Control Commission stripped him of his license. Playboy removed the name from the casino and it was reopened as the Atlantis by the Pritzker family. The name was an unfortunate choice; as with its namesake, the casino became another lost world. They brought in casino executives from Las Vegas, but they were unsuccessful in keeping Atlantis out of receivership, the only casino in the history of Atlantic City to suffer such a fate. Having worked at Playboy and followed its transitions with no little interest, it was disheartening to see it become a case study for Murphy's Law.

The Denial of a Gaming License for Hilton

One of the most respected gaming companies in the world was denied a license by the aforementioned by-the-book Casino Control Commission. Hilton was a company which had been actively courted by three different New Jersey governors; a company which had just completed construction of a $300-million facility; a company which had 3,000 employees eagerly waiting to open the facility; a company which the Division of Gaming Enforcement had recommended for licensure; and a company which had been cleared of a questionable relationship with a labor lawyer in Chicago. By a tie vote when a majority was required, the license was denied. The casino industry responded swiftly by vowing never to develop properties in Atlantic City. This has halted new casino development in the city for the past thirteen years. The Hilton Corporation has gained licensure since the merger with Bally's and now owns two properties on the Boardwalk, Bally's Park Place and the Atlantic City Hilton.

Economic Growth in Atlantic and Cape May Counties

Prior to the passage of the casino referendum, Atlantic and Cape May county residents were suffering through difficult economic times, with an average per capita income under $8,000 per annum. Tax ratables (properties used to establish tax base) were at an all-time low. Unemployment was rampant. Retail sales were only marginal, with income having to be made during the "season." Current per capita income is approaching $30,000 per annum. New housing starts are increasing in both counties, and new malls, restaurants, and businesses are changing the face of their landscape. Poverty has not been eliminated, but a diverse compendium of noncasino jobs is available for those who are willing to work. Attendance at schools and colleges is on the rise, since families are better able to afford personal enrichment programs, job skill upgrades, and their children's education.

The Trump Organization

No one owns more nor has had the staying power of Donald Trump. Three properties carry the Trump name: Trump Plaza, which includes the former Playboy/Atlantis casino, renamed Trump Regency; Trump Marina, formerly the Atlantic City Hilton/Trump Castle; and the Trump Taj Mahal. The Trump organization has had a roller-coaster existence in Atlantic City. From the "king of Atlantic City" to eminent financial insolvency to the "comeback kid," from the legendary battles with Bally's and Steve Wynn to his legendary battle with Ivana at the Castle to the battle with Steve Wynn's anticipated return to Atlantic City, Donald Trump always seems to not only survive but flourish. One casino executive, who shall remain nameless, said that Donald Trump typifies the casino industry in the Northeast—tough, aggressive, and, above all, a survivor.

THE FUTURE

Atlantic City is currently the number two gaming market in the United States. It may never attain the number one status currently held by Nevada. It is, however, the top destination resort in the United States and has been for the past three years. With 25 percent of the population of the United States living within a 300-mile radius, unless a mass migration occurs, the outlook is bright. Competition is springing up in surrounding states, but major casino companies such as Mirage, MGM, and Circus Circus read the same demographic reports, which show that Atlantic City's 32 million visitors averaged four trips per year, so, in reality, only 8 million different visitors were attracted. That leaves plenty of new visitors to attract. There is an old adage in real estate: the most important asset is location! location! location! Atlantic City has that. It also has less competition than the myriad of casinos in Las Vegas.

SUMMARY

Atlantic City started gaming out of necessity—economic necessity. It has far exceeded even the wildest expectations of the Committee to Rebuild Atlantic City. The fact that the city and state were ill prepared to deal with the phenomenal success is not the fault of the "experiment," neither is the picture entirely positive. It has taken nearly twenty years for implied and promised benefits to begin to develop in the city. State law forbids casino personnel from holding a position in or influencing local government. So the casino industry, with its wealth of management talent, is precluded from assisting the city in solving problems. Atlantic City has found, as have other cities with successful corporate citizens, that having a lot of money does not ameliorate the problem. In fact, in many cases, it only makes matters worse.

For many of the citizens of Atlantic and Cape May counties, their lot has improved. For some, it has not. For others, it may have become worse. Casino gaming is not a panacea. Living in these counties during the time that progaming presentations were made— and I attended quite a few town meetings—I never heard claims that were not met. I will tell you that the expectations of many of my neighbors could never be met. A big business has come to South Jersey, replete with all of the positives and negatives inherent to such a business.

I view the Atlantic City experiment as a "work in progress."

Chapter 3

History, Development, and Legislation of Native American Casino Gaming

William N. Thompson

Gambling in Native American casinos commands 25 percent of all winnings from casino gambling in the United States. There are 281 gaming facilities on reservation lands in thirty-two states; most offer casino games. These facilities produced winnings of $5.4 billion in 1996. Of this amount, $4.7 billion was won at casino gaming. A large share of the revenues go to pay the salaries of approximately 100,000 individuals.

Table 3.1 shows the number of facilities offering casino-style games located in each state, along with numbers of employees, table games, and machine games. Overall, there are 160 casino facilities in twenty-three states. They have 94,500 employees, and they collectively offer gaming on 89,313 machines and at 5,126 tables.

Several of the Native American casinos are as large as any on the Las Vegas Strip. Indeed, one, the Mashantucket Pequot casino (called Foxwoods) at Ledyard, Connecticut, is the largest casino in the world. It has facilities with nearly 250,000 square feet of gambling space, over 5,500 slot machines, and 200 table games as well as a bingo hall. It is estimated that the casino wins over $1 billion each year from its customers—more than twice the winnings of the premier Las Vegas casinos.

NATIVE POPULATIONS: SOME UNHAPPY PERSPECTIVES

The history of Native American nations has not been a happy one, especially since the time of contact between the nations and the conquistadors, explorers, and settlers from the European continent.

TABLE 3.1. Native American Facilities in Each State

State	Number of Employees	Tables	Machines	Facilities
Arizona	7,394	273	6,271	16
California	12,041	1,093	14,961	28
Colorado	460	21	597	2
Connecticut	16,287	492	7,858	2
Florida	1,533	106	1,285	4
Idaho	200	0	480	1
Iowa	1,549	78	2,444	3
Louisiana	4,350	148	4,547	3
Michigan	7,018	313	9,167	13
Minnesota	12,518	465	13,198	16
Mississippi	2,000	96	2,800	1
Montana	115	0	291	4
Nebraska	130	4	116	1
Nevada	525	21	751	1
New Mexico	4,355	190	4,416	12
New York	2,000	148	1,000	1
North Carolina	180	0	874	1
North Dakota	1,073	61	1,390	4
Oregon	3,075	111	3,091	6
South Dakota	1,489	91	1,910	9
Texas	360	32	210	1
Washington	8,251	552	1,578	16
Wisconsin	7,597	831	10,078	15
Totals	94,500	5,126	89,313	160

Source: Jensen (1997).

Note: This is not an official listing. There is also some class III gaming in Kansas. Not all the casinos listed above are operating under approved negotiated Class III compacts.

There were once over 500 sovereign Native American nations, and they occupied lands expanding over the entire North American continent. It has been estimated that their numbers were as few as two million or as many as 15 million at the time of contact on the lands that are now the United States. The numbers decreased to under 200,000 at the beginning of the twentieth century. National policies of assimilation sought to eliminate the tribal identities of the peoples. Lands were taken from the nations by various means, often devious, and the people were pushed onto reservations, which in turn were reduced in size as non-native peoples sought to control all the productive lands of the continent. Nonetheless, the native peoples have persisted, and today they are poised to restore many of the conditions of sovereignty and self-reliance that they had when Europeans first came to America. Gaming is the most important tool that they have in their quest for national renewal.

The general U.S. Census reported that Native Americans numbered 1,959,234 in 1990 (Bureau of the Census, 1993). This number included both Alaskan and Hawaiian natives. Native Americans represent just under 1 percent of the total population (248.7 million). Nearly 35 percent live on native nation trust lands, called reservations.

In the forty-eight contiguous states, approximately 325 tribes have trust lands. In addition, Alaska has over 200 native communities; however, these communities do not have the same legal status as the reservations of the forty-eight states. No native trust lands exist in Hawaii. The reservation lands are found in thirty-three states (Thompson, 1996).

The current Native American lands consist of over 54 million acres, or approximately 90,000 square miles. This is comparable to the land area of Utah and represents about 2.5 percent of the land base of the United States (Hirschfelder and Kreipe de Montano, 1993).

The history of nation-breaking policies pursued by the United States against native peoples has taken its toll. At the beginning of this decade, Native American peoples were collectively the poorest ethnic group within U.S. borders. The Census Bureau reported that in 1990, 27 percent of native families were living below the poverty line, compared to 10 percent of all families in the United States. The U.S. Census reported Native American median family income was $21,750, compared to $32,225 for the total population, and over 20 percent of the reservation families lacked plumbing facilities (Bureau of the Census, 1993).

The poverty conditions of Native American life are related to education and employment characteristics. Native peoples' educational levels were much lower than national averages. For Native Americans living on reservations, the proportion of high school (or higher) graduates was only 54 percent, compared to 75 percent for the general population over age twenty-four (Bureau of the Census, 1993).

The Bureau of Labor Statistics reported that the 1991 unemployment rate among Native Americans was 45 percent. The overall American population "suffered" an 8 percent rate. On some reservations, the number of unemployed adults exceeded 80 percent (Hirschfelder and Kreipe de Montano, 1993).

Native Americans are much more likely to die young, with 37 percent dying before age forty-five, compared to 12 percent of the total population. Deaths also are more likely to result from violent actions. Moreover, certain diseases take a greater toll on native peoples. The rate of death from diabetes is 2.6 times the rate for non-natives; from tuberculous, five times as great. Liver disease is three times as likely to claim native peoples, and deaths directly attributable to alcoholism are five times more likely than among the general population of the United States (Hirschfelder and Kreipe de Montano, 1993; Utter, 1993).

PROMOTING TRIBAL SELF-SUFFICIENCY: THE PROMISE

The direction of federal policy regarding native peoples took a decided turn in the 1960s, as the administrations of Presidents John F. Kennedy, Lyndon Johnson, and Richard Nixon all advanced initiatives calling for self-sufficiency and autonomy for native peoples. Most important, the policy thrust recognized that the people should have their cultures and identity preserved and that they should not be forced into programs of assimilation with the general non-native populations.

The 1961 Area Redevelopment Administration Act allowed Native Americans to buy lands and facilities for industrial and commercial use. The notion that the lands of the Nations could expand was a unique departure from Euro-American policies dating back to 1492. The message conveyed was that Native Americans could and should develop their natural resources.

When Lyndon Johnson assumed the presidency, he proposed a new policy that would erase "old attitudes of paternalism" and promote "partnership self-help." Johnson stressed the need for Native American leadership and involvement with the federal government to improve health, education, economic growth, and strength of community (Johnson, 1969; Cohen, 1982).

President Richard Nixon took the self-determination concept and defined it as "progress through participation." He proposed that tribes control their own schools and direct the use of funds given them by the federal government. An Indian Education Act was passed in 1972, and the Indian Financing Act was passed in 1974, providing funding mechanisms for Native American business ventures (Prucha, 1990).

The Indian Self-Determination and Educational Assistance Act was passed in 1975 soon after Nixon left office. The Jimmy Carter administration also oversaw the passage in 1978 of the American Indian Religious Freedom Act, the Tribally Controlled Community College Assistance Act, and the Indian Child Welfare Act. Native American cultural autonomy was further recognized with the Archaeological Resources Protection Act of 1979 (Prucha, 1990).

Presidents Ronald Reagan and George Bush also endorsed the notion of native self-reliance. Nevertheless, the bottom line of three decades of federal programs "for" Native Americans was seen in the statistics reported at the beginning of the 1990s. Whatever had been tried simply did not work—at least in a way that impacted native communities nationwide in positive ways. Reservations were still lacking basic amenities such as electricity, plumbing, water, adequate housing, and medical care. Very little economic development had occurred, an essential element in achieving any measure of self-sufficiency for native peoples (Thompson, 1996).

However, by the beginning of the 1990s, a new element had asserted its presence. It did not come about by any designed federal program; it came about because some native tribes explored an opportunity that was generated from their special status as political units within the fabric of the federal system of the United States of America.

GAMING: BEGINNING TO REALIZE THE PROMISE

Although Native Americans had traditionally participated in various kinds of games that included prizes and could be considered gambling activities, commercial gaming operations were not found on reservations until very recently. Not unrelated is that very few commercial gambling operations were anywhere until very recently. However, with the restoration of government-sponsored lotteries in the 1960s, the public began to demand the operation of games to benefit charities of one kind or another. Soon many states were permitting churches and other nonprofit groups to conduct bingo and other lower-stakes games to raise revenues.

In the 1970s, many Native American tribes began to participate in charity gaming in accordance with state rules regarding how the games would be played and the types of prizes that could be offered. Then, in 1978, the Florida Seminole Nation decided to do things differently at their bingo hall. Faced with competition from other charities, they threw aside the state's prize limits and began a high-stakes game with prizes in the tens of thousands of dollars. Players flocked to the Miami suburb of Hollywood where the Seminole bingo hall was located. Rival bingo games run by charitable groups took a major hit. Their sponsors were not amused.

Nor were state and local government officials. The Broward County sheriff, Robert Butterworth, filed criminal charges and sought to close down the Seminole bingo game. His actions led to a series of law cases, culminating in the 1981 approval of games without state limits by a federal court of appeals (*Seminole Tribe of Florida v. Butterworth*, 1981). In 1982, the U.S. Supreme Court refused to review the ruling (*Seminole Tribe of Florida v. Butterworth*, 1982). Key to the case was that in Florida, bingo was legal and could be played. The tribes were only violating the manner in which the games were played.

Tribes across the United States took notice of the gaming activities and especially of legal cases that affirmed the special status tribes enjoyed in this realm of economic enterprise. Gaming began to appear on most of the reservations in America. However, except for internal tribal regulations, there was almost no supervision of the gaming activities. And the activities involved large sums of money.

EFFORTS TO REGULATE NATIVE AMERICAN GAMING

Problems arise when there is little independent regulation of large-scale gaming. In regard to Native American bingo games, some cases revealed that non-Indian managers were setting up games and taking the bulk of the revenues. Members of organized crime families made their presence felt on some reservations. Also, some unscrupulous tribal members used gaming for personal advantages in ways adverse to their tribe's interests. As the 1980s progressed, the need for independent oversight of Native American gaming was recognized. Congress began to explore the manner in which the gaming could be regulated.

The first bills to regulate tribal gaming were introduced in 1984. Hearings were held over the next three years; however, no consensus developed over the manner of regulation that should be set into place. State governments wanted federal authorization for them to oversee the regulation or, alternatively, to have federal regulations that incorporated all the state rules on non-native gaming. The tribes opposed the notion of any state control over their gaming. An impasse ensued.

The impasse could not be resolved easily because during this same time, a case was wending its way to the U.S. Supreme Court. The case essentially was designed to gain a review of the earlier Florida case. State interests were optimistic that the Court would overturn the earlier ruling and allow state rules on gaming to apply to the tribes. They were not about to make any compromises in Congress while the case was pending. The tribes, on the other hand, were leaning toward concessions that would allow some federal regulation.

The political formula changed when, in February 1987, the Court ruled in a 6-3 vote that the earlier decisions would stand—that states could not impose their civil regulations on Native American gaming operations. Moreover, the Court endorsed gaming as being consistent with federal policies designed to promote self-sufficiency for tribes. They pointed out that the Bureau of Indian Affairs had actually given grants for construction of some gaming facilities and that gaming revenues "provide the sole source of revenues for the operation of tribal governments, and the provision of tribal services. They also are major sources of employment on the reservations." The Court added, "self-determination and economic development are not within reach if the Tribes cannot raise revenues and provide employment for their members. The Tribes' interests obviously parallel the federal interests" (*California v. Cabazon Band of Mission Indians,* 1987).

The Court added that regulation by any nontribal entity could take place only if a specific act of Congress called for such measures. The states besieged members of Congress to act. Tribal interests were less inclined to endorse congressional action, as the status quo was quite acceptable to them. However, they agreed to a compromise. The Indian Gaming Regulatory Act (IGRA) was passed and signed into law by President Reagan on October 7, 1988 (IGRA, 1988).

Two tribes, the Minnesota Red Lake Band of Chippewa and the Mescalero Apache Tribe of New Mexico, immediately challenged the constitutionality of the act, claiming that it was an infringement upon their sovereignty. However, federal courts denied their claim, and the Supreme Court refused to hear their appeal (*Red Lake Band v. Swimmer,* 1990). That was not the end to constitutional challenges to the act, however.

THE INDIAN GAMING REGULATORY ACT OF 1988

Overview of the Act

Congress identified the purpose of the act as establishing a "statutory basis for the operation of gaming by Indian tribes as a means of promoting tribal economic development, self-sufficiency, and strong tribal governments." Congress further recognized the need to shield tribal interests from organized crime and to ensure that tribal members received the gaming revenues.

The IGRA established a three-member National Indian Gaming Commission. Two of the members were Native Americans. The commission was empowered to regulate bingo-type games on reservations and to promulgate general rules for Native American gaming pertaining to contracts with outside companies. Casino-type gaming was to be regulated in accordance with rules established in negotiations between the tribes and the state governments. If the states refused to negotiate in good faith, they could be mandated to do so by federal courts.

Starting in 1989, many court mandates prompted states to enter into negotiations allowing casino gaming on reservations. However, on March 27, 1996, in a 5-4 vote, the U.S. Supreme Court ruled that the provision of the act which allowed tribes to sue states in federal courts over the lack of good faith negotiations was unconstitutional because of the Eleventh Amendment. The amendment implies that states are sovereign units and cannot be sued in federal courts except by other states, foreign countries, or the federal government.

The Court did not rule the entire act unconstitutional, nor did the Court address how negotiation impasses would be resolved in the future—whether states could simply say "no" to tribes, or whether tribes could go to the secretary of the interior for relief.

Classes of Gaming

The IGRA delineated three classes of gaming. Class I gaming consists of small prize games between tribal members. It also consists of games traditionally played by tribes in ceremonies or celebrations. These activities are regulated entirely by the tribes. No issues have arisen over Class I games since the passage of the act.

Class II gaming encompasses bingo in its various forms, as well as pull-tab cards, punch boards, and tip jars. Certain card games such as poker also are included as long as the games are nonbanking, that is, do not involve bets between the casino and the player, rather only bets among players.

In four specific states—Michigan, North Dakota, South Dakota, and Washington—banked card games, specifically blackjack games, were to be regulated as Class II games if the games were played in the tribal casinos before the act passed. Elsewhere, blackjack and other banked card games were to be regulated as Class III games.

Tribes can conduct Class II gaming as long as the game involved is permitted in the state to be played "for any purpose, by any person, organization or entity." The tribe must first pass an ordinance to offer Class II games. The ordinance must be approved by the commission chairman, and the commission then conducts background investigations on the gaming facility and its employees.

The commission regulates the gaming for a period of three years, after which the tribe can apply for permission to self-regulate the Class II games. Most tribes have successfully won permission for self-regulation. The permission can be revoked if the commission believes that the self-regulation efforts are inadequate. While the commission regulates the gaming, it may assess the tribes a fee for the cost involved.

Class III gaming consists of all forms of gaming not covered by Class I and Class II definitions. Basically, the Class III category covers all casino-banked games, including blackjack, baccarat, roulette, craps, and all slot machines. Class III also includes lottery games as conducted by state governments and pari-mutuel racing wagers. As with Class II games, the Class III games may be played only if the tribe has an ordinance permitting them and if the games are permitted "for any purpose, by any person, organization or entity" in the state where the tribal facility is located.

Also, for Class III gaming to be permitted, the tribe must enter into a compact with the state. The compact will provide a detailed provision on games allowed in the facility, the manner of offering the games, and the regulatory structures for oversight of the games. If a state refused to enter into negotiations in good faith for Class III games, the tribe was authorized to seek federal court mandates for negotiations. After the mandates were issued, if the state continued to refuse to negotiate, the court could appoint a mediator, who would be empowered to select a proposed compact offered by either the tribe or the state. The secretary of the interior would then certify the compact as being in force.

The complications placed upon the process by the Supreme Court's ruling that the tribes could not seek relief in federal courts if the states refused to negotiate in good faith linger. Secretary of the Interior Bruce Babbitt has sought comments on a procedure that would allow the tribes and states to directly present their proposed compacts to the secretary's office for approval, in effect, bypassing the court process altogether. Such a procedure may be attempted in the near future, but the concern is whether the secretary would or legally could force a compact upon an unwilling participant in the process—be that a tribe or state.

Management Contracts

Tribes may negotiate with nontribal members to run gambling operations on their lands. Outside management groups may not receive more than 30 percent of the net proceeds of the gaming operations—Class II or Class III. Their portion may be increased to 40 percent if they make major capital investments for the gaming facilities. The 30 percent share may be paid for up to five years. The agreements may be renewed. If the agreement involves capital investments, an amount up to 40 percent may be paid to the outside company for up to seven years.

Enforcement, Taxation, and Revenues

The Class III compacts may provide very specific authority for tribal and nontribal (whether county, city, or state) law enforcement agencies to supervise and enforce provisions of the gaming agreements. Without such authority, all enforcement activities regarding gaming on Indian lands remains in the hands of the tribal government and the federal government. In other words, without a compact, even if tribes are permitting games the state believes to be Class III games, the state cannot enforce the law. The state must wait for federal district attorneys and marshals to make all enforcement actions. State governments may not tax the native gaming facilities. However, as with the federal government, the state may charge the tribes sums of money to cover the actual costs of state regulation of the facilities.

The tribe's share of net revenues must go for tribal purposes. If the tribe shows that it is meeting its obligations to provide for the social welfare of its members, it may authorize up to 40 percent to go to individual members in a per capita distribution. One small Minnesota tribe has given its members as much as $700,000 each as their annual share of gaming proceeds.

Implementation Hurdles

The IGRA has many vague qualities. Much difficulty has arisen over the compact process for negotiating tribal-state agreements on

Class III gaming. Congress was happy to come upon this solution, as it transfers much of the difficult decision making over to the tribes, the states, and, for several years, the federal courts. The compacting process was the key compromise that permitted the act to win majority support in both houses of Congress (Thompson and Dever, 1997).

One major difficulty is the question of just who negotiates for the state. Perhaps Congress assumed the governor would negotiate, but that was not made clear in IGRA. In Kansas and New Mexico, Governors Joan Finney and Gary Johnson, respectively, negotiated in good faith and signed agreements with tribes. In the case of New Mexico, Secretary of the Interior Bruce Babbitt actually ratified an agreement and declared it to be in force. Tribal casinos were built and opened. After the agreements were made in each state, other state officials claimed that they were void because state procedures were violated. A state court in New Mexico actually voided the agreement that was approved by the secretary of the interior in accordance with IGRA—the national law. The ultimate irony of states nullifying federal action was avoided, as a new compact was ultimately signed according to state procedures in both states.

Compacts in many states reached an impasse over the issue of slot machines. The impasse remains in California. Governor Pete Wilson has refused to sign an agreement for slot machines on native lands; however, in excess of 10,000 machines are in operation. Arguments over whether California permitted machines for any purpose were complicated when the state lottery began using machines for its keno games. Later, the state courts ruled that the lottery (a government agency) was violating California law by having machines. While the tribes and governor argued, federal officials in the Justice Department played cat-and-mouse games over enforcement activities. Although California might be obligated to negotiate compacts, it was clear that, without compacts, the machines were illegal. Nonetheless, no federal official moved to close them down. Periodically, they issued warnings that the machines must be stopped by a certain date. Then the dates were extended. At one point, they said the illegal machines could continue operation only if 16 percent of them were removed. Why 16 percent? No one knew.

As mentioned, the most successful Native American casino is in Ledyard, Connecticut. Governor Lowell Weicker had refused to negotiate agreements, claiming casino games were illegal in the state. However, the state did permit table games for charities on special "Las Vegas Nights." The tribe won a court mandate ordering the governor to negotiate. He refused. A mediator was appointed. The tribe and governor both submitted proposed compacts. The governor's proposal actually included provisions for allowing table games. The mediator selected the governor's proposal. Then the state appealed the selection, asking the secretary of the interior to reject its own proposal. The secretary of the interior instead signed the proposal, and it became the compact (*Mashantucket Pequot v. Connecticut*, 1990).

Clearly, the state of Connecticut did not permit anyone to have slot machines. Also, the IGRA clearly says states cannot tax tribal gaming. Nonetheless, in 1993, the state and its governor reached a "side agreement" with the tribes to allow them to have as many slot machines as they wanted, providing they paid the state 25 percent of the revenue from the machines. The agreement was never approved by the secretary of the interior (how could it be, since it was patently illegal?), but the casino offers slot machines—5,500 of them—for its customers. The 25 percent tax was called a monopoly fee. It would go to the state only as long as the Mashantucket Pequots had a monopoly on the machines (how could they possibly be permitted to others under the circumstances?). The monopoly ended in 1996 when a second tribe opened a casino, and the 25 percent share was renegotiated with the governor's office, without the approval of federal authorities. The state of Connecticut received approximately $160 million a year as its share of the slot revenues.

In Minnesota, Governor Arne Carlson refused to negotiate an agreement for table games. However, the tribe persuaded the federal court authorities that a law allowing social gaming in homes among friends constituted permitted gaming. When ordered to negotiate, the governor signed an agreement allowing blackjack in tribal casinos. Next, they asked for slot machines on the basis that recreational slots were in taverns and winners could win free new games. The governor signed an agreement to allow video gaming machines.

In Wisconsin, a strange series of events found tribes and Governor Tommy Thompson at an impasse. Federal Judge Barbara Crabb ordered that the state allow the tribes to have casinos. No one else in the state was permitted to have any casino games. However, in the past, casino gaming had been outlawed on the basis of a state constitutional provision banning lotteries. But in April 1987, state voters removed the constitutional ban. The legislature then created a state lottery authority and authorized it to offer games of consideration, chance, and prize—a general definition that covers almost all casino games. The lottery only offered regular lottery-type games, but Judge Crabb ruled that the statute was written to permit casino games if the lottery desired to have them (*Lac du Flambeau Band v. Wisconsin*, 1991).

She ordered the governor to negotiate an agreement allowing casino games. He promptly appealed the decision. Almost as promptly, he offered to let the tribes have machines and blackjack as the Minnesota casinos had. The 1993 compacts had a five-year limit. Most of the tribes agreed, and casinos began in earnest on the Wisconsin reservation. The court appeal lapsed when the state did not meet certain filing deadlines. Now the issue is, what will happen in 1998? After the governor signed the agreement, the voters plugged the "lottery loophole." Lotteries were defined very specifically to be traditional lotteries, and just as specifically, all casino-type games were banned. The governor is the same individual who negotiated agreements before. Can he renew the agreements? Can he refuse to do so? Must he refuse to allow native casino gaming? Can the secretary of the interior approve a new agreement for casino games if they are so clearly banned by state law?

THE FUTURE OF NATIVE AMERICAN GAMING

Many questions remain, making the policy arena for Native American gambling a puzzling one. A new factor has come into the process since it first began. Many Native American tribes are now very powerful players in the political process. The Mashantucket Pequots have a very active lobbying force in Washington, DC. They gave considerable amounts to many political candidates in both parties. They were among the leading three contributors to President Clinton's reelection campaign. The Sault St. Marie tribe in Michigan was the leading contributor in state elections in 1996. This new power arises out of tribal resources gained from gaming operations. The money is focused upon policymakers who have to consider questions involving Native American gaming. It can be safely concluded that Native American gaming is here to stay for quite a while.

THE BOTTOM LINE: DOES GAMING HELP OR NOT?

The Positive Answer

In assessing how the goals of Native American gaming have been met, or are being met, we can look at several areas (Thompson and Dever, 1997).

Social advantages. Money from gaming activities on native lands has been placed into food, housing, and health programs that were suffering severe budget cuts at the hands of federal authorities (Raymond James Associates, 1992). Gaming revenues are used for abuse treatment and also prevention programs (Woods, 1993).

Gaming has brought jobs to Native Americans and others—over 100,000 of them. The jobs have given Nation members an incentive to return to their homelands and renew their native nationalism. The jobs have offered career hopes as well, training members for advancement.

Nongaming enterprise. Money from gaming opportunities has been invested in nongaming enterprise to gain a diversity of employment and to secure a stable economic basis for the future. Arnold Sowmick, the late chief of the 900-member Saginaw Chippewa Tribe in Mt. Pleasant, Michigan, indicated that, with gaming, his Nation is "branching into manufacturing" and other ventures. "It's a whole new ballgame. . . . You can see it all around, but where I like to look is at our young people. They're outgoing and confident and they present a positive image. It hasn't always been that way. . . . People will listen to us now who wouldn't before. That old saw about 'money talks' is true." He added that the Nation had gained credibility by demonstrating that they can operate businesses (BeVier, 1988, p. 1N).

The Oneida Casino of Wisconsin has used gaming money to construct a $10-million hotel, establish a "300-head cattle farm, an environmental testing laboratory, a printing company, a 32-acre shopping center, and several convenience stores" (Stanley and Spivak, 1992). The Minnesota Mille Lacs tribe purchased a bank and formed the first native-owned bank holding company in the United States (Vinge, 1996).

The money made possible by gaming has allowed the First Nations to choose the direction of economic development. Before they had the opportunity to secure gaming funds, the Nations felt pressured to accept any economic opportunity. Accordingly, they were enticed to have their lands strip-mined and gutted of mineral resources, grazed or timbered in nonecological manners, polluted with garbage and industrial wastes. Efforts have even been made to use the lands as dumping grounds for nuclear waste materials (Richert and Barker, 1991). One Nation even seriously explored the prospects of having a brothel on their lands (Reaves, 1984).

Lance Hughes, Director of the Tahlequah, Oklahoma-based Native Americans for a Clean Environment, said that forty Nations across the United States had been approached by the waste disposal industry. "It's big money. It's the biggest money there is right now. . . . They pick on the poorest of the tribes" (Zizzo, 1991, p. 27-A).

Educational opportunities. Gaming money gives Native Americans greater educational opportunities and, with those, greater chances for training for a variety of economic opportunities. A Milwaukee, Wisconsin, bingo hall operated by the Potawatomi Nation of Crandon, Wisconsin, utilized funds for books, computers, new desks, a roof, remodeled halls, and plumbing for the Native American community school—where bake sales formerly were needed just to hold things together. The school serves the urban First Nation population of Milwaukee with both cultural and vocational education (Marchione, 1992). Several other gaming facilities devote profits to Nation educational functions.

Regaining native lands. Money allows Native Americans to quest for a return of their original land bases. The Mashantucket Pequots were, at the time of contact, a Nation of 13,000 thriving on a land area of 2,000 square miles. Contact was not kind to the Nation. Disease and massacres left the Nation with only 200 members and 213 acres of land. Gaming revenues have been utilized to hire archaeologists to help identify traditional lands. Thus far, the Nation has been able to purchase back 1,500 acres of the lost land (Carbone, 1992).

Cultural restoration. Native gaming funds have been focused upon cultural restoration activities. The Pequots plan to spend millions of dollars on a museum that will chronicle their history. Many other Nations are taking similar steps with gaming funds. Nations also are turning funds to educational programs to reestablish their languages.

Political power. As indicated earlier, the money from gaming has allowed Nations to assert all manner of legal issues in courts and in front of other policymakers. The costs of court cases on gaming negotiations have been secured in many cases from gaming operations. Native Americans now have powerful lobbying groups, and they are among the leading contributors to political campaigns (Christiansen, 1997).

Economic benefits. Economic power is directed at state and local government treasuries. The IGRA precludes state or local taxing of native gaming. However, with the wealth of gaming funds, tribes have brought several economic benefits to local and state governments. Employment of tribal members and others has resulted in reduced welfare rolls. Also, the employees of the gaming operations do pay taxes, as do people who have gained employment indirectly as a result of the gaming operations.

Equality. The IGRA has lent itself to an expansion of native sovereignty by requiring American state governments to deal one on one with the Nations on an equal basis. The decades and centuries of subordination of the Nations to the political power wishes of the states may be coming to an end, once and for all.

Some Other Answers

The benefits of gaming, however, do not come without some disadvantages (Thompson and Dever, 1997).

Exploitation. Native gaming presents new opportunities for exploitation. If outsiders are not closely watched and guarded against, they can become a force that will destroy the gaming opportunity for the tribes.

One of several examples of the white man's greed in native gaming was reported by Lynn Waddell of the *Las Vegas Sun:*

> They own a casino, but have no control over who runs it. They watch thousands of people pour coins into their slot machines, but never see a quarter roll their way. They gave $15 million to a developer to build a gambling hall that a county assessor values at $188,000. (Waddell, 1993, p. D-5)
>
> Tribal members claim that they "don't know how much the casino cost" or where "the money goes." Tribal leaders secretly entered into agreements with unscrupulous entrepreneurs. (Waddell, 1993, p. D-5)

Criminal activity. Native Americans must be aware that any gaming enterprise can be a magnet for scam artists and thieves of all sorts. The crooks will work outside of the gaming halls and inside too—as employees, if given the opportunity, or as players. The answer to this problem is control. However, expressions heard at several gaming conferences that there is no crime at native gaming facilities should be a red flag for those concerned about sovereignty. If members of tribes ever think they are immune from criminal activities, they may relax controls, and they will be hurt. Although the overall record of native gaming is good, some evidence suggests that thievery has occurred at gaming facilities (Waldman, 1992).

Less sovereignty. Gaming operations can mean less sovereignty if the tribes, in their quest for economic resources, willingly yield authority to nontribal governments. Many tribes vigorously opposed federal legislation in 1952 that allowed state police officials to have jurisdiction on their lands in six states. Now negotiated agreements provide the same access for outsiders.

Gaming operations can tear apart tribal cultures and thereby block efforts to build up sovereignty. Several Nations have resisted gaming operations because gambling itself violates their religious beliefs and the operations would be seen as a desecration of their lands. Others share those attitudes but allow the gambling anyway because they desire the economic rewards.

Gaming also opens up tribal lands to outsiders. After all, successful gaming requires that thousands of outsiders enter the lands to spend their money. But, as they come, they also bring their society with them. They come in buses and automobiles that cause traffic congestion and pollution. They also bring drinking and drug abuse behaviors. And they engage in gambling. These behaviors may serve as model behaviors for members of native Nations, especially the young, if the behaviors are endorsed as part of tribal enterprise. Yet these are not the behaviors that the Nations desire their members to have.

Gaming jobs may not be the best building blocks for sovereignty. Many of the jobs do not require intensive training—which may be good; however, the skills of the jobs may not be readily transferrable. Unless gaming revenues are utilized to develop a diversified economic base, the concentration on gaming jobs may create trained incapacities for tribal members. At some future time, when gaming may not be a viable enterprise, their members will not be able to compete for other jobs or help in the creation of other enterprises.

Internal divisiveness. Although gaming operations have brought native peoples together and improved their political functioning abilities, gaming also has torn some tribes apart. It can be a divisive issue, as many members of Nations oppose the gaming for a variety of reasons—economic, social, and cultural. The Meskwaki Nation of Tama, Iowa, saw the issue of gaming create considerable division among their people in the 1980s. A series of votes had to be taken before an ordinance for bingo was approved. Traditional methods of deciding matters on a consensual basis had to yield to Euro-American methods of resolving questions by majority rule. Then there was considerable agony over how the bingo hall was being managed and how the money was accounted for. Divisive debate was renewed when the Nation considered introducing slot machines and casino games to the facility (Erb, 1991).

Another tribe found that members who lived in the district close to major highway access points wished to separate and form a new reservation because they could reap a greater share of the casino benefits by being a smaller reservation. The collective good was being set aside in their thinking because gaming had placed a financial opportunity in front of them.

Much internal divisiveness regarding gaming in the Nations centers around the issue of how to distribute the gaming profits. If Nations neglect collective social concerns—education, health, housing, substance abuse—and instead direct the bulk of the revenues to per capita distribution programs, they may not be building sovereignty. Indeed, in some cases, they could be encouraging unemployment and other personal values antithetical to the notions of true self-determination. The issue of per capita distributions also engenders divisions over just who is included or should be included in the distribution (Young, 1991; Trautman, 1992).

Outsider resentment. Native gaming can invite a backlash. Outsiders have a five-century track record of taking any benefit they see in the hands of native peoples. The outsiders are generally possession oriented and can be quite jealous of others who have possessions. Gaming competitors do not like the position of sovereignty that permits tribes certain gambling advantages. Success in native gaming has brought out, and will continue to bring out, those who wish to strip away the advantages achieved with new litigation and new federal legislation. In the long run, they may be successful if tribes do not recognize the advantages of building good relations with their outside neighbors.

REFERENCES

BeVier, T. (1988, January 17). Gambling spurs business for state tribes. *The Detroit News*, pp. 1N-2N.

Bureau of the Census (1993). *We the Native Americans.* Washington, DC: Author.

California v. Cabazon Band of Mission Indians (1987). 480 U.S. 202.

Carbone, G. (1992, February 9). Economic, cultural stakes high in Conn.: Tribe's casino opening. *The Providence Journal Bulletin* (Providence, RI), pp. A1, A8.

Christiansen, E. (1997). U.S. gaming faces new growth challenges. *International Gaming and Wagering Business* (Supplement, August).

Cohen, F. (1982). *Handbook of federal Indian law* (Second edition). Charlottesville, VA: The Michie Company.

Erb (1991, March 3). Gambling is risky business for some tribes. *Des Moines Register*, p. 6B.

Hirschfelder, A. and Kreipe de Montano, M. (1993). *The Native American almanac: A portrait of Native America today.* New York: Prentice Hall.

Indian Gaming Regulatory Act (IGRA) (1988), U.S. Statutes at Large. §102: 2467ff (passed October 17).

Jensen, L. (1997, July). Guide to North American casinos. *Casino Executive 3*(7), 39-69.

Johnson, L.B. (1969). *1968-1969 public papers, Part I.* Washington, DC: U.S. Government Printing Office.

Lac du Flambeau Band v. Wisconsin (1991), 770 F. Supp. 480.

Marchione, M. (1992, March 3). Indian school thrives on bingo cash. *The Waukesha Journal* (Milwaukee, WI), pp. 1, 5.

Mashantucket Pequot v. Connecticut (1990), 737 F. Supp. 169 (Dist. Ct. Conn).

Prucha, F.P. (1990). *Documents of United States Indian policy.* Lincoln, NE: University of Nebraska Press.

Raymond James Associates (1992, October 28). *Native American casino gaming—A national perspective.* St. Petersburg, FL: Author.

Reaves, J.A. (1984, February 25). Paiutes pin hopes of better economy on brothel issue. *Las Vegas Review Journal*, p. 10B.

Red Lake Band v. Swimmer (1990), 740 F. Supp. 9.

Richert, K. and Barker, R. (1991, February 6). Collision course: Anders tribes try to block nuclear waste. *Post Register* (Idaho Falls, ID), pp. A1, A4.

Seminole Tribe of Florida v. Butterworth (1981), 658 F. 2d. 310.

Seminole Tribe of Florida v. Butterworth (1982), 455 U.S. 1020.

Stanley, G. and Spivak, C. (1992, March 25). Gambling lifts tribes out of poverty. *Milwaukee Sentinel.*

Thompson, W. N. (1996). *Native American issues.* Santa Barbara, CA: ABC-Clio.

Thompson, W. N. and Dever, D. (1997). Gambling enterprise and the restoration of Native American sovereignty. In W. Eadington and J. Cornelius (Eds.), *Gambling: Public policies and the social sciences* (pp. 295-315). Reno, NV: Institute for the Study of Gambling, University of Nevada, Reno.

Trautman, M. (1992, March 1). Tribal rift threatens casino plans. *Argus Leader* (Sioux Falls, SD) pp. 1F, 2F.

Utter, J. (1993). *American Indians: Answers to today's questions.* Lake Ann, MI: National Woodlands.

Vinge, D. (1996). Native American economic development on selected reservations. *American Journal of Economics and Society, 55*(4), 427-442.

Waddell, L. (1993, August 29). Poor accountability troubles tribal casinos. *Las Vegas Sun*, p. D-5.

Waldman, H. (1992, May 6). Thievery shows its hand at new casino. *Hartford Courant* (Hartford, CT).

Woods, W. (1993, April 19). American Indians discover money is power. *Fortune, 127*(8), 137-138.

Young, S. (1991, May 1). Members living off reservation are losing out. *Argus Leader* (Sioux Falls, SD).

Zizzo, D. (1991, February 10). Tribes urged to beware of trash. *Daily Oklahoman* (Oklahoma City, OK), p. 27-A.

Chapter 4

History, Development, and Legislation of Riverboat and Land-Based Non-Native American Casino Gaming

Cathy H. C. Hsu

Riverboat casinos and land-based non-Native American casinos, excluding Las Vegas and Atlantic City, started in the late 1980s and have grown rapidly in the 1990s. Several reasons explain the rapid development common to some states. The reason most cited to rationalize gaming is economic development. In the 1980s, state governments were forced to absorb many costs that formerly were paid for by the federal government. Many states experienced budgetary shortfalls and shrinking revenue sources due to the decline of traditional industries such as agriculture and mining. Gaming was seen as a solution to provide the much needed employment opportunities and tax revenues.

The popularity of Native American casinos was a catalyst for the development of riverboat and other land-based casinos. The success of many Native American casinos indicated the acceptance of gaming by a large number of American people. Gaming tax, additional income and sales taxes, and increased property tax revenues local and state governments "could have" collected, if those were non-Native American casinos, prompted initial discussions on gaming legislation.

Regulations of gaming vary greatly among states, as do tax structure and revenue distribution. In addition, gaming was introduced by legislative initiative in some states and citizen initiative in others. This chapter provides an overview of the development and current regulations of gaming in states with riverboat and land-based non–Native American casinos. Tables 4.1 and 4.2 provide a summary of casino legislation and revenue collection and distribution, respectively, of various states for easy comparison and contrast. Figure 4.1 shows the locations of all riverboat and land-based casinos, excluding Las Vegas and Atlantic City.

RIVERBOATS

Riverboat gaming was prevalent in the 1880s on the Mississippi and Ohio Rivers. All states eventually banned all forms of gaming due to corruption and criminal activities. One hundred years later, most river communities use paddlewheelers as a tourist attraction to showcase their history and scenic vistas. Riverboats were the choice for gaming locations for several reasons. When state legislatures introduced gaming, riverboats seemed to be an "easier sale" than land-based locations because of the nostalgic and romantic feelings most people have about riverboats. People also have the perception that riverboat casinos are easier to control because of the limited space and restricted locations; therefore, it is possible to have a low-crime gaming environment that attracts respectable patrons. Residents were more at ease thinking their communities would not turn into a Las Vegas or Atlantic City overnight. In addition, development of riverboat casinos usually means the redevelopment of downtown and waterfront economy and infrastructure, which fit into many downtown revitalization projects (Harrah's Entertainment, Inc., 1996).

Currently, six midwestern and southern states have riverboat casinos. The riverboat gaming industry collectively has become the third largest gaming destination in the country, after Nevada and Atlantic City ("A Threat to Nevada?", 1993). The development and legislation of riverboat casinos in each state is summarized next.

Iowa

The farm crisis and economic recession in the early 1980s caused many heavy farm machinery manufacturers to close down or leave

TABLE 4.1. Casino Regulations of Various States

	Riverboat						Land-Based				
	IA	IL	MS	LA	MO	IN	SD	CO	LA	IA	MI
Year of legislation	1989	1990	1990	1991	1992	1993	1989	1990	1992	1994	1996
Year gaming began	1991	1991	1992	1993	1994	1995	1989	1991	—	1995	—
Bet limits	—	—	—	—	—	—	$5	$5	—	—	—
Loss limits	—	—	—	—	$500/cruise	—	—	—	—	—	—
Operating hours	24 hr	24 hr	24 hr	24 hr	24 hr	24 hr	24 hr	Closed 2-8 a.m.	24 hr	24 hr	24 hr
Min. slot machine payout	—	—	—	—	80%	—	80%	80%	—	—	—
Player credit	No	Yes	Yes	Yes	No	Yes	No	No	Yes	No	Yes
Min. gaming age	21	21	21	21	21	21	21	21	21	21	21
Min. employment age	18	18	21	21	18	18	21	21	21	18	18
Total licenses/casinos allowed	—	10/20	—	15/15	—	11/11	—	—	1/1	—	3/3
Max. percent of facility for gaming	—	—	—	60%	50%	—	—	35%	—	—	—
Max. square feet	—	—	—	30,000	—	—	—	—	—	—	—
Local referendum required	Yes	No	Yes	Yes	Yes	Yes	No	No	No	Yes	Yes
Cash wagering allowed	5¢, 25¢	No	Yes	No	No	No	Coins	Yes	No	5¢, 25¢	No
Type of vessel	Historic	Historic or cruise ship	—	Historic, new construction	Historic	Historic on Ohio River					

TABLE 4.2. State Casino Taxes, Fees, and Revenue Distribution

State	Taxes[a]	Fees[b]	Distribution
Riverboat			
Iowa	5% on first $1 million 10% on next $2 million 20% on all over $3 million	Admission fee of $5,666 per week per boat License fee of $5 per person capacity Distributor fee of $1,000 Manufacturer fee of $250	0.5% to city 0.5% to county 0.3% to Gamblers' Assistance Program Balance to the General Fund
Illinois	20%	Admission fee of $2 per passenger Owner fee of $25,000 initially, $5,000 thereafter Supplier fee of $5,000	$1 admission fee to municipality or county 25% to municipality or county Appropriation made by the legislature to the Dept. of Revenue and Dept. of State Police for administration and enforcement of the Riverboat Gambling Act Balance to the Education Assistance Fund
Indiana	20%	Admission fee of $3 per passenger License fee of $25,000 initially, $5,000 thereafter Supplier fee of $5,000 Occupational license fee set by commission	Varies by waterway; see text
Louisiana	15%	License fee of 3.5% plus $50,000 per vessel initially, $100,000 thereafter Permit fee to conduct racehorse wagering of $1,000 Manufacturer fee of $5,000 for slot machines; $2,500 for other gaming devices Supplier fee of $1,500 for gaming devices, $250 for suppliers of other than gaming devices or equipment Employee license fee of $100 per employee	1%, not to exceed $150,000, to the Compulsive and Problem Gaming Fund Taxes to General Fund Fees to Riverboat Gaming Enforcement Fund •Expense of the Riverboat Gaming Enforcement Division •Amount up to 1/7 of 3.5% license fee to the Riverboat Gaming Commission •Balance to the office of State Police

State	Taxes[a]	Fees[b]	Distribution
Riverboat (*continued*)			
Mississippi	4% on first $50,000 per month 6% on next $84,000 per month 8% on over $134,000 per month	License fee of $5,000 Device fee of $50-$4,800 per establishment, based on the number of games operated Distributor fee of $500 Manufacturer fee of $1,000	State General Fund, approx. 25% of which goes to a bond sinking fund for highway construction related to gaming
Missouri	20%	Admission fee of $2 per passenger License fee of $25,000 Supplier fee of $5,000 Occupation fee of $50	Taxes: • 10% to city or county • Balance to Gaming Proceeds for Education Fund Fees: • $1 admission fee and 10% of taxes to city or county • Administrative costs of Commission • $500,000 to cities and counties with matching fund • Balance to Veterans' Commission Capital Improvement Trust Fund until July 1, 2000 • Balance to State General Fund after July 1, 2000

TABLE 4.2 (continued)

State	Taxes[a]	Fees[b]	Distribution
Land-Based			
Colorado	See Figure 4.2	Retail license fee of $1,250 Device fee of $75/gaming device Manufacturer, distributor, or operator license fee of $1,000 Key employee license fee of $250 initially, $200 thereafter (effective for 2 years) Support employee license fee of $175 initially, $150 thereafter (effective for 2 years)	Operating expenses of the Commission and Division of Gaming Two months of operating expenses of Commission and Division of Gaming in escrow 50% to State General Fund 28% to State Historical Fund[c] 12% to counties in proportion to gaming revenue generated 10% to cities in proportion to gaming revenue generated
Iowa	5% on first $1 million 10% on next $2 million 22% on all over $3 million, beginning January 1, 1997; there will be a 2% increase each succeeding calendar year until the rate is 36%	Admission fee of $.50 per visitor License fee of $1,000 Distributor fee of $1,000 Manufacturer fee of $250	Same as riverboat
Louisiana	18.5% or $100 million, whichever is higher		Operating expenses of the Corporation Dividends to the state Legislative appropriation
Michigan	18%	License fee of $25,000 Supplier fee of $5,000 Occupational fee to be determined	55% to city 45% to State School Aid Fund

68

State	Taxes[a]	Fees[b]	Distribution
Land-Based (*continued*)			
South Dakota	8%[d]	Operator fee of $1,000 initially and $200 thereafter	40% to General Fund
		Retail license fee of $250 initially and $100 thereafter	10% to county
		License stamp fee of $2,000 per gaming device	Operating and administration expenses of the SD Gaming Commission
		Manufacturer and distributor fees of $1,000 initially and $250 thereafter	Repayment of the funds appropriated for the start-up of the Commission
		Key employee license fee of $150 initially and $75 thereafter	Balance to City of Deadwood Historical Restoration and Preservation Fund[e]
		Support employee license fee of $50 initially and $25 thereafter	

a   Taxes are based on the adjusted gross receipts (total amount wagered less winnings paid) unless otherwise noted.

b   Fees listed are on an annual basis.

c   Of this, 20 percent goes to preservation and restoration of the three cities and 80% to the preservation and restoration of historical sites throughout the state.

d   Initially set by the legislature. After June 1990, the Commission has the option of adjusting the tax within a range of 5 to 15%.

e   Historical restoration and preservation is broadly defined to include street, water, sewer, and low-interest programs for both commercial and residential property.

FIGURE 4.1. Non-Native American Land-Based and Riverboat Casino Locations

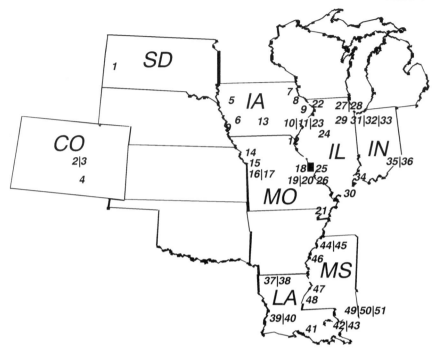

Location (No. of Units)	Location (No. of Units)	Location (No. of Units)	Location (No. of Units)
South Dakota	**Missouri**	**Indiana**	**Mississippi**
1. Deadwood (90)	14. St. Joseph (1)	31. East Chicago (1)	44. Robinsonville (9)
	15. Riverside (1)	32. Gary (2)	45. Lula (1)
Colorado	16. North Kansas City (1)	33. Hammond (1)	46. Greenville (3)
2. Black Hawk (19)	17. Kansas City (3)	34. Evansville (1)	47. Vicksburg (4)
3. Central City (12)	18. St. Charles (1)	35. Rising Sun (1)	48. Natchez (1)
4. Cripple Creek (23)	19. Maryland Heights (1)	36. Lawrenceburg (1)	49. Bay St. Louis (1)
	20. St. Louis (1)		50. Gulfport (2)
Iowa	21. Caruthersville (1)	**Louisiana**	51. Biloxi (8)
5. Sioux City (1)		37. Shreveport (1)	
6. Council Bluffs (3)	**Illinois**	38. Bossier City (3)	
7. Marquettee (1)	22. East Dubuque (1)	39. Westlake (2)	
8. Dubuque (2)	23. Rock Island (1)	40. Lake Charles (2)	
9. Clinton (1)	24. East Peoria (1)	41. Baton Rouge (2)	
10. Bettendorf (1)	25. Alton (1)	42. New Orleans (2)	
11. Davenport (1)	26. East St. Louis (1)	43. Harvey (1)	
12. Burlington (1)	27. Aurora (1)		
13. Altoona (1)	28. Elgin (1)		
	29. Joliet (2)		
	30. Metropolis (1)		

eastern Iowa river communities (Cooper, 1996). The area once known as the "Detroit of the farm belt" suddenly faced the economic crises with an unemployment rate higher than 10 percent (Iowa Workforce Development, 1996). Between 1980 and 1985, Iowa lost a higher percentage of its population to out-migration than any other state. Eight million square feet of industrial floor space lay empty (Cooper, 1996). Proponents of riverboat casinos sold gaming as a way to revive economically depressed river communities by boosting local tourism and tax revenues.

Iowa was the first state to legalize riverboat gaming in April 1989. The five-member Iowa Racing and Gaming Commission is in charge of licensing and regulating riverboat gaming. Only nonprofit organizations may be issued a license to conduct gaming activities on a riverboat; however, commercial entities are eligible to be licensed to operate such a boat for a fee and/or a percentage of the gaming revenues. Features of the 1989 Iowa Excursion Boat Gambling Law (Excursion Boat Gambling, 1991) include the following:

- Betting limits are a maximum bet per hand of $5 and a total loss of $200 per passenger per visit.
- Casinos are required to close at 2:00 a.m. daily, and requirements of cruising and loading and unloading of patrons must be met.
- Boats must have a capacity of 500 persons.
- There must be twenty slot machines for each gaming table.
- Boats are required to reserve 70 percent of their floor space for nongaming activities, including areas designed for entertainment of minors.
- Riverboats must have scheduled cruises lasting a minimum of three hours from April through October. During winter months, the commission sets the rules limiting times of admission to boats operating dockside.

In April 1991, three floating casinos were launched from Mississippi River communities. Two more boats joined the competition in June 1991. The five riverboat casinos served a total of nine eastern Iowa communities: Bellevue, Bettendorf, Burlington, Clinton, Davenport, Dubuque, Fort Madison, Keokuk, and Muscatine. Sioux

City, a western Iowa community, was the first Missouri River community to have a riverboat casino, commissioned in January 1993.

Two boats left the state of Iowa in July 1992 and a third in April 1993 due to betting limits and regulations. By July 1993, only three riverboat casinos remained in Iowa. In April 1994, the Iowa Legislature revised the gaming law, which included the following major changes (Gambling—Excursion Boats and Racetracks, 1996):

- There are no bet or loss limits.
- There is no limit on the amount of space that may be occupied by a casino.
- Boats are allowed to open twenty-four hours a day.
- Boats must have a capacity of 250 persons.
- Passengers may embark or disembark at any time while casinos are operating dockside.
- The commission defines the excursion season and the duration of excursions.

The revised customer-friendly law allows riverboats in Iowa to remain competitive. Riverboats now cruise just once a day in the summer session for a minimum of 100 days at a minimum of two hours each cruise and operate as dockside casinos at all other times. To date, nine riverboats exist in the state. A tenth license has been issued to a boat to be opened on a lake. In addition to the aforementioned regulations, the Iowa gaming law includes the following important components:

- Before a license is granted, an operator of a riverboat shall work with the Iowa Department of Economic Development to promote tourism throughout Iowa.
- A substantial amount of resources and goods used in the operation of riverboats should come from Iowa and a substantial amount of services and entertainment should be provided by Iowans.
- A section of the riverboats should be reserved solely for activities and interests of persons under the age of twenty-one and staffed to provide adequate supervision.
- A section of the riverboats should be reserved for promotion and sale of arts, crafts, and gifts native to, and made in, Iowa.

- It is the intent of the general assembly that employees be paid at least 25 percent above the federal minimum wage level.
- Credit cards shall not be accepted to purchase coins, tokens, or other forms of credit to be wagered.
- Local referendums should be revoted in 2002 and in each subsequent eight-year interval.
- A city or county may adopt an admission fee not to exceed $0.50 for each person boarding the riverboat docked within the city or county.
- If local voters approved gaming and later disapprove by a second referendum, the licenses issued by the commission shall remain valid and are subject to renewal for a total of nine years from the date of original issue.
- When a gaming proposal is defeated through a local referendum, another referendum shall not be held for at least two years.

During the 1998 legislative session, the Iowa Senate discussed a stop to the issuing of gaming licenses in Iowa for the next five years. If passed, the bill also would ban indefinitely casino gaming licenses for waterways other than the Mississippi and Missouri rivers. After many heated debates, the five-year moratorium on licenses did not pass. To the contrary, a gaming license was issued to allow a riverboat casino on the West Lake in central Iowa.

Illinois

Historically, Illinois has been the manufacturing and financial center of the Midwest. Many major operating and manufacturing facilities and company headquarters were based in Chicago and its suburbs. Recessions in the early 1970s and early 1980s caused a decline in the automobile, chemical, and heavy machinery production industries. The loss of those jobs resulted in higher welfare expenses and higher unemployment rates than the national average (Nevada Gaming Control Board, 1990). Since Iowa boats attracted a major share of their customers from Illinois, the Illinois Riverboat Gambling Act was passed in February 1990. The act was intended to benefit the people of Illinois by assisting economic development and promoting tourism. The five-member Illinois Gaming Board established under the act, within the Department of Revenue, is responsible for licensing and regulating riverboat gaming. The first two riverboat casinos opened during fall 1991 in Alton and Peoria. The riverboat in Rock Island opened in March 1992, and two more opened in Galena and Joliet in June 1992. Currently, ten riverboats are operating in nine Illinois communities.

Important elements of the Illinois Riverboat Gambling Act (1991) include the following:

- The board must issue five owner's licenses to become effective no earlier than January 1, 1991. Of the five initial licenses issued, three must authorize riverboat gaming operations on the Mississippi River, of which one must authorize gaming from a home dock in the city of East St. Louis, and the other one must authorize operations on the Illinois River south of Marshall County (Peoria).
- The board may issue five additional owner's licenses to become effective no earlier than March 1, 1992. One of these licenses must authorize riverboat gaming operations on the Des Plaines River in Will County (Joliet). The remaining four licenses may be issued for operation on any navigable stream within the state at the discretion of the board, except that no vessel may be permitted to conduct gaming activities on Lake Michigan or within a county having a population of three million, thus outlawing casinos in Chicago and suburban Cook County municipalities.
- In selecting docking locations, the board shall consider the economic benefits to the state and give favorable consideration to economically depressed areas and applicants who currently operate nongaming riverboats in Illinois and whose plans provide significant economic benefits to a large geographic area. The board also should disperse docking locations across the state.
- Each owner's license is allowed up to 1,200 "gaming participants" on one or two boats.
- Boats on the Mississippi River and the Illinois River must have a capacity of at least 500 persons; boats on other waters must have a capacity of at least 400 persons.

• Casinos are required to cruise year-round; excursions may not exceed four hours in duration; and gaming activities may not be conducted while the vessel is docked.

The decision by the state of Illinois not to have bet or loss limits gave Illinois boats a remarkable competitive advantage over the Iowa boats in the early 1990s. The success of the Illinois riverboats allowed the state to become a model for other states working on riverboat gaming laws (Raymond James and Associates, Inc., 1993). The ten gaming licenses authorized by the Illinois Riverboat Gaming Act were awarded to ten gaming firms in nine communities. Three of the nine riverboats dock near Chicago (Joliet, Aurora, and Elgin) and two in the St. Louis area (Alton and East St. Louis). To conform with the act, all regions of the state are represented.

Mississippi

The declining oil and gas industry, the need to create jobs, and the shifting of national opinions about gaming even changed the mentality about gaming for people in some of the Bible Belt states ("A Threat to Nevada?", 1993). In the late 1980s, Mississippi ranked near the bottom of most lists of economic and social indicators and had state budget deficits of hundreds of thousands of dollars. The severe budget deficit, combined with the introduction of riverboats to Iowa, record levels of unemployment and economic depression—especially in the "delta" region between Vicksburg and Memphis, and a declining tourism industry losing out to Alabama and Florida, accelerated the gaming legislation process. With the passage of a series of amendments to existing state law, Mississippi became the third state to legalize riverboat gaming in June 1990. Mississippi offered the first "dockside" casinos in the country. No cruising is required; all riverboats are floating, but permanently moored to the dock. Most of the riverboats are actually partial structures built atop dockside barges. Prior to September 1993, the State Tax Commission was the regulator of Mississippi casinos. Since October 1993, the three-member Mississippi Gaming Commission has had the authority to regulate the gaming industry.

The first three casinos opened in Biloxi in August 1992. Over the next two years, more than twenty casinos opened in nine of the fourteen eligible counties. Three major casino clusters have emerged over the years: Harrison County (especially Biloxi), Tunica County, and Vicksburg in Warren County. Intense competition within the two largest clusters led to the closing of two Biloxi casinos and five Tunica casinos and the relocation of one Tunica casino to Coahoma County, where the market includes a small but steady stream of patrons from Arkansas (Meyer-Arendt, 1995). Of the twenty-nine casinos currently operating, eighteen are along the Mississippi River, with ten in the Tunica cluster, and eleven along the coast, with eight in the Biloxi cluster.

Mississippi patterned its law on the Nevada Gaming Control Act. Important aspects of the Mississippi Gaming Control Act (1972) include the following:

- Gaming is allowed only in counties bordering the Gulf Coast or having navigable waters of the Mississippi River or its tributaries running through them.
- Local municipalities and counties may impose a monthly fee of 0.4 percent on the first $50,000, 0.6 percent on the next $84,000, and 0.8 percent on gross revenue over $134,000. When licensees are located in a municipality, the local government fees are allocated based on the proportion that municipality's population is of the total population of the county, according to the most recent federal census. Balance of the fees are allocated to the county. When licensees are not located within a municipality, all fees go to the county in which the licensee is located.

Because local governments receive only 0.8 percent of gross gaming revenues, most cities have levied their own casino tax and license fees. Almost all local governments levy a 3.2 percent tax to increase the local receipt to 4 percent. No statutory provisions in the act instruct municipalities or counties as to how to utilize local taxes and fees. The 1994 amendment of the Mississippi law dedicated 25 percent of the 8 percent gaming tax collections to retiring bonds issued for certain highway construction or reconstruction. The allocation is for the period of July 1, 1995 to June 30, 2002. All tax collections will go to the state general fund after June 30, 2002.

Louisiana

Riverboat gaming became legal in the state of Louisiana in July 1991, with the passage of the Louisiana Riverboat Economic Development and Gaming Control Act. The purpose of the act was to authorize, license, and control legislated gaming activities on riverboats on designated waterways to stimulate and promote growth of Louisiana's economy. The act stated that the development of a historic riverboat industry will assist in the continuing growth of the tourism industry. Although each parish had the option of passing reactive local referendums by March 15, 1992, to prohibit riverboat gaming in the parish, none chose to do so. The riverboat gaming is regulated by the seven-member Riverboat Gaming Commission in conjunction with the Riverboat Gaming Enforcement Division. Both the commission and the division were created within the Department of Public Safety and Corrections.

Due to the requirement that riverboats be new constructions built after January 1992, the first casino did not open until October 1993. As of October 1997, Louisiana has thirteen boats, with three in Bossier City and two each in Baton Rouge, Lake Charles, New Orleans, and Westlake. Harvey and Shreveport both have one.

The following major provisions are included in the Louisiana Riverboat Economic Development and Gaming Control Act (1989):

- A limit of fifteen vessels is permitted on the Mississippi, Red, Calcasieu, Mermentau, and Atchafalaya Rivers; the Sabine River north of the Toledo Bend Reservoir Dam; the Mississippi River Gulf Outlet; Bayou Bienvenue; Bayou Segnette within the city limits of Westwego; Lakes Pontchartrain, Maurepas, and Charles; and the Intercostal Waterway, except the portion within the borders of Terrebonne and Lafourche parishes.
- No more than six riverboats may operate in any one parish.
- Replicas of nineteenth-century paddlewheel Louisiana riverboats must be constructed beginning on or after January 1, 1992, with the approval and supervision of the commission.
- Dockside gaming may only be conducted during periods of inclement weather or for periods of time less than forty-five minutes between excursions. Dockside gaming is permitted on a portion of the Red River between Ropides and Caddo par-

ishes. However, the governing authorities of these parishes may call an election to prohibit dockside gaming in their parish.

- Cruises must be a minimum of three hours, but no longer than eight hours in duration.
- A parish or municipality may levy an admission fee of up to $2.50 per passenger. In Bossier and Caddo parishes, an admission fee of up to $3.00 may be levied. Allocation of admission fees specified in the act varies among parishes and municipalities. Generally speaking, admission fees are used for economic development, education, social services such as youth shelters and multicultural centers, road improvement, and police efforts.
- Appointed public officials and their families are not prohibited from engaging in business activities, such as providing goods and services for profit to riverboat casinos, with licensees.

Missouri

In November 1992, 63 percent of Missouri voters approved a statewide referendum governing riverboat gaming excursions and dockside casino operation. In January 1994, the Missouri Supreme Court ruled that the 1992 referendum did not remove the constitutional ban against games of chance. Therefore, Missouri's original riverboat casinos featured only poker, video poker, blackjack, and craps. Voters in a subsequent referendum in April 1994 narrowly rejected a constitutional amendment that would have repealed that ban. However, in November 1994, voters decided to lift the ban on games of chance, so Missouri's riverboats now offer a full range of games, including slot machines.

The regulatory responsibility of Missouri gaming rested in the Tourism Commission, a body designed to promote visits to the state, prior to April 29, 1993. Since then, a five-member Missouri Gaming Commission was created to regulate all gaming activities (Gaming Commission, 1994). The first casino was in operation on May 27, 1994. Casinos are only permitted along the Mississippi and Missouri Rivers (Excursion Gambling Boats, 1994). Currently, four riverboats are on the Mississippi River, with three in the St. Louis area and six on Missouri River, in or near Kansas City. Dockside gaming is permitted year-round along the Mississippi River near downtown St. Louis and during the winter (November through March) in the rest of the state; the Gaming Commission is authorized to permit year-round dockside gaming in locations other than St. Louis.

Taxes and fees collected are distributed separately as indicated in Table 4.2. The $500,000 fees allocated to cities and counties are appropriated on a per capita basis. Local governments must provide matching funds to receive the allocation, and the money must be used for the homeless and to deter gang-related violence and crimes. The money transferred to the Veterans' Commission Capital Improvement Trust Fund is used for the construction, maintenance, or renovation of veterans' homes and cemeteries in the state. An outpatient center for compulsive gambling treatment may be established. However, funding must come from gaming taxes distributed to cities or counties.

Indiana

Indiana is the sixth riverboat gaming state and also the first state to permit riverboat gaming on the Great Lakes. The intent of the Indiana Riverboat Gambling Act also was to promote tourism and assist economic development. The Indiana gaming law took effect July 1, 1993, but legal challenges to the law's constitutionality delayed its implementation. The first riverboat casino did not open until December 1995, in Evansville on the Ohio River. Currently, Indiana has seven riverboats, four on Lake Michigan and three on the Ohio River.

The seven-member Indiana Gaming Commission is responsible for the administration, regulation, and enforcement of the riverboat gaming act. In determining navigable waterways, the commission must consider the economic benefit that riverboat gaming provides to Indiana and ensure that all regions of Indiana share in the economic benefits of riverboat gaming. In addition, the commission must consider the impact of the navigation and docking of riverboats upon the environment and scenic beauty of Patoka Lake, which is on the western edge of the Hoosier National Forest.

Important items of the Indiana Riverboat Gambling Act (1996) include the following:

- A maximum of eleven licenses may be issued: five for boats along Lake Michigan, five for boats on the Ohio River, and one for a boat on Patoka Lake.

- Riverboats are required to cruise unless due to specific weather, water, or traffic conditions; passengers may play games thirty minutes before and after the actual cruise. Excursions may not exceed four hours.
- Licensed owners must conspicuously display the toll-free telephone number for addiction information on each admission ticket to a riverboat and on a poster or placard on display in a public area of each riverboat.
- In granting a license, the commission may give favorable consideration to economically depressed areas of Indiana and to applicants presenting plans that provide for significant economic development over a large geographic area.
- The license applicant must construct or provide for the construction of a hotel with a minimum of 250 rooms and with meeting and banquet facilities and theaters. In lieu of building a hotel, the applicant can demonstrate that the riverboat will cause economic development that will have an economic impact on the city exceeding that which the construction of a hotel would have.
- Local city or county referendums are required other than for the city of Gary, where only approval of a local legislative body is necessary.

Gaming taxes and fees allocation varies between riverboats docked on Lake Michigan and the Ohio River and those on Lake Patoka. For riverboats docked on Lake Michigan and the Ohio River, $1.00 of the $3.00 admission fee is allocated to the city or county where the boats dock, $1.00 to the county where the city is located, $0.10 to the county convention and visitors bureau or promotion fund, $0.15 to the State Fair Commission, $0.10 to the Division of Mental Health, and $0.65 to the Indiana Horse Racing Commission. The Division of Mental Health is required to allocate at least 25 percent of the funds received to the prevention and treatment of compulsive gambling.

For riverboats docked on Patoka Lake, $1.00 of the $3.00 admission fee is divided equally among counties contiguous to Patoka Lake; $1.00 goes to the Patoka Lake development account administered by the Department of Natural Resources; $0.40 goes to the resource conservation and development program serving Patoka Lake; $0.50 goes to the state general fund; and $0.10 goes to the Division of Mental Health, with 25 percent allocated for treatment of compulsive gambling.

As for all other taxes and fees, 25 percent is allocated to the home city or county for riverboats docked on Lake Michigan or the Ohio River. For the riverboat on Patoka Lake, 25 percent of other taxes and fees is equally divided among all counties contiguous to the lake. The other 75 percent is paid to the Indiana lottery and gaming surplus account.

LAND-BASED NON-NATIVE AMERICAN CASINOS

Non-Native American casinos are legalized on land in five states other than Nevada and New Jersey. South Dakota and Colorado turned historical mining towns with failing economies into limited-stakes casino hosts. "Limited-stake gaming" is defined as a maximum single bet of $5.00 on slot machines, blackjack, and poker games. Louisiana also approved a land-based casino in addition to the riverboats. Iowa legislature allowed slot machines at money-losing race tracks. Michigan is the newest player in the game.

South Dakota

Limited casino gaming became legal in Deadwood in 1989 in an attempt to revitalize a crumbling economy and restore the town's historic culture, of which gaming was well known to play a role. With a population of 1,800 (Bureau of the Census, 1993), Deadwood had seen the loss of jobs and local services as well as out-migration of residents. In April 1989, 75 percent of South Dakota voters approved limited-stakes gaming within the city limits of Deadwood. Gaming began on November 1, 1989, and slot machines, blackjack, and poker are allowed. As of August 1997, approximately ninety casinos are in operation. Each casino must offer a second business, such as gift and craft stores, restaurants, or taverns. The five-member South Dakota Commission on Gaming, attached to the Department of Commerce and Regulation for reporting purposes, is responsible for licensing and regulating limited-stakes casino gaming in Deadwood. No member of the commission may be a resident of Lawrence County, in which Deadwood is located.

The following are key regulations of the South Dakota Limited Card Games and Slot Machines Act (1991):

- Each retail license is allowed up to thirty total gaming devices (slots and card games). The number of gaming devices may not exceed thirty per building.
- No person may have a financial interest in more than three licensed locations, and a person licensed as a retailer or a slot machine operator must be a "bona fide resident and citizen of South Dakota."
- The City of Deadwood may own or lease up to fifty $.05 slot machines for placement within licensed locations. These machines are exempt from license fees, and the entire net proceeds generated by the machines are remitted to the South Dakota commission fund.

The South Dakota legislature proposed a bill in 1993 to expand gaming in Deadwood. The bill would have allowed more gaming devices and changed the distribution of additional future revenues by allocating more to the state general fund. The legislation was defeated by a 58 to 42 percent citizen vote in September 1993.

Colorado

The success of limited-stakes gaming in Deadwood, South Dakota led the state of Colorado to follow suit and authorize limited-stakes gaming in three small mining towns. The twin towns of Central City and Black Hawk, forty-five miles west of Denver, and Cripple Creek, forty miles west of Colorado Springs, had suffered major economic decline and infrastructure decay over the previous two decades. Mining, gaming, and tourism had been the mainstay of their economy for over 100 years. Mining died at the turn of the century, gaming was put to rest in the 1940s, and tourism had experienced decline for many years. The 1990 census reported populations of 227, 335, and 580 for Black Hawk, Central City, and Cripple Creek, respectively (Bureau of the Census, 1993).

The Colorado Limited Gaming Act was enacted in June 1991 following a 57 percent voter approval of a statewide constitutional amendment legalizing limited casino gaming in November 1990. To change the location of gaming in Colorado, to increase the betting limits, or to change the types of games allowed would require a change in the constitutional amendment through a statewide vote of the people. Six initiatives to expand gaming to other locations have appeared on the ballots since 1992. All six were defeated (Turner, Burmania, and Hammer, 1996).

Gaming started in Colorado on October 1, 1991, with eleven casinos statewide. At the end of 1992, seventy-six casinos with 12,000 devices were in operation. Since gaming began, more than twenty casinos closed due to competition, financial problems, and mismanagement (Long, Clark, and Liston, 1994). At the end of August 1997, Colorado had fifty-four casinos, with twelve in Central City, nineteen in Black Hawk, and twenty-three in Cripple Creek.

The Colorado Division of Gaming, within the Department of Revenue, and the Colorado Limited Gaming Control Commission, within the Division of Gaming, are responsible for the regulation and control of limited-stakes casino gaming activity in the state. The commission is responsible for establishing the gaming tax rate on an annual basis. The gaming tax shall never exceed 40 percent of the adjusted gross proceeds. In setting the tax rate, the commission considers the cities' need for historical restoration and preservation and gaming's impact on infrastructure, law enforcement, and environment. The tax rate has decreased dramatically over the past six years as gaming volume increased (see Figure 4.2).

The following regulations are included in the Colorado Limited Gaming Act (1991):

- A retail gaming license may only be granted to a retailer.
- A maximum of 35 percent floor space in a given building and 50 percent of any one floor of a building can be used for gaming.
- No one person can own an interest in more than three retail gaming establishments.

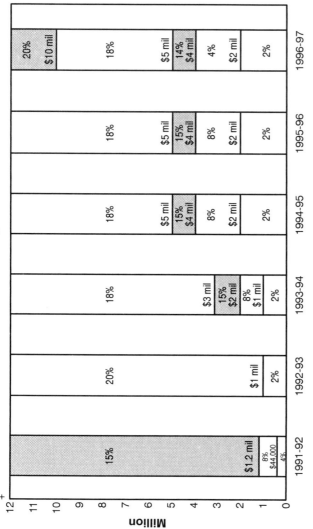

FIGURE 4.2. Colorado Gaming Tax Rates

Sources: Adapted from *Win, Lose, or Draw? Gambling with America's Small Towns* (p. 29), by P. Long, J. Clark, and D. Liston, 1994, Washington, DC: The Aspen Institute; and *Gaming in Colorado: Fact Book and 1996 Abstract* (p. 7), by G. Turner, D. Burmania, and C. Hammer, 1996, Lakewood, CO: Colorado Division of Gaming.

* Percentage of adjusted gross proceeds

Central City, Black Hawk, and Cripple Creek imposed an annual device fee ranging from $750 to $1,200. Fees collected are at the disposal of the city governments. Colorado has a unique Contiguous County Limited Gaming Impact Fund that receives at least 9 percent of the 50 percent gaming taxes distributed to the state general fund. The eight counties immediately surrounding Gilpin (Black Hawk and Central City) and Teller (Cripple Creek) counties receive allocations from the Contiguous County Impact Fund. The fund helps offset financial impacts associated with increased highway traffic, higher law enforcement incidents, and increased demands on social services caused by gaming. Half of the fund is distributed directly to the counties, based on the number of casino employees residing in the respective counties. The other half is distributed on a competitive basis to political entities within the counties, based on applications to the Department of Local Affairs (Turner, Burmania, and Hammer, 1996).

A Municipal Limited Gaming Impact Fund was created in 1996 to compensate cities in the Gilpin and Teller counties, other than Central City, Black Hawk, and Cripple Creek, for expenses incurred in response to the limited-stakes gaming. Of the 50 percent share of limited-stakes gaming proceeds to the general fund, 2 percent is transferred to the Municipal Limited Gaming Impact Fund. Another 0.2 percent of the general fund is allocated to the Colorado Tourism Promotion Fund.

Louisiana

The Louisiana legislature decided that gaming activities are a unique economic development tool that can promote general economic development, increase employment, and produce direct and indirect state and local revenues. To prevent customers from patronizing privately owned casinos, the legislature decided to monopolize the market by establishing an official gaming operation in a large metropolitan area. Part of the rationale for doing so is to stimulate the overall economy of the metropolitan area and its tourism and hospitality industry.

The Louisiana Economic Development and Gaming Corporation Law (1989) was enacted in 1992. Neither a citywide nor a statewide referendum on the proposal was held. The law allows an official gaming establishment in a parish having a population of 490,000 or more, according to the latest federal census. The Louisiana Economic Development and Gaming Corporation was created and empowered to grant an exclusive contract to operate a casino and to regulate the casino. The affairs of the corporation are supervised by a nine-member board.

The site selected for the 100,000-square-foot, or larger, city-owned land-based casino was the Rivergate Convention Center in New Orleans. The Rivergate is adjacent to the French Quarter, the Mississippi riverfront, the New Orleans Convention Center, the Aquarium of the Americas, and numerous shopping outlets and hotels. The license allows for twenty years of exclusive operation, with one ten-year renewal option. The casino must be free-standing and not physically connected to a hotel.

The corporation and its operations are exempt from taxation by the state, including but not limited to state sales tax, income tax, corporation franchise tax, and occupational license taxes, if any. After the repayment of any appropriated funds provided to the corporation by the state, the corporation is self-sustaining and self-funded. All money received is deposited into a corporate operating account. The corporation transfers 1 percent of its operating account, not to exceed $150,000 annually, to the Compulsive and Problem Gaming Fund. The corporate operating account will pay necessary expenses of the corporation and dividends to the state. The balance will be transferred to the Casino Gaming Proceeds Fund. Monies in the fund may be expended only pursuant to legislative appropriation (Phillips-Hymel, 1994).

Harrah's Jazz Company was selected as the operator of the casino, and a contract was signed. A temporary casino was opened while construction was underway for the permanent location. The Harrah's Jazz Company filed bankruptcy and closed the temporary casino before the new construction was completed. The building, with a completed exterior and incomplete interior, has been standing idle for more than a year while the state and the operator go through a litigation process in federal bankruptcy court. Before the casino project moves forward, either the state legislature has to pass the rectified contract or the governor has to sign the contract. It is safe to say that it will be a while before the casino starts bringing in any revenue or dividends for the state.

Iowa

Due to increased variety of available gaming options, Iowa's dog and horse racetracks faced declining revenue and increasing financial troubles. Bankruptcies were filed and bonds were issued to help racetracks survive, to no avail. The Iowa legislature revised the Iowa gambling law in 1994, allowing any licensee holding a valid license to conduct pari-mutuel dog or horse racing on January 1, 1994 to apply for a license to operate "gambling games" that do not include table games of chance or video machines. Before a gaming license is issued, voters in the county where the pari-mutuel racetrack is located must approve the operation through a special election. The first racetrack and casino opened on March 15, 1995. Currently, all three remaining racetracks offer casino gaming. Those racetrack casinos are subject to the same regulations as riverboats in Iowa and are supervised by the Iowa Racing and Gaming Commission.

After paying all taxes, fees, and expenses, licensees should distribute remaining gaming receipts to education, civic, public, charitable, or religious organizations. However, if a licensee has unpaid debt from the pari-mutuel racetrack operations, the remaining gaming receipts should first be used to pay the debt.

Michigan

The Michigan Gaming Control and Revenue Act (1997) was passed by voters in November 1996 and took effect in December 1996. The five-member Michigan Gaming Control Board, within the Department of Treasury, was created to enforce and supervise the administration of the act. One million dollars was allocated for the fiscal year ending September 30, 1997, to fund the operation of the board.

Gaming is allowed in a city having a population of 800,000 or more, located within 100 miles of any other state or country in which gaming is permitted, and a majority of city voters had approved gaming in the city at the time the act was voted on. This leaves Detroit as the only city qualified to have casinos. City government has the option to impose local regulations governing casino operations, occupational licenses, and suppliers as long as local regulations are consistent with the rules promulgated by the board.

As of November 1998, three license applications are in review. Once the licenses are issued, temporary casinos may open while permanent sites are being built. Locations of temporary casinos, with estimated opening dates between summer and fall 1999, have been identified. Permanent locations are expected to open in 2001 or 2002 (Michigan Gaming Control Board, 1998).

Wagering taxes and fees allocated to the city must be used for the hiring, training, and deployment of street patrol officers; neighborhood and downtown economic development programs; public safety programs; antigang and youth development programs; and other programs to improve the quality of life of the city. The allocation to the State School Aid Fund is to provide additional funds for K-12 education. It is specified that funds from the act should not be used to supplant existing state appropriations or local expenditures. In addition to paying the wagering tax and fees, each licensee pays a 1.25 percent municipal service fee or $4 million, whichever is greater, to the city to assist in defraying the cost of hosting casinos.

OTHER STATES

Many other states, such as Montana and South Carolina, allow various types of gaming operations and devices. Some operations promote themselves as casinos. However, those facilities usually have a limited number of games, such as poker, video gaming machines (e.g., keno and bingo), and other nonbank games. The payout of those allowed games also is limited. Traditional games associated with casinos, such as craps, blackjack, and slot machines, are not allowed. Therefore, those states are not discussed in this chapter, even though gaming tax revenues received by local and state governments are quite significant.

REFERENCES

Anonymous. (1993, March). A threat to Nevada? America's heartland sets sail for gaming. *Casino Journal, 6*(3), 14-17.

Bureau of the Census (1993). *1990 census of population and housing*. Washington, DC: U.S. Government Printing Office.

Colorado Limited Gaming Act (1991), 5B Colorado Revised Stat. §§ 47.1-101-1401 (Supp. 1996).

Cooper, M. (1996, February 19). America's house of cards: How the casino economy robs the working poor. *The Nation 262*(7), pp. 11-12, 14-16, 18-19.

Excursion Boat Gambling (1991). 1 Code of Iowa §§ 99F-1-17.

Excursion Gambling Boats (1994). 16A Vernon's Ann. Missouri Stat. §§ 313-800-850 (Supp. 1997).

Gambling—Excursion Boats and Racetracks (1996). 7 Iowa Code Ann. §§ 99F-1-18 (Supp. 1997).

Gaming Commission (1994). 16A Vernon's Ann. Missouri Stat. §§ 313-004 (Supp. 1997).

Harrah's Entertainment, Inc. (1996). *An overview of riverboat gaming in the United States: March 1996*. Memphis, TN: Author.

Illinois Riverboat Gambling Act (1991). Smith-Hurd Illinois Ann. Stat. §§ 120-2401-2423 (Supp. 1992).

Iowa Workforce Development (1996). *Labor force summary*. Des Moines, IA: Author.

Long, P., Clark, J., and Liston, D. (1994). *Win, lose, or draw? Gambling with America's small towns*. Washington, DC: The Aspen Institute.

Louisiana Economic Development and Gaming Corporation Law (1989). 17 West's Louisiana Stat. Ann. §§ 27-5-201-286 (Supp. 1997).

Louisiana Riverboat Economic Development and Gaming Control Act (1989). 17 West's Louisiana Stat. Ann. §§ 27-4-41-113 (Supp. 1997).

Meyer-Arendt, K.J. (1995). Casino gaming in Mississippi: Location, location, location. *Economic Development Review 13*(4), 27-33.

Michigan Gaming Control and Revenue Act (1997). Michigan Compiled Laws Ann. §§ 432-201-216.

Michigan Gaming Control Board (1998, November 24). *What's next? . . . A timeline* (On-line). Available: http://www.state.mi.us/mgcb/timeline.htm.

Mississippi Gaming Control Act (1972). 17 Mississippi Code 1972 Ann. §§ 75-76-1-281 (Supp. 1996).

Nevada Gaming Control Board (1990, May). *Legalized gaming in the state of Illinois*. Carson City, NV: Author.

Phillips-Hymel, S. (1994). *Louisiana gaming: A state budget perspective*. Baton Rouge, LA: Office of Fiscal Affairs and Policy Development, Louisiana Senate.

Raymond James and Associates, Inc. (1993, January). *New life on the Mississippi—and elsewhere: The promising potential of modern riverboat gaming*. St. Petersburg, FL: Author.

Riverboat Gambling (1996). 1996 Replacement Volume Burns Indiana Stat. Ann. Code Edition. §§ 4-33-1-15.

South Dakota Limited Card Games and Slot Machines—Gaming Commission (1991). 12B South Dakota Codified Laws. §§ 42-7B-1-62.

Turner, G., Burmania, D., and Hammer, C. (1996). *Gaming in Colorado: Fact book and 1996 abstract*. Lakewood, CO: Colorado Division of Gaming.

SECTION II:
ECONOMIC IMPACTS

Chapter 5

Casinos in Las Vegas:
Where Impacts Are Not the Issue

William N. Thompson

INTRODUCTION

The spread of legalized casino gaming from two states at the beginning of the 1980s to over one-half of the states today prompted Congress to establish a national commission to study the impacts of gambling on society. The implication, of course, was that many negative social impacts are attached to gambling. The lobbying force behind the idea of having a study commission came from antigambling groups.

As the commission came together, high on its agenda was a schedule of visits around America to check things out and to hold hearings. The commission debated just where they should go. Only as an afterthought did they conclude that they should visit Las Vegas. Well, maybe they shouldn't have scheduled Las Vegas for a visit. In Las Vegas, the impacts of gambling are simply not an issue. In Las Vegas, the issue is, "Can we keep what we have going, going? What roadblocks are in the way of achieving more and more of what we are achieving? Can we grow forever?" In Las Vegas, the impacts of gambling are viewed collectively as positive ones—at least the net effects of the impacts are positive. Given that consensus, the only issues worthy of discussion are issues of strategy— how best to maintain the status quo and achieve even more gambling activity for the community.

Of course, such a consensus is rather Pollyannaish. Somehow, Las Vegas has not escaped the anguish that is attached to having a large number of compulsive gamblers in its midst. Las Vegas does have casino-gaming-related crimes. Yet, even if we accurately calculate the direct costs associated with the social problems of having gambling in our community (which we could do, but it would be expensive), we very likely would find that they add up to numbers that are insignificant when compared with the direct economic benefits from having a casino gambling establishment in Las Vegas and Nevada. This is not to suggest that gambling does not have nonquantifiable effects on quality of life which may make Las Vegas an unpleasant place for many people. Still, the positive economic effects of gambling in Las Vegas can be rather impressive. Indeed, Las Vegas is one of the very few places where casinos are recognized as beneficial to the economy, and that issue is not debated. This chapter examines the economic engine that is Las Vegas casino gambling and looks at factors that should be considered in assessing whether that engine can maintain.

THE SUCCESS STORY THAT IS LAS VEGAS

Las Vegas is the world's Mecca of gambling. I am not sure that our Muslim friends would appreciate the phrase "Mecca of gambling," as their religion discourages people from gambling. However, similar to the great Mecca in Saudi Arabia, the shrines and temples of the Las Vegas Strip attract pilgrims from the farthest reaches of the earth.

More money is wagered on games in Las Vegas than in any other city on Earth. When I first wrote this, I wrote "more money is gambled here than anywhere else," but then I realized that the New York, London, and Tokyo Stock Exchanges do have more wagering activity. Las Vegas gambling is not risk-taking on business ventures, but merely playing simple games.

Las Vegas (the term is used here to apply to Clark County, Nevada, which encompasses both the Las Vegas Strip and the city of Las Vegas) has the biggest resort complexes in the world. They are, of course, built around gambling floors. Thousands and thousands of hotel rooms are in each resort. Las Vegas now has over 100,000 hotel rooms, more than any other city in the world. The largest hotels have over 4,000 rooms each; the MGM Grand has

5,009 rooms. Thirteen of the fourteen largest hotels in the world are in Las Vegas, and they are located on, or next to, one street: the Las Vegas Strip (Las Vegas Boulevard South). Plans are underway to build another 10,000 rooms, and more plans have been made for another 10,000 rooms beyond those (Jensen, 1997; Nevada Development Authority, 1997).

The hotel rooms on the Strip are usually full. Occupancy rates across the Las Vegas Valley have exceeded 90 percent, compared to rates two-thirds as high throughout most of the country. The hotels attract tourists—over 30 million last year. Approximately one-half that number arrive and depart through McCarran International Airport. Of those visitors, 3 million come for conventions (Schwer, 1997) (see Tables 5.1 and 5.2).

TABLE 5.1. Clark County Hotel Rooms and Gaming Revenues: 1980-1996

Year	Total Gaming Revenue	Hotel Rooms	Occupancy Rate
1980	$1,646,354,726	45,815	77.0%
1981	$1,736,161,802	49,614	76.0%
1982	$1,786,029,460	50,267	70.0%
1983	$1,949,892,289	56,394	73.0%
1984	$2,153,889,838	54,904	72.5%
1985	$2,295,199,685	55,564	79.8%
1986	$2,568,112,367	58,435	81.4%
1987	$2,831,308,478	62,440	83.4%
1988	$3,176,289,715	66,334	85.1%
1989	$3,568,546,606	67,391	85.2%
1990	$4,035,500,404	73,700	84.7%
1991	$4,159,817,290	76,900	80.3%
1992	$4,381,116,000	74,700	83.9%
1993	$4,729,093,000	86,053	87.6%
1994	$5,431,475,000	88,560	89.0%
1995	$5,720,390,000	90,046	88.0%
1996	$5,783,567,876	99,072	90.4%

Source: Schwer (1997).

TABLE 5.2. Clark County Visitors and Convention Information: 1970-1996

Year	Visitor Volume	Visitor Revenue	McCarran Air Traffic	Number of Conventions	Convention Attendance	Convention Revenue
1970	6,787,650	$1,182,543,972	4,086,973	296	269,129	$63,598,020
1971	7,361,783	$1,356,788,068	4,102,285	320	312,347	$76,221,840
1972	7,954,748	$1,505,660,818	4,608,764	385	290,794	$71,547,900
1973	8,474,727	$1,772,083,169	5,397,017	305	357,248	$90,129,844
1974	8,664,751	$1,891,089,307	5,944,433	339	311,908	$79,388,220
1975	9,151,427	$2,182,565,255	6,500,806	393	349,787	$91,982,560
1976	9,796,354	$2,447,644,172	7,658,175	325	367,322	$97,343,400
1977	10,137,021	$2,922,038,957	7,964,687	352	417,090	$108,388,380
1978	11,178,111	$3,279,205,986	9,110,842	421	607,318	$193,081,755
1979	11,696,073	$4,136,680,954	10,574,127	356	637,062	$218,328,450
1980	11,941,524	$4,755,879,064	10,302,106	449	656,024	$227,025,265
1981	11,820,788	$4,798,027,273	9,469,727	515	719,988	$324,477,067
1982	11,633,728	$5,184,774,011	9,438,646	518	809,779	$590,672,696
1983	12,348,270	$5,935,050,380	10,312,842	463	943,611	$652,163,666
1984	12,843,433	$6,308,817,877	10,142,744	499	1,050,916	$792,388,609
1985	14,194,189	$6,901,178,440	10,924,047	480	1,072,629	$866,305,752
1986	15,196,284	$7,461,375,444	12,428,748	564	1,519,421	$1,042,279,651
1987	16,216,102	$8,602,965,887	15,582,302	556	1,677,716	$1,197,168,704
1988	17,199,808	$10,039,448,236	16,231,199	681	1,702,158	$1,242,227,536
1989	18,129,684	$11,912,941,021	17,106,948	711	1,508,842	$1,140,912,624
1990	20,954,420	$14,320,745,600	18,618,781	1,011	1,743,194	$1,358,243,318
1991	21,315,116	$14,326,553,719	20,171,557	1,655	1,794,444	$1,482,327,551
1992	21,886,865	$14,686,644,065	20,913,654	2,199	1,969,435	$1,693,074,125
1993	23,522,593	$15,127,266,781	22,492,156	2,443	2,439,734	$2,253,526,873
1994	28,214,362	$19,163,212,044	26,850,486	2,662	2,684,171	$3,034,267,004
1995	29,002,122	$20,686,800,160	28,027,239	2,826	2,924,879	$3,359,162,165
1996	29,636,361	$22,533,257,750	30,459,965	3,827	3,305,507	$3,943,105,480

Source: Schwer (1997).

Las Vegas also has gambling complexes with smaller hotels or no hotels at all. These casinos cater to local residents. In addition to the casinos, slot machine parlors are in bars and taverns, in convenience stores, and even in grocery stores. It is very difficult to go anywhere in Las Vegas and not see a gambling machine, and on every street, big signs advertise the gambling. Without doubt, people who live in Las Vegas gamble more than people living anywhere else. Still, over 90 percent of the gambling activity comes from tourists and visitors, not residents. About 13 percent of the gambling dollars comes from foreign tourists. The leading tourist countries are Germany, Great Britain, Canada, and Japan. Foreign tourists stay longer than other tourists, but overall, tourists spend three nights and four days in Las Vegas. This means that tourists have ample time for nongambling activities and spend considerable amounts of money on a wide range of activities. Actually surveys show that the average tourist who gambles spends only four hours a day inside the casinos (Las Vegas Convention and Visitors Authority, 1996).

Nearly $6 billion comes to Las Vegas casinos each year as the result of losses from players. Overall, tourist spending brings in $22 billion to the Las Vegas economy. The impact on the economy is even greater, as the money will typically circulate two times before it leaves Las Vegas—most likely for California, where Nevadans buy most of their products. The gambling and tourist dollars mean that Las Vegas has tremendous economic growth, and that means jobs—about 1.6 jobs for each hotel room.

Over 167,000 people work in the casinos and hotels in Clark County. This represents over one-third of the labor force. The largest hotels employ more than 5,000 workers each. The jobs are good jobs: the workers have unions, they receive higher than minimum wages, and many (e.g., dealers, cocktail servers, and valet parking attendants) receive most of their income from tips. The workers receive good benefit packages, including full health insurance coverage.

A noteworthy fact is that the jobs in casino hotels are available for people who have become unemployed due to labor reductions in manufacturing businesses in the United States. Also, the person who has been unlucky in finding work can often turn that luck around in Las Vegas. Many of the jobs in Las Vegas do not require high skill levels initially. A low-skill person can start the job and learn while working, often in a short time.

Steady job growth means many jobs outside the casinos too. The annual private job growth in Nevada is 8.7 percent. This year,

23,000 new jobs in the service sector also have spawned 14,400 new jobs in trade, 12,400 in construction, and 4,000 in the government sector. Overall the casino-hotel jobs have a 1.7 multiplier effect, which means, for each hotel job, the local economy picks up .7 of another job. This is actually a low multiplier because Las Vegas is not a manufacturing center and most items in the casino hotels, with the exception of slot machines, must be imported (Schwer, 1989).

Two kinds of new workers are present in Las Vegas. Skilled tradesmen work constructing the new palaces of gambling wonder. (At this time, the Las Vegas skyline is punctuated by more cranes, the state "bird," than in any other city in North America.) The other workers come into town with very few job skills, many with very bad work habits as well. They are at the lower end of the socioeconomic scale. For many, English is not their first language. They are the "second chance" seekers. And Las Vegas has always been a place where if you have a dime in your pocket, you have another chance.

The new job winners and new job seekers are from out of town. All the people in Las Vegas who want or can hold a job have one already. These new workers come mostly from California, but also from everywhere else. Construction workers rotate from site to site, but the others are taken in by casino hotels who really want to hold on to them.

The personnel director of one of the largest casino companies said that when he looks for personnel supervisors, he looks for people with the qualities of a probation officer. He commented that the new workforce desperately needs very close supervision for the initial work period to ensure that they get on the pathway toward honest self-sufficiency. With that close supervision and with programs in such mundane things as personal habits, consistency in work performance, customer interactions, and the English language, the workforce with this particular company has achieved success beyond expectations. In an industry where yearly employee turnover can approach 50 percent, his company now has a turnover rate of less than 15 percent. Now other operations at the newer, larger properties are competing with similar performances. Las Vegas doesn't just hire; Las Vegas trains, instructs, supervises, and gives effective incentives to make sure not only that the workers work but that the workfare program works.

The Las Vegas workfare program is not just a warmed-over liberal attempt to have another Works Progress Administration, Job Corps, Americorps, Comprehensive Employment Training Administration, or whatever. Las Vegas jobs are real jobs in the private sector. These are jobs where success is based upon serving real paying customers with genuine customer service. Indeed, although these jobs carry full benefit packages, including good health care coverage, many have compensation tied to tips, hence requiring good service.

The jobs in Las Vegas also are good for the employment market because the people with the jobs spend money from their salaries in Las Vegas. The spending of the casino hotel workers supports other workers. For each two casino hotel workers, another new job is created. The economic impact of casino hotels also spills over into the government. The gambling industry is directly responsible for over one-half of the taxes in Las Vegas and in the state of Nevada. As a result, the Las Vegas area has some of the lowest residential and business taxes in the country.

No other city in the world is so tied to one industry as Las Vegas is to the casino industry. Las Vegas leads the world in gambling, and for general tourism, it shares the national lead with Orlando. Las Vegas is big, and it is growing. The city's low tax policy—the lowest gambling taxes of any casino jurisdiction in the world—encourages casinos to expand and to build new facilities. Gaming revenues are increasing, hotel rooms are increasing, and the number of visitors is increasing. The population also is increasing; 5,000 new residents come into Las Vegas every month. In 1970, the population of Clark County was 277,000; in 1980, it was 463,000. Today it is approaching 1.2 million, a 300 percent increase since 1970, a 140 percent increase since 1980. In contrast, the national population increased 30 percent since 1970, and 12 percent since 1980. Gambling is responsible for Las Vegas's growth.

The strongest point to be made about Las Vegas is a point that should be made for persons located in other jurisdictions, such as Detroit, Michigan, that are initiating processes for starting casino industries in their communities. If people are creating new gambling sites for the purpose of economic growth and jobs, they *must* look at Las Vegas as their model. There are other gambling cities; there are casinos in other places—Joliet, Illinois; Evansville and Gary, Indiana; Kansas City, Missouri; and Deadwood, South Dakota. If casino planners aim at a very big target and set their goals to be like Gary, Indiana, there is good news and bad news. They *will* succeed. But, they will become another Gary, Indiana.

Gary, Indiana, has two prosperous riverboats. Each makes between $100 million and $200 million a year in gambling revenues. Detroit may easily duplicate the Gary revenues when they open temporary casinos in 1999, if this is what they want to do. However, that accomplishment would not have highly noticeable positive impacts for either the local or the regional economy. On the other hand, a place such as Detroit could aim at a smaller, more difficult to hit target and attempt to model a complex of casinos after the Las Vegas experience. It is very unlikely that Detroit would experience the scope of economic impacts found in Las Vegas. However, Detroit would be aiming in the correct direction, and it is much more likely that the city would realize very noticeable positive economic benefits from having casinos styled after the Las Vegas model.

Las Vegas is doing things right. The main issue in Las Vegas is, "Can the current situation persist?" To be sure, some signs suggest that growth is slowing. Although gaming revenues and the number of visitors still increase, they currently are not increasing as fast as the number of new hotel rooms and amount of gaming floor space. Occupancy rates have fallen off for the non-Strip hotels, and wins per playing spot at the casinos are down. However, before delving into the future and any stumbling blocks ahead for Las Vegas, it would be beneficial to explore the reasons why Las Vegas is where it is today.

WHY LAS VEGAS IS SUCCESSFUL AND GROWING

Some general reasons can explain why Las Vegas is successful and growing, but there are specific reasons for the success. Las Vegas is growing because all gambling is growing in the United States. This is related to the nature of the gambling product and to national demographics. However, Las Vegas is successful for very local reasons. Las Vegas offers a synergism that can come only from having a concentration of gambling casinos in a single location. Also, Las Vegas thinks big, and it offers overcapacity and an overabundance of both gambling and nongambling products. The products all revolve around various kinds of entertainment, both indoor and outdoor, spectator and participant entertainment. Las Vegas offers Caesar's Court; a volcano outside The Mirage and white tigers inside; a movieland theme park; a Treasure Island pirate ship fight, which draws thousands of spectators four times a day; and the Fremont Street Experience, a unique light show spectacular. The architecture is fantastical (a replica of an Egyptian pyramid that is a casino hotel, with a medieval castle motif next door) and set against vistas of snowcapped mountains. Entertainment includes multiple dance/revue shows, as well as the most popular entertainers of the world on stage, along with various sports events, and, for the recreationally inclined, nearly twenty accessible golf courses.

When people visit Las Vegas, they have more than enough to do—enough for several visits, enough for everyone in the family, whether a person wants to gamble or is old enough to gamble. Additionally, because of gambling revenues, much of the entertainment can be offered at lower prices than those offered by nongambling establishments. That gambling is competitive also keeps prices down among casinos.

Gambling is growing nationwide, and indeed worldwide, because the gambling product is in demand. The demand arises because most forms of gambling have been illegal in most places for a long time, if not forever. When gambling becomes available in a convenient and legal format, people wish to try it out. Gambling is part of human nature; we all engage in various risk behaviors on a daily basis. The gambling product, however, stands out from other products. With other products, losers talk and winners stay quiet. If people buy an automobile and it does not work right, or if they received a bad deal or bargain from the dealer, they tell people how dissatisfied they are. Some will tell as many as ten or fifteen other people that their car is no good. On the other hand, if their car is good, they drive their car. They are too busy traveling around to be telling anyone about the car. Actually, the bad service story is told on average to ten people, the good story to three or fewer. If you sell a product, you need twelve satisfied customers to make up for one dissatisfied customer. Not so with gambling. Losers stay quiet: they may be embarrassed; they may not want their spouse to know; they may feel stupid. But if they win, they tell everyone. They feel they are somehow intelligent if the slot machine made them a winner (Thompson, 1995a).

So when you talk to people who go to Las Vegas, if they talk about the weather and how nice the shows were, they probably lost. If they won, that is all they will talk about. For that reason, when people hear about casinos, they think that players are supposed to win. Word of mouth is the best kind of advertising that a business can have.

The population is becoming older. In the United States, the average life expectancy is increasing. We have a generation of "baby boomers," born between 1946 and 1961. This peak population group determines trends in America. Now these baby boomers are entering their fifties. Every day in the United States, 10,000 people turn fifty years old, and this will continue for the next fifteen years. This is the best age to target for marketing gambling products. People in their fifties are at their maximum earning power. They also have the maximum amount of vacation time of all workers. Moreover, their spending needs have been drastically reduced, as their children have left to make their own homes. These are the people who were teenagers and college students in the 1960s and 1970s. This generation supported the protests of the 1960s. They were exposed to drugs; they wanted to try new things. They engineered the sexual revolution. They did everything—then—*except* for one thing: they did not gamble at casinos. First, casinos were not readily available, and second, *then* they would have found gambling offensive to their mores. *Now* it is different. Casinos may be one of the few forms of entertainment left that they haven't already tried. Las Vegas offers gambling with value and with entertainment amenities, and the city will prosper because this baby boom generation will keep visitor numbers up for the next decade or longer. Today the visitors to Las Vegas are already in the older-age categories. Although the average age of the visiting gambler is 49.4 years,

31 percent are over sixty years old, and 70 percent are over forty years old.

The main reason Las Vegas is prospering and will continue to prosper is that the gambling city allows very large facilities, and it allows multiple casinos with different owners. The placing of many large casinos in one location—one city—has resulted in the unleashing of a force known as synergism. Large casinos try to offer more and more services and better pricing of gaming and entertainment products. Actually, they do not directly compete with the other big casinos, rather they work together with them to advertise and sell Las Vegas as a whole. The result is that Las Vegas becomes the tourist experience, rather than gaming at a particular casino.

Certainly, Las Vegas is in a competitive fight, but it is not like the competition faced by riverboats in Joliet, Illinois. The latter have to struggle for patrons who may otherwise go to boats in Gary, Indiana, or Aurora or Elgin, Illinois. In Las Vegas, casino owners have to figure ways to compete for visitors who may think of taking their vacation in Paris or Hawaii instead. Ironically, whereas the riverboats crave national prosperity so local residents have more entertainment money to spend, in Las Vegas, prosperity may have negative consequences, as the visitors can more freely consider vacations overseas. This is one external factor that may contribute to suppressing Las Vegas's growth in the late 1990s.

The Las Vegas experience is one in which everything the tourist expects is available in abundance. Casinos are so large that they are rarely so crowded that a player cannot find a place at a game he or she wishes to play. Shows are abundant enough that the person coming to Las Vegas knows he or she can get into some show. A survey of visitors found that 97 percent made plans to see a specific show *after* they arrived in Las Vegas. Entertainment is the real game of Las Vegas. In fact, 66 percent of visitors said they came to Las Vegas for pleasure and vacation, while only 5 percent said they came to gamble. Actually, 87 percent did gamble. In addition to shows and gambling, Las Vegas offers swimming pools and golf courses. Of the visitors, 30 percent took tours outside of the city. The largest numbers went to Hoover Dam, followed by the Grand Canyon, Lake Mead, Death Valley, and Bryce and Zion National

Parks. Additional numbers went snow skiing at Mt. Charleston. Las Vegas offers variety and that contributes to gambling success for the city and its casinos.

THE FUTURE ECONOMIC HEALTH OF LAS VEGAS

If Las Vegas can continue to offer its products in the future as it has in the past, success should continue. But things could change. The win-win formula that derives from the fact that winners talk and losers stay quiet has its limits. In fact, some losers will talk loudly under certain circumstances. If they believe the game is dishonest, they do not mind telling others that they were cheated. Second, if they received rude service, they will tell others how they lost all their money and the casino people were unkind to them. It is therefore critical that casino gambling be closely monitored to ensure that all gambling action is honest at all times. More important, it must be fair. The odds or costs of playing games should be reasonable. Slot machines in Las Vegas pay out over 95 percent of the money put into them as prizes for the players. Some casinos, in areas where monopolies exist, may pay out only 80 percent—or even less. Players may realize that the odds are in favor of the casino, but at least they want to be able to play and take chances for a long period of time before all their money disappears. Additionally, the problem of compulsive gambling can destroy the win-win atmosphere. If a casino takes advantage of a player's inability to control gambling, and lends money to the player or tries to get the player drunk, players will talk about this kind of unfairness. Las Vegas has not paid much attention to customer service or to problem gambling in the past; they will have to do so in the future.

Some concern about the competition from new casinos is warranted. However, Las Vegas markets to the world. As long as it does so, new casinos in other places will only cause more and more people to want to come to Las Vegas. On the other hand, if the Las Vegas casinos decide to market only to local players, they will find their revenues decreasing every time a new casino opens.

In Tables 5.3, 5.4, and 5.5, clear evidence is presented that the legalization of gambling around the United States has not hurt Las Vegas. Rather, casinos around the country seem only to train new gamblers and whet their appetites for vacations in Las Vegas. As gambling expanded to new jurisdictions, the proportion of visitors from those regions to Las Vegas remains constant, and actual numbers increase.

TABLE 5.3. Gaming Revenues in Nevada and Elsewhere

Year	Non-Nevada Casinos				Nevada Casinos
	States with Casinos	States with Nontribal Casinos	No. of Casinos	Revenues (Billions)	Revenues (Billions)
1989	7	2	53	$2.778	$4.996
1990	7	2	115	3.563	5.481
1991	11	5	144	4.186	5.569
1992	13	6	196	5.777	5.862
1993	15	7	237	8.914	6.218
1994	16	8	281	9.203	6.990
1995	17	9	300	14.688	7.366

Sources: Adapted from State Gaming Control Board (1990-1996); Christiansen (1990-1996); Thompson (1994).

TABLE 5.4. Visitor Volume to Las Vegas and Economic Impacts

Year	Number of Visitors	Economic Impacts (Billions)	Per Visitor Spending
1989	18,129,684	$11.91	$656
1990	20,954,420	14.32	683
1991	21,315,116	14.33	672
1992	21,886,863	14.69	671
1993	23,552,593	15.13	643
1994	28,214,362	19.17	679
1995	29,002,122	20.60	710

Source: Adapted from Las Vegas Convention and Visitors Authority (1990-1996).

TABLE 5.5. Distribution of Las Vegas Customers by Region

Year	Midwest	East	West	South	Total
1989	18% (4; 1)*	10% (1; 1)	57% (2; 0)	15% (0; 0)	100% (7; 2)
1990	19% (4; 1)	10% (1; 1)	57% (2; 0)	14% (0; 0)	100% (7; 2)
1991	18% (6; 3)	10% (1; 1)	56% (4; 1)	16% (0; 0)	100% (11; 5)
1992	20% (6; 3)	12% (2; 1)	53% (4; 1)	16% (1; 1)	100% (13; 6)
1993	20% (6; 3)	9% (3; 1)	58% (4; 1)	13% (2; 2)	100% (15; 7)
1994	17% (6; 3)	10% (3; 1)	58% (4; 1)	15% (3; 3)	100% (16; 8)
1995	17% (6; 4)	10% (3; 1)	58% (4; 1)	15% (4; 3)	100% (17; 9)

Sources: Adapted from Las Vegas Convention and Visitors Authority (1990-1996); Thompson (1994).

* Number of states with casinos, tribal or nontribal; number of states with non-tribal casinos.

An examination of the tables reveals that from 1989 through 1995, the number of casinos outside Nevada increased from fifty-three to 300, with 247 new casinos. Nevada revenues increased $2.37 billion over the same period of time. With the addition of each new casino, Nevada revenues went up an average of $9.6 million on an annual basis. Over the seven-year span, gambling revenues outside Nevada increased $11.91 billion, while the increase in Nevada was $2.37 billion. For every new $5.02 outside casinos brought in, Nevada casinos brought in one extra dollar. Also for each extra $1 million wagered outside of Nevada, Las Vegas gained 900 new visitors.

Michael Evans (1996), a Professor of Economics at Northwestern University and an author of a study of the favorable impacts of casino gaming throughout the United States, recently spoke to the International Gaming Exposition in Las Vegas. He said this: "There is not a shred of evidence to support the hypothesis that riverboat gambling will take gambling away from Nevada or New Jersey." He is right. It hasn't happened. It won't happen if Las Vegas sticks to its game of offering increasingly better entertainment products along with its casino games.

A CASINO DEVELOPMENT MODEL

To understand the economic effects of casino gaming for a state or region, we need a model. Casino economics can be analyzed by using a bathtub model. In doing so, we can emphasize the simplicity of the analysis. The model is as simple as the operations of a bathtub.

Water comes into a bathtub, and water runs out of a bathtub. If the water comes in at a faster rate than it leaves the tub, the water level rises; if the water comes in at a slower rate than it leaves, the water level decreases. A local or regional economy attracts money. A local or regional economy discards money. Money comes and money goes. If as a result of the presence of casinos more money comes into an economy than leaves the economy, the casinos create a positive monetary effect.

Money comes into casino economies because of gambling. Players lose money to the casino games. Also, players attracted to a location because it has a casino will spend money on food, lodging, transportation, and other items. In the long run, construction money balances out because the money must be taken out of casino revenues. In the short run, it can constitute a major boost for a community. The money coming into the casino economy circulates and recirculates at rates known as multipliers.

Money leaves casino economies for several reasons. First, the money brought to the casino by local residents cannot be counted, unless there is reason to think the money would have been spent in another community if the casino were not there. Other money leaves the casino economy—special taxes on casinos go off to state capitals never to be seen again. Casino supplies may be purchased from sources outside of the area of the casino economy. This is money lost, as are profits that go to casino owners who live outside of the economic area of the casino. Some casino owners may reinvest money in the local economy, but they won't if they are not allowed to expand casino facilities.

Casino economies also lose money due to the costs of government services that are not directly offset by casino contributions: extra police protection outside the casino, better roads to the casino, traffic control in the casino area. The casino also may attract criminal activity, resulting in police and judicial system costs as well as costs of victimization and insurance premiums for those living near the casino. Additionally, the presence of casinos likely will be associated with some increases in pathological gambling behaviors, and these carry costs as well.

The Las Vegas economy has witnessed phenomenal growth. This has occurred even in the face of competition from around the nation and the world, as more and more locations offer casinos and casino gambling products. The Las Vegas economy is strong because the overwhelming amount of gambling money (over 90 percent) brought to the casinos comes from visitors. Figure 5.1 indicates the spending patterns of the 30 million visitors to Las Vegas each year.

FIGURE 5.1. Summary of Economic Impact Factors

Days stayed (average)	4.7
Nights stayed (average)	3.7
Proportion of respondents who stayed overnight	99%
Proportion of respondents who stayed in a hotel or motel room (among those who stayed overnight)	89%
Lodging expenditures (average per night, hotel/motel overnight visitors only—excludes package and tour/travel group visitors)	$58.04
Proportion of visitors who bought a hotel or airline package or were traveling as part of a tour/travel group where accommodations were included (among those who stayed overnight in a hotel or motel)	27%
Average cost of package per person (among package/tour group visitors)	$507.08
Number of room occupants (average—hotel/motel only)	2.1
Average trip expenditures for food and drink	$110.92
Average trip expenditures for local transportation	$38.35
Average trip expenditures for shopping	$63.51
Average trip expenditures for shows	$27.62
Average trip expenditures for sightseeing	$7.04
Proportion who gambled while visiting Las Vegas	87%
Average trip gambling budget (among those who gambled)	$580.90

Source: Las Vegas Convention and Visitors Authority (1996).

Despite visitor spending, money escapes the Las Vegas economy as well. However, state taxes are very low, and much of the profit remains because owners are local, or if not, they see great advantages in reinvesting profits in expanded facilities in Las Vegas. Las Vegas is not a manufacturing nor an agricultural region so most of the purchases, except for some gambling supplies, result in expenditures to other economies. Las Vegas also has several gambling locations (e.g., bars, 7-Eleven stores, and grocery stores), that represent very faulty bathtubs—bathtubs with huge leaks, as almost all of the gamblers at these sites are local Las Vegas residents.

Other leakages do occur in Las Vegas, as costs attached to compulsive gambling and crime caused by gamblers or because gambling is in Las Vegas. However, since over 90 percent of the gamblers come into town for only a short time as visitors, their opportunities to develop compulsive behaviors are fewer, and for those who do, the problems are shifted to other communities. The crime costs due to gamblers also are shifted for the same reason. Nonetheless, there are costs to Las Vegas. Yet, in no way will the costs in economic terms offset the positive benefits casinos bring to Las Vegas.

SOME DOWNSIDES FOR THE LAS VEGAS ECONOMY

Older Casinos

Not all casinos in Las Vegas are profitable. The overbuilding has caused some immediate grief for older properties that cannot offer new "must-see" awe-inspiring entertainment products. Four such properties fell prey to the destruction ball and were imploded in events that only added to the glamour of Las Vegas—two towers at the Dunes were blown up, as was the Sands, the Landmark, and the most spectacular implosion was the New Year's Eve display of the destruction of The Hacienda.

A Bit of Joliet in Vegas

Another genre of casinos is in trouble: the locals-oriented casinos. Their markets consist essentially of local residents and drive-in trade—overnight and weekend tourists from California and Arizona. A person visiting one of the casinos must come by automobile or by special buses that go to apartments and neighborhoods. These casinos have expanded faster than the population growth. In a sense, they represent qualities found on the riverboats of the Midwest. They compete by being newer and having cheap, but good, food. Still, their basic product is gambling, and their gambling is no different from that found at the next casino down the road. They have good odds on games so that the local residents know not to go to the Strip if they just want to gamble. In their appeals to local gamblers, they seek to get repeat visits several times a week from the same players. With their come-ons, they appeal to people who have, or are inclined to develop, gambling problems. Unfortunately for Las Vegas, players who have gambling problems in these casinos don't go back to Columbus or Indianapolis or Pittsburgh, where their economic costs may be dispersed and where they also may escape "the fever" by being many hours removed from other casinos. These problem players stay in Las Vegas. They live here.

The Essential California Market—
From There to Here: How?

Las Vegas relies upon a base of high, middle, and low rollers who make frequent visits from California. California furnishes approximately 30 percent of the visitor base. The 20 million people who live in southern California include some very good gamblers. Gamblers of Asian origin seem to enjoy the excitement of gambling and Las Vegas more than other people. The population of southern California may double in the next twenty-five years. Many newcomers to the area will be Asian, although more will be Hispanic. This may be a good market to sustain Las Vegas.

However, Las Vegas has a current crisis. Only one major interstate highway goes into southern California, Interstate 15. It extends about 300 miles, ending in the center of Los Angeles. Typically, the drive takes 4.5 hours each way. However, weekend and holiday excursions to Las Vegas on Interstate 15 take much longer. On Labor Day weekend, the typical rush hours (Friday to Las Vegas, Monday to Los Angeles) took nine hours.

There is no passenger train service between Los Angeles and Las Vegas. McCarran airport is very crowded. Combined with the lack of seats on scheduled airlines is the problem of the Californian getting to one of the four airports of the Los Angeles area. McCarran has added twenty-six gates to handle many more flights (nearly 1,000 per day already); however, the help will be for only the next few years. The Las Vegas area needs new air facilities, and the Los Angeles-Las Vegas corridor needs an effective passenger rail link, as well as new multiple lanes on Interstate 15 (much of the route has only two lanes each way).

Other Infrastructure Concerns

The Las Vegas Valley needs more water capacity. Actually, the water is available, in northern Nevada, in the Colorado River, in the Pacific Ocean. Getting the water requires overcoming major political and economic problems. Actually, the problems are mainly economic. The political aspect of the problems revolves around a willingness to spend the money and a formula for allocating the costs. There also is a growing air pollution problem, caused essentially by automobiles, but also by construction areas that do not use enough water to dampen dust distribution. Automobile-related pollution will not be helped by more cars coming from California, nor by the extra internal traffic from growing numbers of residents. Mass transit systems can be developed for the Strip and casino areas, but the local residents are not at all amenable to using mass transportation. Leaders must develop systems that appeal to locals. A convenient, reliable, and frequent system would help, but no one seems able to plan one that is cost-effective.

THE BOTTOM-LINE UPSIDE

Even with all these problems, Las Vegas should prosper well into the twenty-first century. Other casino communities—Joliet, Illinois; Deadwood, South Dakota; and Tunica, Mississippi—are forced to think about whether they will make it through next year. Las Vegas has the luxury of more long-term thinking. The demographics of the

United States are with Las Vegas. Moreover, the Las Vegas casino industry, especially the large casino industry on the Strip, has effective leadership that recognizes the communities' needs, a leadership that is willing to deal with problems to ensure that the community will remain strong economically. There is little concern about gambling's impacts in Las Vegas. It is the model of casino success (Thompson, 1995b).

REFERENCES

Christiansen, E. (1990-1996). The gross annual wager. *International Gaming and Wagering Business*, (August-September Issues).

Evans, M. (1996, October). The economic impacts of casinos in the United States. Paper presented at the meeting of the International Gaming Exposition, Las Vegas, NV.

Jensen, L. (1997, July). Guide to North American casinos. *Casino Executive 3*(7), 39-69.

Las Vegas Convention and Visitors Authority (1990-1996). *Las Vegas visitor profile study*. Las Vegas, NV: LCVA.

Nevada Development Authority (1997). *1997 Las Vegas perspective*. Las Vegas, NV: Metropolitan Research Association.

Schwer, R.K. (1989, January 31). Why the Las Vegas multiplier is less than 3. *Las Vegas Metropolitan Economic Indicators*, 1-4.

Schwer, R.K. (1997). *Historical perspective of southern Nevada*. Las Vegas, NV: University of Nevada, Las Vegas, Center for Business and Economic Research.

State Gaming Control Board (1990-1996). *The Nevada gaming abstract*. Carson City, NV: State of Nevada, Gaming Control Board.

Thompson, W.N. (1994). *Legalized gambling: A reference handbook*. Santa Barbara, CA: ABC-Clio.

Thompson, W.N. (1995a, November). To keep the winning formula. *Casino Executive 1*(8), 58-59.

Thompson, W.N. (1995b). Gambling will continue to benefit Nevada's economy. In C.P. Cozic and P.A. Winters (Eds.), *Gambling: Current controversies* (pp. 116-121). San Diego, CA: Greenhaven.

Chapter 6

Economic Impacts of Casino Gaming in Atlantic City

Dan Heneghan

The introduction of casino gambling to Atlantic City in 1976 sparked an economic revolution that continues today. Casino gambling was the economic catalyst that converted one of New Jersey's poorest cities into its richest. It turned around years of decay and attracted billions of dollars of new investment and created a boom that has had a dramatic impact on the entire state. But to fully understand the magnitude of the revolution, one has to study what Atlantic City was before casinos and how it got there.

THE QUEEN OF RESORTS

Atlantic City is a town that the railroads built. Prior to the construction of the Camden and Atlantic Railroad, only a handful of people lived in what would become Atlantic City. But once the railroad starting bringing people the sixty miles from Philadelphia in 1854, the city began to blossom. Since these earliest beginnings, Atlantic City has been a tourist/resort town.

By the start of the twentieth century, Atlantic City had become a grand seaside resort. It boasted many magnificent hotels, such as the Chalfonte-Haddon Hall, the Marlborough-Blenheim, the Traymore, and others. They were elegant sandcastles at the seashore, palaces where people could be pampered and could soak up the medicinal benefits of hot and cold running, fresh and salt water in their bathtubs. But the city didn't cater only to the rich. It's side streets were lined with smaller hotels and rooming houses, enabling working people to spend time at the shore, stroll along the Boardwalk, and rub elbows with the wealthy.

The city attracted top-name entertainment of the day to entertain those people from Philadelphia and New York City who made Atlantic City their summer home. Early in the century, it was the likes of John Philip Sousa, George Gershwin, and Enrico Caruso who entertained on the Boardwalk and in the hotels. Later came the Dorsey brothers and their bands, along with Harry James and Benny Goodman, Dean Martin, Jerry Lewis, and Frank Sinatra. In one of its last shining moments, Atlantic City even hosted the Beatles. Vicki Gold Levi described it well in her book on Atlantic City's history, *Atlantic City: 125 Years of Ocean Madness* (1979):

> If it hadn't been for unique opportunities in Atlantic City, the American public might never have heard of John Philip Sousa, W.C. Fields, Paul Whiteman, and, for better or worse, Abbot and Costello. (p. 119)

It was a city where Prohibition never really took effect and where vice was a way of life. In the 1930s, when the city was in its heyday, houses of prostitution, gambling clubs, and speakeasies operated openly and helped the city earn its reputation as a "wide-open" town. Gambling was commonplace in the city in the 1920s and 1930s:

> Thus it is that Atlantic City old-timers smile when asked how casino gambling will change their town. The fact is, Atlantic City has long been a bettor's paradise, less publicized than it is today, certainly less legal, but where there has never been a shortage of frantic action. (Levi, 1979, p. 192)

The city's population peaked in 1930 at more than 66,000 people. But things changed. The development of the interstate highway system and the start of America's love affair with the automobile opened up a whole range of new vacation opportunities for Americans. People weren't limited to vacation spots that offered convenient rail service and did not have to rely on resorts that offered transportation to shuttle guests from the train to the inn. In addition, the availability of airline travel made it just as easy for New Yorkers to fly to places such as Miami as it was to take the train or bus to Atlantic City.

THE DECLINE OF ATLANTIC CITY

As travel became easier, other cities developed convention centers to compete with Atlantic City. Fewer people visited Atlantic City, which meant that hotel operators and business owners had less money to reinvest in their facilities. As each year passed, the situation only got worse, but it was a gradual decline that wasn't always obvious to outsiders. Atlantic City continued to live off its reputation, hoping for some miracle that would lure back the big crowds, that would show the world it was still a wonderful place to visit, that would pump enough new money into the city to reverse its decline.

The city got its big chance in 1964 when the Democratic Party agreed to hold its national convention in Atlantic City. Although the city was traditionally controlled by Republicans, powers that be in the city seized on a national political convention as a way to show the nation that Atlantic City was a city on the move, a great vacation resort, and a perfect political town. This was to be Atlantic City's moment to shine.

They couldn't have been more wrong. At a political convention where the outcome was preordained—everyone knew that Lyndon Johnson was going to be chosen to run for the presidency—the media horde that descended on the city had little to report on. Certainly, there were confrontations, such as the competing Mississippi delegations, and emotional highlights, such as Robert Kennedy's moving tribute to his late brother. In the absence of real news, the media focused on the city. What they saw proved to be a major embarrassment.

In his book *The Making of the President, 1964*, Theodore White (1965) summarized how Atlantic City appeared to the outsiders looking in:

> On a six-and-a-half mile boardwalk, once the most fashionable resort of the Atlantic Coast, its old hotels rear themselves like

monuments of another era, a strung-out Angkor Wat entwined in salt water taffy, along a long, curving strand which is still one of the best beaches in the world. Time has overtaken it, and now it has become one of those sad gray places of entertainment that one can find across America, from Coney Island in New York to Knotts Berry Farm in California, where the poor and lower middle class grasp so hungrily for the first taste of pleasure that the affluent society begins to offer them—and find shoddy instead. Frequented now by old people on budget, by teenagers who come for a sporting weekend, by families of limited means trying to squeeze into cramped motel rooms, it is run down and glamourless. (pp. 275-276)

To White and the other journalists who descended on Atlantic City, as well as to the thousands of politicians and officials from around the country, the city was a disaster. Officials used to white-glove treatment were booked into motels that provided guests with paper towels. Party leaders, for whom a telephone was an umbilical cord through which the lifeblood of information flowed, were frustrated by hotel switchboards which were swamped by the demand or which simply shut down by 11 p.m., leaving guests cut off from the world. "Never have a town and chamber of commerce made a greater effort only to end by exposing themselves to ridicule" (White, 1965, p. 277).

As Heneghan noted, "What local officials thought would be the beginning of the city's rebirth was instead perhaps its most humiliating moment. From that point on, the whole world knew that the 'Queen of Resorts' was virtually comatose" (Heneghan, 1988, p. 23).

From that point on, the city's decline accelerated dramatically. In the decade before casinos were legalized, Atlantic City lost approximately 6,000 hotel rooms. Gone were grand old facilities such as the Breakers, the St. Charles, and the Ambassador. Buildings such as the Ritz-Carlton and the President were converted to apartments, while the Dennis and the Claridge slid into bankruptcy and were shut down just before the casino referendum. By the time citizens around the state voted on casinos, slightly more than 3,200 "first-class" hotel rooms were left in Atlantic City. The city counted among its finest hotels the Holiday Inn and the Howard Johnson's Regency.

All indicators showed that Atlantic City was an economic basket case. Unemployment in the city averaged just over 20 percent in 1975 and passed 24 percent in the winter. For the entire county, the rate was 13.6 percent. By the time the first casino opened in 1978, the city's population was well below the 1910 level of 46,150 (Economic Research Associates, 1976, p. III-4). Between 1960 and 1975, the city's population dropped by almost 27 percent to only 43,695.

The value of real property in the city was declining year after year. In 1972, the total taxable value of property in Atlantic City was $333.96 million. By 1976, that had slid to $308 million (Atlantic County Board of Taxation, 1972-1976). Meanwhile, according to a study commissioned by the Atlantic City Housing Authority and Urban Redevelopment Agency, the number of conventions and conventioneers visiting Atlantic City was on the decline. Between 1970 and 1975, the number of conventions that came to Atlantic City dropped from 485 to 358. The number of people attending those conventions plunged from approximately 479,000 to 360,000 (Economic Research Associates, 1976, p. III-25)

In 1976, the year New Jersey voters legalized casino gambling in Atlantic City, Atlantic City had no future. Its beachfront was littered with broken-down sandcastles of another era and a past filled with failed attempts at urban renewal. One by one, the grand old hotels that lined the Boardwalk closed their doors. The lucky ones, such as the Traymore, were demolished, while others, such as the Ambassador or the Morton, became decrepit hulks—abandoned and decaying.

Joseph Lazarow, who served as mayor of Atlantic City in the mid-1970s, was a practicing attorney prior to running for public office and his specialty was bankruptcy law. "Bankruptcy was a big business," he said in a 1988 interview with the author (Heneghan, 1988, p. 24). For Atlantic City, bankruptcy was perhaps the only alternative to casinos.

ATLANTIC CITY TURNS TO CASINOS

The first talk of legalizing casinos in Atlantic City appears to have occurred in the late 1950s when the Women's Chamber of Commerce pushed the idea. Local residents remembered earlier years when Atlantic City had a reputation as a wide-open town.

Residents and officials alike yearned for the good old days when illegal casino gambling flourished in clubs with names such as Babette's and the Bath and Turf Club—clubs that operated under the watchful eyes of corrupt local officials.

However, the effort to amend New Jersey's constitution and permit legal casino gambling didn't gain much steam until the 1970s. Backers finally were able to get a measure on the ballot in 1974. Although the original concept was to bring casinos to Atlantic City, the referendum would have permitted state-owned casinos anywhere in the state that the people wanted them. But the people didn't want that. The thought of a casino in some of the state's tonier neighborhoods frightened away supporters, and the measure failed.

Although the referendum was defeated in 1974, local residents didn't give up. Within months, they mounted a new campaign to legalize casinos. A group of local business, civic, and political leaders was formed—the Committee to Rebuild Atlantic City, or CRAC. Committee members embarked on an aggressive fund-raising campaign to help sell the state on casinos. This time the measure would limit casinos to Atlantic City alone and the gaming halls would be privately owned while strictly regulated by the state. To make the measure more palatable to voters, supporters promised that the taxes on gambling revenues would be dedicated to programs that would benefit the state's senior citizens and people with disabilities. It was an effort to turn the moral question of legalizing gambling into a mom-and-apple-pie issue of helping senior citizens. A campaign was mounted with the slogan "Help Yourself. Help Atlantic City."

With the prospect of another effort to legalize casinos on the horizon, the Atlantic City Housing Authority and Urban Redevelopment Agency commissioned a study that would project the impact that casino gaming would have on the city. Economic Research Associates (ERA), a Virginia-based consulting firm that had done earlier studies for the city and the housing authority, was retained to estimate the impact. The 126-page report ERA submitted in June 1976 became the basis of the campaign promises made to the people of New Jersey.

In the report, ERA spelled out the plight of Atlantic City. Virtually every economic indicator showed that the city was either stagnating or on the decline. Population of the city was down; the number of hotel rooms was down; convention attendance was down; real estate values were down; traffic in and out of the city was down; luxury tax collections were down. But casino gambling could turn that all around. According to ERA, "If this amendment is enacted, the subsequent development of Atlantic City as a destination attraction for casino gambling will have a major impact on the city's primary economic base" (ERA, 1976, p. II-1).

PROMISES MADE

The projected impacts identified by ERA appeared monumental. But in hindsight, they were quite conservative. Here are just a few of ERA's conclusions:

- A minimum of 1.4 million additional visitors to Atlantic City can be expected annually when casino facilities are in place.
- Each new visitor will spend approximately 3.8 days in Atlantic City.
- New casino hotels and renovated hotel facilities in Atlantic City will receive revenues in excess of $800 million annually.
- When completed, the new casino hotels will employ between 21,825 and 29,100 new workers. . . . This added employment will generate in excess of $213 million to $284 million in new payrolls.
- Based on the present level of gaming taxes found in Nevada, it is estimated that the state of New Jersey will receive approximately $30 million annually in casino tax revenues.
- Additional property tax revenue generated by the new casino hotels will approximate $29 million annually to Atlantic City.
- Between 4,900 and 9,700 hotel rooms will be constructed to accommodate new visitors to Atlantic City at a cost of between $436.5 million and $698 million from 1977 through 1985. (ERA, 1976)

The projections were incorporated into campaign literature developed by the Committee to Rebuild Atlantic City. Campaign literature urged voters to "Help Yourself. Help Atlantic City. Help New Jersey." It promised that a "yes" vote on the casino referendum would "balance taxes, create jobs, boost the economy, cut down on street crime" (Committee to Rebuild Atlantic City, 1976).

However, the projections proved to be way off. It is easy to point to a variety of sources which show that the promises turned out to be extremely conservative. One source was a pair of reports prepared for the Casino Association of New Jersey by the accounting firm of Touche Ross in 1987 and 1988: "In reviewing the original projections made for the casino industry a decade ago for the year 1985, the results have far exceeded original projections" (1988, p. 3).

AN EXPLOSION OF GROWTH

ERA's projections probably most missed their mark in the area of visitation (see Table 6.1). ERA had estimated that the introduction of casinos would result in an additional 1.4 million visitors and those visitors would stay an average of 3.8 days in the city. Those figures were based, in part, on the experience reported by Las Vegas and the Bahamas.

As the casinos developed, it turned out that ERA was far too conservative on the number of visitors and far too optimistic on the

TABLE 6.1. Comparison of ERA Projection and Actual Casino Contribution

	ERA Projection 1976-1985	Actual Contribution by 1985
Number of visitors per year	1.4 million	29.3 million
Average length of stay	3.8 days	shorter
Hotel revenue	$800 million	$2.4 billion
Number of new jobs	21,825-29,100	40,000
New payrolls	$213-284 million	$658.6 million
Casino tax per year	$30.3 million	$169.2 million
Property tax per year	$29 million	$37.4 million
Number of hotel rooms	4,900-9,700	6,342
Hotel construction cost	$436.5-698 million	$2.3 billion

Sources: Economic Research Associates (1976); Touche Ross (1987, 1988).

length of stay. ERA didn't take into consideration that people had to make a significant commitment to visit Las Vegas or the Bahamas. In the first year of casino gaming, the city's one gaming hall helped to attract slightly more than 7 million visitors. By 1985, the end of the projection period used by ERA, the number of visitors was more than 29.3 million! However, it turned out that most of those visitors never spent the night in Atlantic City. More than 12.5 million of those visitors came to the city by bus. They generally stayed only six hours and then went home. In addition, since Atlantic City is located in the heart of the most heavily populated area of the country, many of the 15.7 million people who drove into the city lived close enough to drive in, gamble, and drive back home on the same day (South Jersey Transportation Authority, 1997).

ERA estimated that the casinos would generate revenues of $800 million by 1985. Figures from the casino industry and the state regulators show that casinos passed that level by 1981, when the gaming halls took in over $1.27 billion. By the target date of 1985, casinos were generating $2.4 billion in total revenue. The growth trend continued every year, and by 1996, total revenues exceeded $4 billion. Revenues from the casino operations alone accounted for most of that. In 1981, gaming activity accounted for $1.1 billion. That increased to $2.1 billion by 1985 and to $3.8 billion in 1997 (see Figure 6.1).

MORE JOBS THAN EVER IMAGINED

Supporters claimed that casino gambling would create between 21,825 and 29,100 new jobs for Atlantic City by 1985. "The gaming program would certainly contribute substantially to resolving the chronically high unemployment rate in the area by providing a stable source of year-round employment and by generally providing a strong stimulus to the overall economic revitalization of Atlantic City" (ERA, 1976, p. VII-7).

Those projections were so conservative that the low end was passed by the end of 1980. By mid-1982, the number passed the upper end of the range. In a study for the Federal Reserve Bank, Professor Thomas Hamer (1982) commented on the enormous impact:

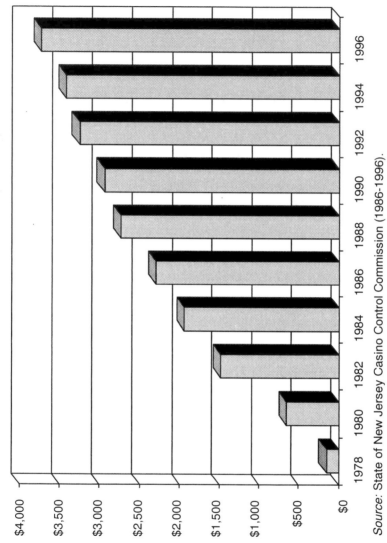

FIGURE 6.1. Atlantic City Casino Revenues (in Millions)

Source: State of New Jersey Casino Control Commission (1986-1996).

Compared to what would have been, then, legalized gambling has created a boom in Atlantic County. Employment has grown vigorously instead of stagnating, and unemployment insurance claims have remained stable instead of rising. (p. 12)

By the target date of 1985, some 40,000 people had full-time jobs in casino hotels. In the second quarter of 1997, more than 50,000 people were employed in Atlantic City's casino hotels. With the potential for significant additional investment and the construction of another four or five casino hotels, the number of casino employees will continue to increase.

The effects on payroll were equally impressive. As shown in Figure 6.2, the ERA study estimated that casino employees would earn anywhere from $213 million to $284 million in salaries and wages by 1985. By 1985, they actually earned $658.6 million—more than two to three times the original projection. As of 1996, the total salaries and wages exceeded $1 billion (State of New Jersey Casino Control Commission, 1996).

TAX REVENUES SOAR

ERA and CRAC projected that by 1985, casinos would generate $30.3 million a year in taxes on the casino revenue alone. Figures from the industry and the state regulators show that the gross revenue tax passed the $30-million mark in 1979—the first full year of casino gambling. In 1985, the state actually collected $169.2 million. In 1996, the amount collected passed $303 million, ten times the amount forecasted by ERA and CRAC just twenty years before.

However, those aren't the only taxes casinos pay. As owners of the most valuable real estate in Atlantic City, the casinos pay the lion's share of the real estate taxes in Atlantic City. In 1976, backers projected that the casinos would contribute an additional $29 million a year to the city through real estate taxes. By 1985, casinos paid $37.4 million in taxes to support the city government—or 72 percent of the amount raised from all property owners. In the same year, they also paid $12 million to support the city's school system and another $14.2 million to pay the cost of county govern-

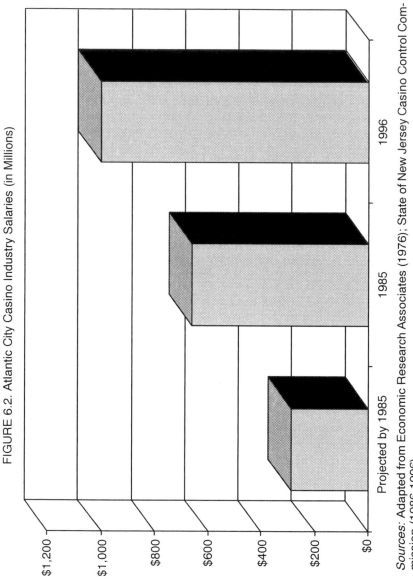

FIGURE 6.2. Atlantic City Casino Industry Salaries (in Millions)

Sources: Adapted from Economic Research Associates (1976); State of New Jersey Casino Control Commission (1986-1996).

ment. By 1996, those figures had increased to $80.8 million for city government, another $35.4 million for the schools, and $22.6 million for county government, according to figures reported to Atlantic City and Atlantic County tax offices.

Casinos also pay corporate taxes, Social Security taxes, unemployment taxes, and others. They also collect taxes from patrons on hotel rooms, parking, and other items. When added together, the taxes and other payments to government entities exceed $700 million a year.

BILLIONS INVESTED

The number of hotel rooms built by casinos fell in the middle of the range estimated by ERA. By the end of 1985, casino hotels had a total of 6,342 rooms. However, the amount spent by casinos to build those rooms far exceeded the projections. Instead of investing between $436.5 million and $698 million, the casino industry had invested nearly $2.3 billion. And it didn't stop in 1985. By 1996, casinos had invested more than $6 billion, and companies were poised to invest another $4 billion to $5 billion in several new projects on the drawing board. The existing casino hotels had more than 11,000 rooms, and at least that many more rooms were in new casinos and expansions proposed by Mirage Resorts, Circus Circus Enterprises, Boyd Gaming, MGM Grand, Sun International, and other operators.

As a result of the massive investments by casinos, the value of all the city's taxable real estate soared. As shown in Figure 6.3, from a nadir of $318 million just before casinos, the city's tax base soared to more than $6.3 billion (Atlantic County Board of Taxation, 1976; 1996). That made Atlantic City, once dependent on special state urban aid, the wealthiest city in the state. All of the property in Newark, the state's largest city, every square inch of land and every building on it, was worth just over $5 billion in 1996. Newark is about 23.8 square miles, while the developable land in Atlantic City only comprises about four square miles.

In comparing the size of Atlantic City's tax base with other areas, one has to realize that Atlantic City is a very small geographic area. The city is only forty-eight blocks long—shorter than Central Park

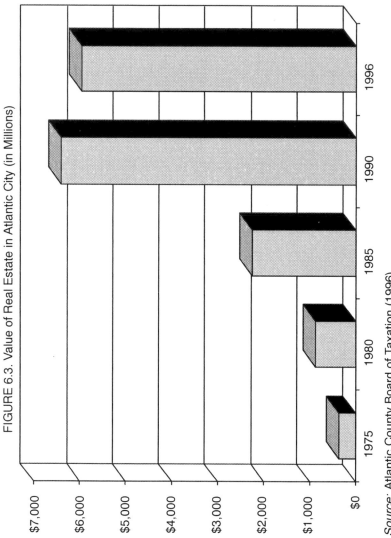

FIGURE 6.3. Value of Real Estate in Atlantic City (in Millions)

Source: Atlantic County Board of Taxation (1996).

126

in Manhattan. And in some areas, the developable land isn't much wider than Central Park. Since the area is so small—only 2,500 acres of developable land in the city—the economic impacts of casino gaming could not be confined to Atlantic City alone. Throughout the greater Atlantic City area, enormous new housing developments have been built within a twenty-five mile radius of Atlantic City since casino gaming was introduced.

One of the criticisms leveled at the gaming industry is that only about one in four or one in five of all the jobs went to residents of Atlantic City. The ratio of local employees was correct, but it over-looked how small the city's population was. As of late 1997, just over 50,000 jobs were available in Atlantic City's casinos, but only about 37,000 residents live in the city. The casino industry employed more than half of the city's workforce. Even with Atlantic City's chronically high unemployment rate, the concentration of casino hotel employees in the city is overwhelming.

If you look at the county surrounding Atlantic City, you find that more than 35,000 of the jobs are located there. In addition, casinos buy an enormous amount of goods and services from companies in Atlantic County. In 1996, casinos spent $2.53 billion buying goods and services. Of that, $966 million went to companies located in Atlantic County.

CASINO BENEFITS FOR ALL OF NEW JERSEY

In addition to the direct employment created by casinos, a variety of indirect economic impacts have benefited the state and regional economy. Casinos now spend more than $1.5 billion annually buy-ing goods and services from companies within the state of New Jersey. In the decade from 1987 through 1996, casinos spent more than $19 billion buying goods and services. Of that amount, $12.67 billion was spent on companies in New Jersey (State of New Jersey Casino Control Commission, 1987-1996).

A study done for the Casino Association of New Jersey in 1988 tried to identify the economic impacts of the industry, both direct and indirect. That report concluded that the casino industry "has had a major effect on the state, county and city in areas such as employment, capital investment, and taxes. . . . In less than ten years, the casino industry has clearly become one of the state's major employers, generating more than 65,044 jobs for New Jersey residents" (Touche Ross, 1987, p. 2).

The actual secondary employment impacts are difficult to pin down, and over the years, several different estimates have been made. For example, the Touche Ross studies in 1987 and 1988 utilized a multiplier of 1.5 for casino hotel jobs based on an input-output model developed by Dr. Jong Keun You of the Office of Economic Policy and Planning for the New Jersey Department of Commerce (Touche Ross, 1987). Using that multiplier, for every two jobs in casino hotels, one other job was created elsewhere in the state's economy.

But Hamer, in a 1995 study commissioned by the Casino Association of New Jersey, utilized a much higher multiplier, based on an input-output model from the U.S. Department of Commerce, Bureau of Economic Analysis. He estimated that the proper multiplier was 2.0858—"for every job in the casino industry, an additional 1.0858 jobs are generated in all other industries in the state" (Hamer, 1995, p. ii). Applying that multiplier to an average monthly employment in the Atlantic City casino industry of 43,900 full-time equivalent positions, Hamer estimated that 47,700 jobs were created elsewhere in the state's economy.

Hamer estimated in 1995 that Atlantic City's casinos accounted for 73 percent of all private sector jobs in Atlantic City. In addition, he estimated that the payroll from casino jobs accounted for almost one-third the total nonfarm payroll for the entire county.

SOME SOCIAL PROBLEMS ADDRESSED, NOT CURED

Casino gaming certainly hasn't solved Atlantic City's unemployment problems. The New Jersey Department of Labor reported that the unemployment rate in Atlantic City stood at 14.3 percent in 1996. In fact, the rate increased sharply several years ago and has slowly declined. But the unemployment rate can lead to a false conclusion that casinos aren't hiring local residents. The gaming halls employ approximately 11,000 Atlantic City residents, or well over half of the city's entire workforce.

Another measure of the success of the casino gaming experiment is the number of recipients of Aid to Families with Dependent Children. In 1978, the number of recipients in Atlantic County peaked at 7,019. That represented 4.82 percent of all recipients around the state. As casinos opened, the number of families receiving this aid declined rapidly. By 1984, when Atlantic City's industry was thriving, recipients numbered only 3,863, and the number of clients in Atlantic County represented only 2.9 percent of the total cases statewide. The number of recipients in the county started to rise slowly at that point until it reached 5,081. Although that was a substantial increase, the total still only represented 3.92 percent of all cases in the state. By 1996, the number declined again, dropping to 3,506, or 3.21 percent of the state total (Hamer, 1995).

GAMING HELPS SENIORS

Although jobs and investment often are viewed as the major impacts, the casino industry in New Jersey is unique in that the tax revenue is dedicated to programs that benefit the state's senior citizens and people with disabilities. Of the total casino revenue, 8 percent is paid into the state's Casino Revenue Fund. The money then goes into a variety of programs that are unique to New Jersey. For example, any senior citizen who qualifies from an income standpoint can participate in the Pharmaceutical Assistance to the Aged and Disabled program. Participating seniors only have to pay $5 to have a prescription filled; the rest is effectively paid for by Atlantic City's casinos. It is a program that has allowed more than 200,000 of the state's seniors and people with disabilities to afford prescription drugs.

Another program is Lifeline Credit. Qualifying seniors can get a credit toward their utility bills of $225 a year. A myriad of other programs also are financed through the Casino Revenue Fund. Casinos help to subsidize real estate tax rebates for seniors and fund transportation programs that bring seniors to social functions, medical appointments, and even to their neighborhood supermarkets. Taken together, those programs offer seniors and people with disabilities a range of services apparently unavailable in any other state, and they have had a significant impact on the quality of life for several hundred thousand New Jersey residents:

> As to the benefits, it is generally acknowledged that when legalized gambling is proposed, it is linked to some worthwhile purpose. For example, an 8 percent tax on casino revenues is designated for programs for the elderly and disabled, and another 1.25 percent is earmarked for redevelopment projects in Atlantic City and across the state. The 8 percent tax has raised more than $1 billion to date, while the reinvestment requirement is expected to gross more than $1.5 billion over 25 years. (Governor's Advisory Commission on Gambling, 1988, p. 4)

REINVESTMENT IN NONGAMING SECTORS

When the Casino Control Act was first passed in 1977, it included a provision that required casinos to reinvest 2 percent of their revenues into real property in Atlantic City and gave operators five years within which to make those investments. Only casinos that took in more money than they had invested in their property were required to make the investment, and if they failed to do so, they had to pay an additional 2 percent gross revenue tax.

For a variety of reasons, the requirement didn't work. Astute accountants quickly realized the reinvestment obligation could be put in the bank for five years and earn interest, after which the additional tax could be paid. The casino could then receive a credit against federal taxes for the additional state tax paid. That made it much cheaper for a casino to delay making any reinvestment in real property.

The inability to capitalize on the enormous investment made by casinos also was the result of a variety of factors, many of which casinos could not control. Interest rates in 1980 were near 20 percent, and the national economy was in shambles. High interest rates and land speculation that was effectively fueled by local government made it economically impossible for any new housing to be built in the city.

The reinvestment program was revised in 1984 to counter criticism over the failure to rebuild Atlantic City. That, after all, had been one of the primary goals of legalizing casino gambling. It was the Committee to Rebuild Atlantic City that was formed to push for passage of the casino referendum in 1976. But for years after the first casino opened, much of Atlantic City continued to look like an enormous slum. The introduction of casinos created a dozen pockets of enormous wealth in what had been an economically depressed area.

The reinvestment provisions were changed to require casinos to reinvest 1.25 percent of their gaming revenues through the Casino Reinvestment Development Authority (CRDA). If they failed to do so, the casino would have to pay an additional tax of 2.5 percent, thereby eliminating the financial incentive to not reinvest. To garner enough support in the state legislature for the change, some of the money was earmarked for other areas of the state instead of concentrating it in Atlantic City. Although the CRDA got off to a slow start, it quickly amassed hundreds of millions of dollars, which it put to use to help rebuild the city.

A CITY REBUILT

"The Casino Reinvestment Development Authority, one of the most unique public agencies for urban redevelopment ever created by government, utilizes revenues generated by Atlantic City's casino industry to finance capital improvement projects which enhance the hospitality industry and residential neighborhoods throughout the resort," authority chairman Frederick P. Nickels wrote in one of the authority's brochures. He added that the use of reinvestment funds to build hotel rooms, visitor attractions, cultural facilities, and infrastructure creates construction jobs and permanent jobs, makes Atlantic City a more livable community, and has a rollover effect that supports local businesses (CRDA, 1997, p. 2).

In the twenty years since gambling was legalized, almost 5,000 new housing units were built in Atlantic City, according to officials at the Atlantic City Housing Authority and Urban Redevelopment Agency. That is an enormous amount of housing for a city with a population of only 37,000. Since the population was declining slowly for much of the period, the housing largely went to replace dilapidated structures. Large sections of blighted neighborhoods were razed and replaced with new townhouses and mid-rise apartments through the CRDA. Casino reinvestment funds also have gone to programs to help encourage people to move into the new housing. For example, police officers who live in the city get extremely low interest mortgages and can get a police car that they can take home with them and park on the street to help deter crime.

In addition, casino reinvestment funds were used to rebuild much of the city's infrastructure. Heavily traveled roads have been widened, rebuilt, and realigned with casino funds. After the state agreed to build a $268-million convention center in Atlantic City, some of the reinvestment funds were used to stimulate the construction of even more hotel rooms. That started a mini-construction boom and the opening of several thousand new hotel rooms. The boom was chronicled in the annual report of the CRDA. "As gaming industry revenues are reinvested, virtually every segment of the community reaps the benefits. Neighborhoods have been improved and redeveloped, and new construction is providing attractive, affordable housing and ownership opportunities previously unavailable" (CRDA, 1996). Through the CRDA, Atlantic City is building a minor league baseball stadium and a marine life education center—projects designed to enhance the city's attractiveness as a place to live, work, and visit.

Reinvestment funds also have gone to help finance projects around the state of New Jersey. As of 1996, tens of millions of dollars had gone to build housing, provide low-interest loans to farmers, and finance a much-needed hospital parking garage. CRDA funds helped pay for the state's Vietnam Veterans Memorial, as well as a minor league baseball stadium in Trenton. Through reinvestment funds, casinos helped to build a supermarket in Union City and provided all of the funding for a day care center in Woodbury.

In the national debate over gaming, it is too easy for people to focus on the $45 billion that gamblers lost in Atlantic City over a twenty-year period at the slot machines and gaming tables and to point to it as the negative economic impact of gaming. It is easy to look around Atlantic City and see the glitzy gambling palaces that conjure up images of great corporate greed. But, an overwhelming percentage of that $45 billion has gone back into the pockets of employees and vendors and has helped to build a vibrant economy for the region.

REFERENCES

Atlantic County Board of Taxation (1972-1976; 1996). *Abstract of rateables.* Atlantic City, NJ: Author.

Casino Reinvestment Development Authority (CRDA) (1996). *Annual report, 1996.* Atlantic City, NJ: Author.

Casino Reinvestment Development Authority (CRDA) (1997). *Agenda 2001.* Atlantic City, NJ: Author.

Committee to Rebuild Atlantic City (1976). *Help yourself. Help Atlantic City. Help New Jersey* [Brochure]. Atlantic City, NJ: Strathmore Press.

Economic Research Associates (1976, June). *Impact of casino gambling on the redevelopment potential of the uptown urban renewal site and the economy of Atlantic City.* Atlantic City, NJ: Author.

Governor's Advisory Commission on Gambling (1988). *Report and recommendations of the governor's advisory commission on gambling.* Trenton, NJ: Author.

Hamer, T. (1982, January-February). The casino industry in Atlantic City. *Business Review,* 3-16.

Hamer, T. (1995). *Economic impact of the New Jersey casino industry.* Glassboro, NJ: Rowan College.

Heneghan, D. (1988, May). Atlantic City B.C. (before casinos). *Casino Gaming,* 4(5), 22-23.

Levi, V.G. (1979). *Atlantic City: 125 years of ocean madness.* New York: Clarkson N. Potter.

South Jersey Transportation Authority (1997). *Annual visitor-trips.* Atlantic City, NJ: Author.

State of New Jersey Casino Control Commission (1986-1996). *Annual report.* Atlantic City, NJ: Author.

Touche Ross (1987). *The casino industry's economic impact on New Jersey.* Atlantic City, NJ: Author.

Touche Ross (1988). *The casino industry's economic impact on the Atlantic City region.* Atlantic City, NJ: Author.

White, T.H. (1965). *The making of the president, 1964.* New York: Atheneum Publishers.

Chapter 7

Economic Impacts of Native American Casino Gaming

Carl A Boger Jr.
Daniel Spears
Kara Wolfe
Li-Chun Lin

BACKGROUND

Expansion from the Florida Seminole bingo hall in the late 1970s to the massive construction of the Mashantucket Pequot's 200,000-square-foot Foxwoods casino in Connecticut demonstrates the growth of Native American casinos throughout the United States. In the Foxwoods example, the casino was opened by the Mashantucket Pequot tribe in February 1992 (Carmichael, Peppard, and Boudreau, 1996). In two short years, this casino had approximately 10,000 employees with revenues over $600 million. This casino is presently the largest in the world. The casino location is excellent, with a strategic location between New York City and Boston, and has a monopoly position on gaming within the state (Leiper, 1989).

This region of the Northeast faced reduction in the defense industry and manufacturing downsizing, which became a crisis situation in the late 1980s. The U.S. State Department of Statistics shows that from 1988 to 1993, the region lost 10,000 jobs overall, including nearly 4,800 high-income manufacturing jobs (Connecticut Labor Department, 1994). The Foxwoods Resort Casino brought in many high-paying service industry jobs to a depressed economy that needed immediate assistance in economic development.

Nationally, Native American gaming is bringing in needed revenue to many rural communities and, in some cases, to blighted urban areas. In 1993, over 170 tribes had some form of legalized gambling, with 145 tribes in twenty-four different states having Class III Native American gaming, with over 160 signed compacts. These compacts are agreements between the states and Native American tribes that allow the Native Americans to have casinos within the states. "Native American gambling only accounts for approximately 5 percent of total United States gaming revenues and it is growing by more than 200 percent annually" (Turner, 1993, p. 62). In 1995, it was estimated that $30 billion was wagered in Native American casinos, generating revenues of $2.8 billion. By 1997, these figures grew to $40 billion wagered and revenues of $5 billion to $6 billion.

Individual gaming facilities also have generated millions of dollars in revenue. For example, Mystic Lake casino on Shakopee Sioux land in Minnesota reported over $177.7 million of revenues, while Foxwoods Casino is generating over $500 million annually (Long, 1995).

HISTORY OF THEIR ECONOMIC DEVELOPMENT

A study was conducted to examine the economic development of twenty-three reservations using 1970, 1980, and 1990 census data. The poverty standard for the year 1970 was $3,743 for a nonfarming family of four (Vinje, 1996). These twenty-three reservations had a total of 52.2 percent of their members falling under the poverty line, compared to Native Americans living outside the reservation, with 33 percent falling under the poverty line.

In the 1960s, the Bureau of Indian Affairs (BIA) became a dominant player in determining the economic development on tribal lands. During this period, tribal authorities, the BIA, the Economic Development Administration, the Office of Economic Opportunity, and the Department of Labor developed proposals to attract private, labor-intensive firms to these reservations. This strategy was extremely expensive for both the tribal and federal governments (Vinje, 1985). By the 1970s, private wages and salary employees represented 47 percent of those who were employed on reservations. Manufacturing represented 47 percent of the employees; agriculture, 11.1 percent; and services, 43.6 percent.

The next decade brought about the issue of self-determination, when Native Americans took control of their own financial welfare and direction. The Indian Financing Act of 1974 and Education Assistance Act of 1975 provided financial assistance to Native American tribes in terms of loans, grants, and collateral to develop new reservation economic activities and to provide educational opportunities to Native Americans. For the first time in decades, Native Americans regained control of their economic destiny. During the same period, raw natural resources on Native American land became increasingly valuable due to price fluctuations of natural resources. Economic situations on Native American reservations improved, and the poverty rate decreased from 52.2 percent in 1970 to 44.1 percent in 1980. Employment opportunities for Native Americans also improved on reservations. In 1970, 41.3 percent of the people were employed, and by 1980, employment grew to 66.8 percent (Stuart, 1990).

The 1980s were extremely difficult for Native Americans living on reservations due to the idea that self-determination should be extended to a "new federalism," which emphasized a reduction in the BIA operations. Federal grants and loans were diminished, and those which were given required that 75 percent of the money be provided by private or tribal sources. This was a total reversal of what occurred in the past, when 75 to 100 percent of the funds came from the federal government. A decrease of 34 percent of federal Native American grants and a 28.1 percent decrease in funds for job training occurred. The only sector of federal expenditures for Native Americans that increased during this period was related to Native American health care, with an average increase of 3.5 percent (Stuart, 1990). The reduction of federal aid and collapse of natural resource markets caused Native Americans to seek other economic development avenues for their people.

The number of families below the poverty line increased to 48.8 percent by 1990, which represented an increase of 4.7 percent since 1980. Employment also decreased from 60.8 to 51.8 percent during the same time period. These economic pressures caused Native Americans to examine gaming as a possible solution to their economic crisis.

What caused these economic problems on reservations? Native Americans are very proud and hardworking people, but, due to reservations being placed on throw-away lands having very little economic value, Native Americans were placed in a situation in which their survival was dependent on aid from the federal government. The majority of tribal lands are barren and isolated and are unsuitable even for growing crops (Turner, 1992). Native Americans have been called the "forgotten people" because of the federal government's broken promises and treaties during budgetary downsizing and shifting emphases at the federal level.

Another dilemma is that 80 percent of tribal lands being held in trust by the U.S. government cannot be used as collateral for the needed capital to invest in businesses and property. The old saying "We mortgage the farm for our families' future" is not true for the Native Americans because the federal government does not allow them to use their lands as collateral. Risk is an inherit factor when individuals, communities, or nations are seeking economic prosperity. Without capital, there is no infrastructure, economic development, or hope for a better way of life for future generations. The question then becomes, what type of businesses could be developed on barren lands without any financial resources or collateral that could have a significant impact on the reservations?

Gaming was seen as one of the few opportunities that could attract outside investors without collateral. Nevada provided an example of how gaming almost entirely supported the local and state economies. The land was barren, but legalized gaming provided the incentives to attract outside investors to build casinos in a near wasteland environment (Ferber and Chon, 1994). The other possible economic alternative for Nevada was to become the world's largest toxic waste dump. If you were a citizen of Nevada, or lived on a reservation, would you rather have toxic waste dumps or casinos? A secondary benefit of casinos in Nevada is that citizens pay no state income tax.

ECONOMIC AND COMMUNITY IMPACT

The advent of Native American casinos has provided jobs for both Native and non–Native Americans (Boger, 1994). Depending on the number of tribal members, size of the casino, and management agreements with outside entities, Native Americans have served as an advisory group, management, and actual workers in the casinos. It has been reported that in some reservations each tribal member received over $500,000 a year. In these cases, Native Americans usually serve as top management and hire non–Native Americans to manage the day-to-day operations.

How much visitors will spend outside a Native American casino is always a question when attempting to determine the overall economic impact of gaming on a local community. A study titled "Economic, Resource, and Fiscal Impacts of Visitors on Washoe County, Nevada," conducted by Borden, Fletcher, and Haqrris (1996) found that the average visitor spends on average $57.90 outside and $75.61 inside of a casino. The two greatest expenditures outside of the casino were shopping ($23.45) and food ($14.59). It is also interesting to note that, within the reservation, the average visitor only spends $14.18 on food. A concern by many restaurant owners is that Native American gaming will draw business away from them. This study found that is not the case and casinos could actually contribute business to off-reservation restaurants. The quality of the restaurants and shopping in communities probably have more of an effect on lost business than the introduction of a casino into the area. Other tourist attractions also benefited from casino visitors by their average expenditures on entertainment ($6.95), sightseeing ($4.72), recreation ($3.33), and events ($1.32).

TAX BENEFITS

Native American gaming has drawn the attention of local, state, and federal government officials to the opportunity of bringing in additional tax revenues through legalizing non–Native American casinos or through agreements among Native American tribes, state, and local governments. The Mashantucket Pequot tribe provides $100 million of annual fees to have exclusive rights to gaming within the state of Connecticut. Another example is the Ho-Chunk tribe in Wisconsin that contributes $250,000 to the Wisconsin Dells Visitors Bureau to provide tourism advertisement in the winter months (Boger, 1994).

As sovereign nations, Native American casinos are not obligated to pay state and local taxes. However, many Native American tribes are reaching agreements with local and state governments to make "donations" or pay "fees" to support road improvements, gain fire and police services to the casinos, and assist in the economic prosperity of nonreservation communities. The increased wealth of Native Americans is circulating throughout the local and state economies through purchases made outside the reservation and through the activity of the casinos. Nearly one out of every four dollars earned by a casino is used to purchase a variety of goods and services for its operation, and nearly 90 percent of these expenditures are made within state boundaries (Connor, 1993). These non-Native American companies are paying taxes on the dollars being generated through Native American casino purchases. At many casinos, a tribal tax is paid by casino visitors on restaurant and gift shop purchases, because they are independent entities and are able to levy taxes on their reservations.

Income taxes are also being paid by the non–Native Americans who are working on the reservations. For example, the Fort Randall Casino in Wagner, South Dakota, employs 654 people; 66 percent of the employees are Native American. Its annual payroll generates more than $600,000 in federal taxes and has a payroll of 7.3 million dollars (McCulloch, 1994). Casino income taxes represent the largest single payment of income taxes from a single business in many rural communities. As Nelson Rose, law professor and expert on gaming, once said, "Gambling begets gambling" (Rose, 1993). The real pressure on Native American gaming probably will not be from other Native American tribes but rather non–Native American gaming, either through riverboat or land-based operations.

ECONOMIC IMPACT STUDIES

Examining the economic impact of Native American gaming on the local, state, and national levels is difficult since Native Americans do not have to report or make public their financial statements. This requires that data be collected through secondary sources, such as studies that have been commissioned by states or Native Americans themselves, or through universities or private institutions.

Nearly every study makes different assumptions or uses different formulas to measure the direct or indirect impact of Native American gaming on the citizens of these different states and the Native Americans. Therefore, this discussion of the economic impact of Native American gaming will be examined through studies that have been conducted and governmental sources.

It is interesting to note that these studies did include both positive and negative economic impacts of Native American gaming and attempted to use conservative figures when estimating the economic impact. This is probably because the studies were conducted by reputable firms that knew their studies would be intensely scrutinized by local, state, and national leaders.

Foxwoods High-Stakes Bingo and Casino

The Foxwoods Resort Casino is located near Ledyard, Connecticut, which is a quiet, rural part of the state that has been hit hard by defense cuts and steady economic decline. Foxwoods Resort Casino has provided more than 9,500 new jobs, with an average wage of approximately $35,000 when you add in wages, benefits, and tips (Wright et al., 1993). Wages paid at the casino are approximately $2,000 more than other jobs within the area. The Mashantucket Pequot tribe has increased the standard of living for its members while diversifying into other business ventures. The state of Connecticut also has benefited through millions of dollars in contributions.

It has been estimated that every new Foxwoods job supports roughly 1.23 additional noncasino jobs in New London County where the casino is located. This means that 20,017 new jobs have been created in New London County, providing an additional $478.5 million in payroll for the area. These additional earnings within New London County also benefit the entire state of Connecticut through the residents purchasing items from other areas of the state. Each job provided by the casino should create another 0.74 job in other counties of Connecticut, which means that an additional 7,000 jobs are created within the state with an additional $214 million being generated in other Connecticut counties. Overall, with an average salary of $30,500, for every new employee at the casino, an additional $50,355 worth of wages will be generated, either through direct or indirect jobs associated with the expansion of Foxwoods Resort Casino. These additional jobs reduce the dependency on Aid to Families with Dependent Children (AFDC). For every 1,000 jobs created at Foxwoods, approximately 175 recipients of AFDC have been removed from the payrolls. This translates into savings of $369,600 to $624,000 per year in AFDC payments for every 1,000 jobs created (Wright et al., 1993).

Not only does gaming activity assist in increasing wages and decreasing welfare costs, it also assists in increasing the market values of homes. For every 1 percent point decline in the weighted average regional unemployment rate, there is a 7 percent increase in home prices. In other words, as the economy improves, home prices increase. Home prices are expected to increase by a total of $1.177 billion just by Foxwoods' hiring of employees. By the year 2000, home prices are expected to increase by a total of 29.1 percent, or $4.882 billion (Wright et al., 1993).

St. Croix Casino

The St. Croix Casino opened in the village of Turtle Lake, Wisconsin, in May 1992. Turtle Lake is located on the western edge of Barron County, which is adjacent to the Polk County border. The village is approximately 2.5 hours from Minneapolis, Minnesota, and 1.5 hours from Eau Clair, Wisconsin. Population within the village is approximately 800 people, with the area's major industries being agriculture and manufacturing. Polk and Barron counties, similar to other counties in Wisconsin, support recreational tourism and a large number of second-home homeowners (Green, Sroka, and Maney, 1996).

The St. Croix Chippewa reservation consists of discontinuous land across several counties. Four major sites are the Round Lake reservation in Polk County, Maple Plains in Barron County, and Hertel and Banbury in Burnett County. The *1990 Census of Population and Housing* reported that the St. Croix Chippewa had 485 Native Americans living on the reservations. The unemployment rate on the reservation was 40 percent, with the per capita income being $4,300. This means that 50 percent of Native Americans living on the reservation were below the poverty line (Bureau of the Census, 1990).

The direct wages of the casino total $12.32 million, with 561 people working within the casino. Other casino expenditures supported another 137 jobs, which translates into another $3.02 million in additional income. Casino patrons also purchased food, lodging, gasoline, and other items within the two counties, which supported another ninety-four jobs, with an overall income of $1.56 million. In total, the casino generated 791 additional jobs and nearly $17 million of total income for the two counties. The multiplier effect has created additional income for the region that totals over $24 million. Wisconsin's trade and service sectors have experienced tremendous impact from the casino. In the trade sector, 280 jobs are supported by the casino, creating $4.23 million in additional income. The casino also supports 321 service jobs, with $5.66 million being added to the local economy through direct wages. Approximately 76 percent of the jobs created or supported are in the trade and service sectors. The service sector experienced a more constant growth than the trade sector from 1992 to 1994. The service sector employment levels increased by 25 percent over the two years, compared to the trade sector, which had a 17 percent increase from 1992 to 1993 and a 43 percent increase from 1993 to 1994. This resulted in a net increase for the trade sector of 26 percent (Deller, Lake, and Sroka, 1996).

Labor market demands are straining an already tight labor market due to the number of employees at the casino. More people are employed at the casino than the number of working-age people living in Turtle Lake. A recent labor market study in Barron County revealed a countywide labor shortage. The local business people have said the current labor crisis likely will continue into the foreseeable future. The casino has created a situation in which additional jobs are being created and wages within the community are higher due to the labor demand within the county. Also, the lack of quality and affordable housing in Turtle Lake places additional stress on the labor market. Many of the workers who live outside of Turtle Lake have indicated they would be willing to move closer to the casino if housing became available within the community.

Lack of qualified workers in Turtle Lake has created a need for workers to migrate to Barron or Polk Counties to work at the casino. Research (Green, Sroka, and Maney, 1996) suggests that when a large employer enters a small community, at least 50 percent of the workers will have to come from outside of the area. However, only 20 percent of the workers migrated to Turtle Lake. Nearly 50 percent of the casino employees came from other jobs, 36 percent were previously unemployed, and 13 percent of the workers received some form of welfare benefits.

Many of the casino's economic impacts in Turtle Lake can be attributed to the 5,000 people who visit the casino on any given day and the twenty-four-hour nature of the business. Every day, casino patrons gamble approximately $250,000 in the casino and spend additional dollars on other products and services in the local area. The town's infrastructure and public services have been designed to accommodate 800 people, but adding 5,000 visitors a day places an enormous burden on the community. The economic impact related to gaming has created a need for more infrastructure and services.

Since trust lands cannot be taxed by the local government, Native Americans have agreed to make "payment in lieu of tax" (PILT) for the costs incurred by the town as a result of the presence of tribal gaming enterprises. The amount of PILTs collected in Turtle Lake increased by 1,250 percent from 1986 to 1994.

The casino also pays property tax payments to Turtle Lake on nontrust land property, which is equal to approximately 30 percent of all property taxes paid in Turtle Lake. The Chippewa have historically paid for direct service that is needed for the casino and their community through PILT. The information contained in this section is from a comprehensive study of the St. Croix Casino's socioeconomic impacts that was conducted by the University of Wisconsin Extension Service (Deller, Lake, and Sroka, 1996).

Native American Gaming in Minnesota

As of June 1997, eleven Native American tribes were involved in owning and managing casino operations within the state of Minnesota (see Table 7.1). These casinos have approximately 12,900 slot machines, almost 500 table games, and several offer bingo either on a weekly or nightly basis. They also offer a variety of recreational activities, including live entertainment, theme restaurants, nongaming video arcades, and child care. Because many of these facilities are outside a major city, hotels are, or will be, constructed on land adjacent to the casinos (Marquette Advisors, 1997).

TABLE 7.1. Minnesota Native American Tribes with Gaming

Tribe	Facility	City	County
Bois Forte Reservation	Fortune Bay Casino	Tower	St. Louis
Fond Du Lac Reservation	Black Bear Casino Fond Du Luth Casino	Cloquet Duluth	Carlton St. Louis
Grand Portage Reservation	Grand Portage Casino and Lodge	Grand Portage	Cook
Leech Lake Reservation	Northern Lights Casino Palace Bingo and Casino	Walker Cass Lake	Cass Cass
Mille Lacs Band of Ojibwe	Grand Casino Mille Lacs Grand Casino Hinkley	Garrison Hinkley	Mille Lacs Pine
Red Lake Reservation	Lake of the Woods Casino River Road Casino Red Lake Casino	Warroad Thief River Falls Red Lake	Roseau Pennington Beltrami
Prairie Island Sioux Community	Treasure Island Casino	Welch	Goodhue
Shakopee Mdewakanton Sioux Community	Mystic Lake Casino Little Six Creek Casino	Prior Lake Prior Lake	Scott Scott
Upper Sioux Community	Firefly Creek Casino	Granite Falls	Yellow Medicine
Lower Sioux Reservation	Jackpot Junction	Morton	Redwood
White Earth Band of Chippewa Indians	Shooting Star Casino	Mahnomem	Mahnomem

Source: Minnesota Indian Gaming Association (1998).

By year-end 1996, total employment should reach nearly 12,000 people in the Minnesota Indian Gaming Association casinos and their related ancillary facilities. Approximately one of every four employees is Native American, with employment being in several different areas: management, marketing, accounting, security, maintenance, and floor personnel. A misconception is that only Native Americans are in management positions. The majority of the tribes hire Native Americans as well as non–Native Americans for these positions. The Native American supervisory board wants well-qualified individuals to manage its casino operations and is willing to hire the person who is most qualified for that position.

It is interesting to note that gaming counties have higher rates of unemployment than nongaming counties. Many of the gaming counties are in rural areas of Minnesota, and many of the reservations had unemployment rates in excess of 40 percent. Although employment in gaming counties has increased nearly 67 percent faster than in nongaming counties, a greater unemployment rate persists in gaming counties because the rate was significantly higher before the introduction of gaming. In 1990, there was a 6.2 percent unemployment rate in gaming counties, compared to 4.8 percent in nongaming counties. In 1996, this changed to 4.8 percent in gaming counties and 3.6 percent in nongaming counties (Marquette Advisors, 1997).

Native American casinos paid approximately $184 million in wages, with an average annual wage of $16,082 for 1995. This wage is significantly higher than other service positions within the state. Amusement parks paid an annual rate of $14,789; motion picture theaters paid $14,066; lodging places paid $11,830; and eating and drinking places paid $8,704 (see Table 7.2). Additionally, several of the facilities set aside funds for employee benefits and pension funds, with an estimated payment of $4.5 million to cover the cost of these benefits. In 1995, Native American casinos paid over $25 million in Social Security and Medicare taxes (Marquette Advisors, 1997). Additional tax revenues were generated through PILT, since the local municipalities have no authority to tax either the Native Americans or the reservation lands. In many instances, Native Americans agree to fee-for-service arrangements to gain access to these services.

TABLE 7.2. Leisure Industry Wage Comparison, 1995[a]

Industry	Wage/Job Oregon	Wage/Job Minnesota
Indian Gaming Facilities	$15,721	$16,082
Amusement and Recreation Services[b]	$14,654	$14,789
Motion Picture Theaters	$14,990	$14,066
Lodging Places	$11,723	$11,830
Eating and Drinking Places	$9,414	$8,704

Source: Marquette Advisors (1996; 1997).

[a] Wages for other industries based upon 1995 preliminary averages.
[b] Includes both privately and publicly owned facilities.

The reduction of governmental assistance was another economic benefit resulting from Native American casinos. Approximately 12 percent of the workers at these casinos were being paid unemployment, while another 5.7 percent received some form of public assistance and/or welfare. This translates into nearly 2,000 people being removed from assistance rolls or having assistance reduced. Between 1992 and 1995, counties with Native American gaming experienced a 2.1 percent decline in total benefit payments and a 10.9 percent decline in the number of claims, with a 10 percent increase in average monthly payment per claimant. In addition, more than 22 percent of casino workers were unemployed for three months prior to being hired by the casino, while 15 percent were unemployed for six months or longer (Marquette Advisors, 1997).

Expenditures made by the casinos have had tremendous impact on Minnesota business suppliers. Advertising and promotions accounted for approximately $49 million, while food and beverage costs accounted for another $25 million. These expenditures demonstrate the impact that these casinos have on the local and state economy. These casinos are also promoting tourism within the state of Minnesota. Nearly $21.7 million was spent to attract out-of-state visitors to the casinos. This figure is more than 8.3 times the entire marketing budget for the Minnesota Office of Tourism. It is estimated that the casinos attracted 19.6 million patrons, including 3.3 million from outside of the state. Approximately one-sixth of these out-of-state visitors were Canadians. At some of these casinos, the percentage of out-of-state visitors ranged as high as 85 percent. These figures show the impact that Native American gaming has had on tourism not only for Native American casinos but for the entire state as well (Marquette Advisors, 1997).

Casinos in the State of Oregon

Indian gaming in the state of Oregon began with the Cow Creek Band of Uniqua Indians in 1993. Today, six Native American tribes are involved in gaming centers that offer approximately 23,000 video lottery terminals, eighty table games, kenos, and bingo. Similar to many gaming operations, they offer live entertainment, theme restaurants, arcades, child care, and lodging. Five of the six centers in Oregon opened in 1995; the other one opened in 1993. Therefore, the data collected for 1995 can only be considered as preliminary data rather than the whole economic impact that Native American gaming has had on the citizens of Oregon and tribal members.

The enrollment of the six gaming tribes is approximately 14,000, with 4,025 living on the reservations. However, only 536 Native Americans are working in the casinos, while another 1,544 non-Native Americans are employed. This equates to only 26 percent of the employees being Native Americans; however, in areas where a larger Native American workforce is available, Native Americans constitute approximately 65 percent of the total workforce. In 1995, 2,080 people worked in the six casinos, and it was estimated that by the end of 1996, the total would be nearly 2,700. Jobs created by these casinos are not limited to only gaming operations but also restaurants, gift shops, convenience stores, and food and beverage outlets (Marquette Advisors, 1996).

Casinos paid approximately $19.5 million in wages in 1995, and this number is expected to increase to $42.4 million in 1996. These casinos have the highest wages compared to other entertainment establishments (see Table 7.2). Eating and drinking establishments pay approximately $9,414 on a yearly basis, while motion picture theaters pay $14,990. The pay difference at the casino can range from 5 percent to over 50 percent, depending on which occupation a worker chooses. Additionally, even if higher-paying jobs are in the area, many of the current service employees are probably not qualified for those positions. The majority of the employment positions within the casinos are entry level. These facilities are spending the necessary dollars to train and prepare these employees to become productive casino workers and for other positions within their communities (Marquette Advisors, 1996).

In 1995, the six casinos generated approximately $1,772,000 in Social Security and Medicare taxes. By the end of 1997, this amount was in excess of $2.6 billion, according to growth estimates from Robert Whelan of ECONorthwest ("Oregon," 1998). These casinos are required by law to pay half of the total Social Security and Medicare tax revenue. Also, they paid an additional $481,000 for combined state and federal unemployment compensation for 1995. Casinos are also participating in PILT to purchase municipal services, including police and fire protection. In 1995, these payments were $387,000.

In 1993, when the Cow Creek Casino opened, 212,764 people received unemployment assistance. In 1995, when five additional casinos opened, the number decreased to 170,986. This decrease may be attributed to the associated direct and indirect economic impacts of the opening of tribal casinos. More important, the number of Native Americans who were receiving some form of unemployment insurance and benefits dropped from 3,725 in 1993 to 3,493 in 1995. In dollars, this represents a statewide reduction from $534,407,915 to $353,085,696 from 1993 to 1995, a decrease in benefit payments of nearly 34 percent (Marquette Advisors, 1996).

Also noteworthy is that the creation of entry-level positions is critical since welfare reforms are forcing a tremendous number of people off government assistance programs. Native American casinos may help many people who have had a difficult time finding employment become productive workers within our society. In Oregon counties with gaming operations, the number of AFDC cases declined from 41,813 in May 1992 to 33,099 in May 1996, a decrease of 21.9 percent. Total AFDC expenditures changed from $2,429,445 to $1,955,044 during the same time period, a savings of 19.5 percent. At the same time, the average cost per case increased from $427.87 to $440.92 in counties with Native American gaming. An interesting finding was that the number of food stamp cases increased statewide from 1993 to 1996. In counties with Native American casinos, cases increased by 16.4 percent, from 15,713 to 18,285. The dollar amount changed from $2,569,565 to $2,966,721 (13.4 percent) during the same time period. However, counties without Native American gaming experienced a higher rate of increase in expenditures during the same time period, 17.6 percent.

These casinos have also created additional construction projects within their communities. In 1996, $90 million was spent on construction projects. Another $119 million was scheduled to be spent to complete construction on gaming facilities. As these facilities expand, additional expenditures will be made to build supporting infrastructures. Additional dollars are being spent by the casinos on Oregon vendors. Over $10 million is being spent to promote and advertise within the state, and food and beverage operations will purchase another $7.3 million of products within the state. Additionally, $10 million is being spent on nongaming supplies, contract labor and services, lodging, utilities, insurance, and other products.

Impact from out-of-state visitors has become a major issue with the management of Native American casinos. In 1995, the casinos spent $775,000 on marketing, advertising, and promotion specifically directed at attracting out-of-state visitors. In 1996, that amount increased to approximately $1.1 million. In 1995, the casinos attracted an estimated 495,000 visitors from outside the state, and in some locations, this number represented 50 percent of the visitors (Marquette Advisors, 1996).

CURRENT ISSUES AND CHALLENGES

A concern of many hospitality businesses is that Native American casinos are placing an unfair burden on non-Native American businesses because they do not have to pay any income taxes. It has been reported that 38 percent of the Minnesota Restaurant, Hotel, Lodging, and Resort Association members have lost business since the opening of Native American casinos (Meyer, 1993). The question then becomes, did the opening of casinos impact their businesses because Native Americans do not pay taxes, or are visitors substituting one form of entertainment for another? The introduction of a new tourist attraction may actually enhance the appeal of an area by increasing market segmentation (Morrisson, 1996). Market factors, not taxes, are probably the reason why noncasino businesses have lost revenues. Competing in a free-market society creates winners and losers, but it is more stable than when outside forces attempt to control prices and competition.

Native American casinos in rural areas have also caused many other businesses to prosper. Additional expenditures are being made to build houses, schools, and medical facilities for the reservations, while other economic activities are improving the roads and building additional infrastructure to support the increase in tourist activity due to gaming. One study found that areas surrounding Native American casinos, within thirty-five miles, are positively impacted by the casinos (Worthington, 1995).

Location of a Native American casino is another important factor that could affect other businesses (Lue, Crompton, and Fesenmaier, 1993). The spatial placement of a Native American casino can either complement or compete with other businesses. Since gaming is an adult form of entertainment, placing a casino away from family entertainment locations has been extremely effective in attracting new market segments into areas that were previously known as family-only destinations (Boger, 1994).

The labor impact in rural communities is probably one of the greatest impacts on nongaming businesses because many gaming facilities are built in rural communities. The wage scale for agriculture and other nongambling businesses has risen since the introduction of Native American gaming in these communities due to competition for workers. For example, a Native American casino in Turtle Lake, Wisconsin, has less than 1,000 people and employs nearly 30 percent of the community population (Boger, 1994). Any new employers that can capture a 10 percent market share of the labor pool will impact both wages and unemployment in the area.

"If you build it, they will come." This quote from the film *Field of Dreams* (1989) has been a reality for many Native American casinos throughout the country, especially in areas where no other type of gaming facilities existed prior to the construction of these casinos. A majority of Native American casinos are in isolated locations throughout the country, but with the absence of any competition these casinos have prospered. Success breeds competition, and this has caused several states to examine the possibility of legalizing the operation and ownership of gaming facilities off the reservations (Turner, 1992). As more commercial and other Native American casinos are built within an area, the existing Native American casinos will need to become more market driven.

The threat to Native American casinos is not only the competition but their isolated locations. Non–Native American casinos could be built closer to more metropolitan populations. Riverboat casinos in Missouri have placed enormous pressure on the rural Native American casinos in Kansas, which are approximately sixty miles from Kansas City, Missouri. Instead of waiting to become economic victims of competition, many tribes have developed a strategic plan to circumvent outside pressures to build non-Native American casinos closer to metropolitan areas.

As competition threatens the profitability of Native American casinos, the need for diversification will become more apparent to the tribes. Many Native American tribes have used casino revenues to build additional infrastructure, such as roads, schools, and other Native American businesses (DePass, 1994). Some Native American tribes have banded together to assist in the planning of diversification on the reservations. Minnesota has an Economic Development Fund to assist Native American entrepreneurs on reservations.

Unfortunately, since easy dollars are flowing into the tribes, it is extremely difficult to imagine that a financial crisis might ever occur. This influx of money from casinos is also creating greed among tribal members. For years, Native Americans have accumulated very little wealth, but gaming generates the needed wealth for their reservations. Many people believe they may be losing their cultural identity due to gaming. However, as a Native American advocate once said, "They want to preserve their cultural identity, but they also like to eat."

Off-reservation gaming will become a major issue as more competition begins to erode the profitability in rural areas. Another issue is that some Native American tribes have reservation lands that are unsuitable locations for a casino. The Department of Interior has, in the past, created trust lands for cultural or religious reasons, such as a burial ground of Native Americans. They have also created trust lands for Native American tribes with lands having little or no economic value (Turner, 1993). These newly acquired trust lands have provided Native Americans with the ability to survive in a more competitive environment in which commercial gaming operations are being allowed to open near Native American casinos. In conclusion, Native American casinos provide Native Americans with the opportunity to obtain economic freedom that otherwise would not be possible due to the lack of resources previously found on their reservations.

REFERENCES

Boger, C.A. (1994). The effects of Native American gaming on other tourist businesses. *Proceedings of the International Society of Travel and Tourism Educators, 6,* 58-72.

Borden, D.W., Fletcher, R.R., and Haqrris, T.R. (1996). Economic, resource, and fiscal impacts of visitors on Washoe County Nevada, *Journal of Travel Research, 34*(3), 75-80.

Bureau of the Census (1990). *1990 census of population and housing* (Tape File 3A). Washington, DC: U.S. Department of Commerce.

Carmichael, B.A., Peppard, D.M. Jr., and Boudreau, F.A. (1996). Megaresort on my doorstep: Local resident attitudes toward Foxwoods casino and casino gambling on nearby Indian reservation land. *Journal of Travel Research, 34*(3), 9-16.

Connor, M. (1993). Indian gaming: Prosperity, controversy. *International Gaming and Wagering Business, 14*(3), 1, 8-12, 45.

Connecticut Labor Department (1994). *Nonfarm employment, New London labor market area, 1988-1993 annual averages.* Hartford, CT: Author.

Deller, S.C., Lake, A., and Sroka, J. (1996). *The St. Croix casino: A comprehensive study of its socioeconomic impacts.* Madison, WI: University of Wisconsin-Madison Extension.

DePass, D. (1994, February 21). Tribes taking gamble on diversification. *Minneapolis (Minnesota) Star and Tribune* (On-line). Available: http://newslibrary. krmediastream.com/cgi-bin/search/mn.

Ferber, S.R. and Chon, K.S. (1994). Indian gaming: Issues and prospects. *Gaming Research and Review Journal, 1*(2), 55-66.

Green G.P., Sroka, J., and Maney, G. (1996). *Labor market conditions in Barron County.* Madison, WI: University of Wisconsin-Madison Extension.

Leiper, N. (1989). Tourism and gambling. *Geojournal, 19*(3), 269-275.

Long, P.T. (1995). Casino gaming in the United States: 1994 status and implications. *Tourism Management, 16*(3), 189-197.

Lue, C.C., Crompton, J.L., and Fesenmaier, D.R. (1993). Conceptualization of multi-destination pleasure trips. *Annals of Tourism Research, 20*(2), 289-301.

Marquette Advisors (1996). *Economic benefits of Indian gaming in the state of Oregon.* Minneapolis, MN: Author.

Marquette Advisors (1997). *Economic benefits of Indian gaming in the state of Minnesota.* Minneapolis, MN: Author.

McCulloch, A.M. (1994). The politics of Indian gaming: Tribe/state relations and American federalism. *Publius, 24*(3), 99-113.

Meyer, H. (1993). Indian gaming: Is it out of control in Minnesota? *Hospitality Management, 13*(1), 34-38.

Minnesota Indian Gaming Association (1998, November 18). *Minnesota gaming directory* (On-line). Available: http://minnesotagaming.com.

Morrison, A.M. (1996). *Hospitality and travel marketing* (Second edition). Albany, NY: Delmar Publishers.

Oregon: State meets tribes as sovereign nations (1998, November 30). The newsletter of the national gaming industry: Casino Journal's national gaming summary (On-line). Available: http://www.casinocenter.com/summary/sample/html/oregon.html.

Rose, I. (1993). *Gambling and the law: Endless fields of dreams.* Whittier, CA: Whittier Law School.

Stuart, P.H. (1990). Financing self-determination: Federal Indian expenditures, 1975-1988. *American Indian Culture and Research Journal, 14*(2), 1-18.

Turner, B. (1992). *Native American casino gaming: A national perspective.* St. Petersburg, FL: Raymond James and Associates, Inc.

Turner, B. (1993). *Native American casino gaming update.* St. Petersburg, FL: Raymond James and Associates, Inc.

Vinje, D.L. (1985). Cultural values and economic development on reservations. In J. Vine Deloria (Ed.), *American Indian policy in the twentieth century* (pp. 155-177). Norman, OK: University of Oklahoma Press.

Vinje, D. L. (1996). Native American economic development on selected reserva-tions: A comparative analysis. *The American Journal of Economics and Sociology, 55*(4), 427-443.

Worthington, R. (1995, April 12). Study says state loses on casinos. *Wisconsin,* p. 2.

Wright, A.W., Clapp, J.M., Heffley, D.R., Ray, S.C., and Vilasuso, J. (1993, September). *The economic impacts of the Foxwoods high stakes bingo and casino on New London County and surrounding areas.* Hartford, CT: Arthur W. Wright and Associates.

Chapter 8

Economic Impacts
of Riverboat and Land-Based
Non-Native American Casino Gaming

Patricia A. Stokowski

As we approach the millennium, recreational gambling is becoming one of the most popular and fastest-growing components of America's "entertainment economy" (Mandel et al., 1994). Currently, all states except Utah and Hawaii offer one or more forms of legalized gambling, and according to an industry-sponsored survey conducted by Harrah's Entertainment Inc. (1996), most people questioned (91 percent) agreed that gambling was an acceptable form of leisure activity for themselves or others. More than half of those surveyed said they gambled in 1996; about 32 percent of the surveyed households had visited a casino in 1996. In fact, casino gaming is growing more rapidly than any other form of legalized gambling. Until the late 1980s, only Nevada and Atlantic City, New Jersey, offered opportunities for legal casino gambling. By 1995, however, Native American, riverboat, and land-based casinos were available in twenty-six states, while ten states offered non-Native American casino gambling.

In concert with industry expansion, the amount of money bet on all forms of legal gambling has risen dramatically. Americans wagered about $22.4 billion in 1974, a total that rose to about $125 billion in 1982, about $330 billion by 1992, and over $586.5 billion by 1996 (Kallick-Kaufmann, 1979; Christiansen, 1994; Christiansen, 1997; Eadington, 1996). At the same time, gross revenues (revenues after payment of prizes) to gaming industry operators were nearly $48 billion in 1996, up from $10.4 billion in 1982 (Shapiro, 1996; Christiansen, 1997). More than two-thirds of the wagers and revenues are obtained at casinos, an industry sector expecting continued growth and patronage.

Even though gambling venues are expanding, available data indicate that the demographic profile of casino gamblers seems to have remained constant over time. A survey conducted in 1975 for the first federal Commission on the Review of the National Policy Toward Gambling found that "the proportion of people who gamble is higher the higher the income level . . . (and) average outlays for betting tend to rise with income" (Suits, 1979, p. 53). Even with variability in wagering across games, the data showed that games with high take-out rates (such as lotteries) tended to be highly regressive: "Low-income bettors, it would appear, are given to betting on games that promise high potential winnings, but at grossly unfair odds, whereas high-income players appear to seek the most action for their money by playing games that afford small pay-offs at rather better odds" (Suits, 1979, p. 57), such as casino games. More recently, Heubusch (1997, p. 37) described a similar pattern of participation: "Gambling of all types typically increases with income. . . . Participation in the most accessible games, such as bingo and lotteries, is highest for those with middle incomes, while casino gambling peaks with the highest incomes and levels of education." However, current industry trends to maximize casino profits by replacing table games with slot machines make such generalizations more problematic in contemporary analyses of gamblers.

Despite the rapid growth of the gaming industry, debate rages about the magnitude of economic benefits that are said to derive from gambling. Industry spokespersons assert that "The casino gaming industry is clearly an important provider of jobs, wages, and taxes to the U.S. economy," and "secondary impacts further ripple through the economy, ultimately impacting all industries across the length and breadth of the country" (Arthur Andersen, 1996, p. 63), but other researchers remain unconvinced. In particular, some analysts believe that the costs of gambling and gaming development have been inadequately assessed, particularly those costs which emerge over time or which are difficult to quantify. The intent of this chapter is to review the issues surrounding assessment of gaming's economic impacts.

EVALUATING ECONOMIC IMPACTS

Debates about providing gambling opportunities by developing casinos in a community tend to return again and again to the issue of economics. The gaming industry is seen as a source of new and improved job opportunities, increased tax revenues for public projects, or broad-based economic development. Reports from new gaming locales tend to feature stories about substantial investments being made by the industry, the rise in property values benefiting land and building owners who wish to sell, and the huge windfalls of new revenues available to local governments. As most new riverboat and land-based casino locales know, however, the story is not all in the earliest reports. Often a significant lag period exists (Stokowski, 1993) between the start of gaming and the provision of expected gains, but such impacts are rarely considered in traditional, short-term economic impact analyses.

Divergent perspectives about the magnitude of the economic impacts of gambling and gaming development arise for several reasons. First, research about economic impacts tends to be supported through funds provided by agencies (industry or government) that have interests in the outcomes of the research. Although much of this research is likely to be carefully prepared, the interpretation and use made of the data often raise questions. For example, an industry survey claiming that "x percent of Americans gamble" probably refers only to the "x percent" of those sampled. Without knowing details of the survey procedures, readers cannot be certain about who was questioned, how the questions were worded, or whether the sample was biased.

Second, not all economic benefits or costs are likely to be included in any single research study. A community considering whether to adopt casino gaming as an economic development strategy is likely to focus on the local benefits and costs, ignoring impacts that potentially occur beyond its borders, such as traffic congestion on highways leading to the community or spillover crime effects. Moreover, impacts are likely to vary according to the time period considered in the economic assessment. Some impacts peak at early stages of a development, while others evolve over time.

Third, not all data are comparable in their original form, thus introducing many sources of error into models. Data collection may vary across time periods for different agencies: in Colorado, for example, governmental revenues are on a fiscal year basis, although the "gaming year" begins on October 1 each year. Reporting and processing procedures may also vary across time periods (crime data formats are sometimes changed over time in response to an agency's requests, for example, or when new computer systems are adopted).

In general, the study of economic impacts might reasonably be divided into two very broad topic areas: (1) revenues and costs associated with industry growth and (2) economic impacts of gambling and gaming development on individuals, communities, and regions. These topics are examined next, with examples drawn from a variety of land-based and riverboat gaming locales.

GAMING INDUSTRY GROWTH

A variety of indicators are traditionally used to analyze economic growth within the gaming industry. These include (1) initial investment costs paid by companies developing casinos; (2) taxes paid to local governments, usually in the form of property taxes and impact fee assessments; (3) gross wagering (the "handle"); (4) revenues obtained by industry, usually identified as gross proceeds; (5) taxes paid to state governments in the form of casino taxes; and (6) wages paid to casino employees. Other research about casino potential and operations has also considered analyses of citizens' attitudes about gambling and the demographics of gambling participation, as well as measures of casino management and ownership patterns across casino venues.

Although some of the aforementioned indicators may be verified using publicly available data (taxes paid to local and state governments or casino employment, for example), difficulties remain in making comparisons across gaming jurisdictions. Different locales have adopted different forms of casino gaming at different time periods, and the legal frameworks are rarely comparable. Given that much of the industry data is proprietary information, analysts must rely on a limited set of published data and industry-generated reports to draw conclusions. Table 8.1 provides a comparison of industry data from states offering non–Native American casino gaming. This table shows the relative status and growth of the casino industry across jurisdictions.

TABLE 8.1. Arthur Andersen (1996) Study of Non-Native American Casino Gaming

	Year Casinos Legalized	No. Casinos Operating Dec. 1995	1995 Gross Gaming Revenues	% Increase Over 1994 Revenues	No. Employees in 1995
Places with Land-based Casinos					
Nevada	1931	>350	$7.3 M	+5.2%	170,000
Atlantic City, NJ	1976	13	$3.8 M	+9.5%	40,800
Deadwood, SD	1989	87	$46.0 M	0.0%	1,100
Colorado (three towns)	1990	56	$354.0 M	+18.7%	6,500
Places with Riverboat Casinos:					
Illinois	1990	13	$1.2 M	+20.3%	12,000
Indiana	1994	3	$239.0 M	—	1,000
Iowa	1989	9	$455.0 M	+333.7%	3,800
Louisiana	1991	12	$1.1 M	+75.9%	13,600
Mississippi	1990	29*	$1.7 M	+17.1%	27,100
Missouri	1992	8	$466.0 M	+323%	8,200

M = million
*August 1996

Christiansen's (1994) analysis of casino gaming relative to other forms of gambling offers some understanding of trends in this industry. While casinos were generally reporting increasing visitation and revenues between 1990 and 1995, other forms of gambling (greyhound racing and horse track betting) were on the decline, particularly in states with new casino gaming venues, namely Colorado and Iowa. On the other hand, state-sponsored lotteries seemed to be independent of casinos: even with the introduction of casinos, lottery revenues increased in Indiana, Colorado, Iowa, Missouri, and New Jersey. A study of interactions between lotteries and riverboat gambling in Iowa confirmed this idea: McGowan found that "riverboat gambling appears to be a form of gambling that does not cannibalize existing lottery sales" (1994, p. 92).

Riverboat gambling, though, was a more unstable venture. As with land-based casinos, the earliest entrepreneurs in a new gaming locale were usually wildly successful. However, increased competition tended to result in very rapid industry restructuring. Riverboat profits declined when competitors moved into adjacent states, and riverboats were easily enticed to move to other locales when less restrictive gaming regulations and more favorable tax rates, betting limits, and hours of operation were promised. Several Iowa riverboats, for example, sailed to more profitable conditions in Illinois and Mississippi after the first year of gaming (Doocey, 1994). Several of the land-based casino venues also showed signs of being susceptible to competition. Central City fell behind the other Colorado gaming towns with local government indecision and industry-favorable conditions in nearby Black Hawk (Stokowski, 1996). Deadwood, South Dakota, was being called overbuilt and "full of cookie-cutter casinos" (Hevener, 1992, p. 1) as early as 1992, only a few years after gaming opened in November 1989.

By 1997, the gaming industry was shifting attention from rural to urban areas. The bankrupt New Orleans casino notwithstanding, the industry turned its attention to high-visibility, populated markets such as Chicago and Detroit. The trend to focus on urban or near-urban locales was evident. Gaming and entertainment companies were investing heavily in Black Hawk, the smallest of the three rural Colorado communities, but the one closest to Denver and most amenable to continued industry expansion. By late 1998, several large companies were in the process of building theme-based hotel/casino/entertainment complexes in that mountain town (plans included the Isle of Capri's Caribbean-theme tropical paradise casino resort, complete with macaws, and a Swiss-theme casino/resort purported to include a penguin ice castle attraction and a bear pit). Las Vegas entrepreneurs were also looking toward the future, remodeling and rebuilding to develop a new emphasis on children's entertainments, amusements, and spectacles (Heubusch, 1997). The effort to stimulate the family vacation market will likely transfer to other, smaller casino locales that hope to reach gamblers who favor affordable recreational gambling.

Beyond the land-based and riverboat casino venues, the newest trend in gaming is the rapid spread of video gaming terminals. These gaming machines are located in convenience stores, bars, taverns, and at truck stops and service stations in Montana, South Carolina, and other states, and their use constitutes an increasing proportion of gaming revenues (Dworin, 1994). Gaming industry officials also talk about ways to make gambling even more convenient through interactive television, bringing gambling into every home. However, there remains considerable public concern over, and legislative antagonism toward, home gaming at this time.

PUBLIC ECONOMIC IMPACTS

When researchers mention the economic impacts of gambling, they usually are referring to the community and regional consequences of industry growth. The impacts of gambling and gaming development on individuals, communities, and states have often been assessed using indicators that include, among others, (1) initial community investment costs; (2) the patterns of governmental revenues and expenditures that depend on gaming taxes paid by the industry; (3) labor force changes before and after gaming development; (4) retail sales and relationships between business sectors; and (5) property sales, including increases in wealth to property sellers and community changes in property valuation. Regional and secondary impacts of gaming development have received less attention from researchers, and economic costs have been poorly considered in most economic analyses of gambling and gaming development. Some of the more prominent topics related to the economic impacts of gambling and gaming development are discussed in the following material.

Government Revenues

Local and state governments typically profit from gaming development by taxing casino businesses to raise funds that both allay the increased costs of governing and contribute to funding a social good, such as historic preservation or education. At the local level, these special taxes include fees levied on gambling devices (slot machines and tables), fees paid in lieu of providing parking spaces, or other general impact fees; these fees are in addition to the usual property and construction taxes. Beyond the special local fees (which are usually calculated yearly), states often tax each casino's adjusted gross revenues. State casino tax rates vary, with some states enforcing a flat tax rate (for example, South Dakota's gaming tax is 8 percent of adjusted gross receipts) and others using a sliding scale (Colorado revises the tax rate yearly and currently assesses rates from 2 percent to 18 percent).

As current riverboat and land-based casino locales have shown, revenues from a successful gaming venture often prove very lucrative for local and state governments, as well as for casino operators. For example, analyzing ten years of data from Atlantic City, Harrison (1992, p. 113) found that "the casino industry generates 21 percent of the direct income, 28 percent of the direct employment, and 33 percent of the local property taxes," as well as contributing 7 percent of the state's taxes. Braunlich (1996, p. 55) labeled Atlantic City's casino hotels as "an unparalleled economic engine" to attract capital investment, stabilize year-round employment, and attract tourists. Similar patterns of significant economic gains are also seen for the western gaming towns and the new riverboat communities. Madden (1992) found the first year of gaming in Deadwood, South Dakota, to have produced nearly $6.4 million for historic preservation. Riverboats in Joliet, Illinois, were providing that city with about $27 million annually in gambling tax revenues (Chadbourne, Walker, and Wolfe, 1997). The budget for the city of Black Hawk, Colorado, rose from about $300,000 in the year prior to gambling to over $4 million in 1994 (Stokowski, 1996). In Tunica, Mississippi, where the county received 4 percent of riverboat gaming tax revenues, the budget rose from $2.8 million in 1992 to $28 million by 1995 (Schwarz and Schwarz, 1996).

Revenues do not come without costs, though. Local government budgets are affected primarily, according to Evart (1994), in three service provision areas: police, public works, and the judicial system. These were also the three service areas requiring community investment in the Colorado gaming towns, though needs for some new services actually preceded the opening of casinos. This condition has been called a "front end problem" by Cummings, Schulze, and Mehr (1978): communities in transition often need new infrastructure and service improvements, but may have few financial resources to address these needs. The community is then tempted to issue bonds and take on debt to complete desired projects, but poor judgments at this stage have long-term consequences. Central City, Colorado, for example, raised its long-term debt to about $23 million to complete water, sewer, street, and transportation projects before gaming began. Over the first five years of gambling, though, the industry struggled and declined, leaving that community with huge debt but with declining gaming tax revenues to service the debt (Stokowski, 1996).

Employment

Proponents of gaming development describe the industry as "highly labor intensive," providing about 284,100 casino jobs nationwide and stimulating the creation of about 400,000 indirect jobs (Arthur Andersen, 1996). Although casinos certainly bring new jobs into a region, it is not yet clear whether those jobs represent a real increase in overall employment opportunities or replace jobs declining in other sectors of the economy.

Researchers have reported that in many of the newer riverboat and land-based gaming locales, casino jobs tend to be filled primarily by people living outside the affected community. Stokowski (1996) found that in the first four years of gaming, only about 10 to 12 percent of casino employees in the towns of Black Hawk and Central City, Colorado, lived in Gilpin County (the gaming towns of Black Hawk and Central City are the only incorporated places in Gilpin County). Similar patterns have been described in Mississippi's riverboat towns (Schwarz and Schwarz, 1996; Evart, 1994) and in Deadwood, South Dakota (Madden, 1992). Most employees commuted to the casinos from larger towns and cities, a pattern that could change if housing were more readily available for rent or purchase in the gaming communities.

The development of casinos does offer opportunities for local people to accept steady employment, even in small or rural communities with a limited workforce. Yet, even if there is a significant increase in employment on the local level, a regional analysis might conclude that the effect is negligible overall. Grinols (1994, p. 11) concluded about riverboat gambling in Illinois that "a substantial number of jobs were lost elsewhere in the affected markets so that net jobs were a small or zero percent of direct employment on the riverboats. There was little discernable impact on reducing unemployment." The rates of unemployment in Tunica, Mississippi, have not changed dramatically from the pregaming era, even with the very lucrative casino development; most workers commute from outside the community (Schwarz and Schwarz, 1996). Though the regional effects of gaming remain poorly understood, it appears that casino development does have the ability to even out extreme fluctuations in seasonal employment patterns, especially in depressed communities (the Colorado and South Dakota gaming towns are examples).

One issue that has received almost no attention in the gaming research literature is casino employee migration. Stokowski (1996, p. 222) suggested, in her analysis of community child support payments in the Colorado gambling towns, that "there may be a pattern of employment-trained people following gambling jobs from state to state, forming a new kind of migrant worker." Service worker migration is problematic for other kinds of tourism communities, such as ski resort areas and gateway communities near national parks, primarily in relation to governmental needs for affordable housing, social services provision, and child care and school system pressures (Ring, 1995). It may emerge as a significant issue in gaming communities as well.

Business Diversity

The impact of gaming development on a local economy depends to a great degree on the number and size of casinos permitted in an area and the location of casinos relative to other important places in the community (such as the commercial center, historical areas, neighborhoods, schools, or areas defined as "special places" by community members). Rampant property speculation in the mining-turned-gambling towns of Black Hawk, Central City, and Cripple Creek, Colorado, and Deadwood, South Dakota, occurred, for example, because casinos were required to locate in the historical, commercial zones of each town. The rush to buy land and buildings in those business districts favored property owners but had negative consequences for people who rented shops or housing space. Renters were evicted so that casino construction could proceed, while owners rode the wave of speculation to obtain exorbitant prices for selling their properties.

One of the consequences of the free-market "land rush" is that business diversity tends to decrease. Between 1980 and 1994, in the Colorado gaming towns, mining, manufacturing, government services, and retail trade establishments all declined in number, while the proportion of businesses in amusement, recreation, and lodging services and construction increased (Stokowski, 1996). The business structure of Deadwood, South Dakota, also showed similar trends with the introduction of gaming: while total taxable sales increased (primarily from the retail trade sector, with the largest increase in sales in eating and drinking establishments, lodging, and legal services), the number of licensed businesses decreased by a third overall (Madden, 1992). One reason for the decline may be that businesses in the commercial zone are taxed at a rate equal to the "highest and best use" (i.e., casinos), so smaller casinos and other noncasino businesses have a difficult time competing.

The situation is less clear in riverboat gaming areas. Analysts studying riverboat gaming suggest that the boats rarely stimulate increased business activity in other commercial areas because tourists visit primarily to gamble, not to enjoy other local entertainment or to shop in local businesses. When casino facilities include hotels, restaurants, and theaters, local businesses in those sectors tend to decline because gamblers have little reason to explore beyond the casinos. Nevertheless, new restaurants, hotels, and shops have apparently opened in Joliet, Illinois, and several Iowa locales, after riverboats were introduced (Chadbourne, Walker, and Wolfe, 1997). In many historic towns, attendance at community festivals, visits to museums and historic sites, and nongambling tourism activities declined after the start of gaming; some, such as the opera and historic museum in Central City, Colorado, have seen their attendance return to pregaming levels when special arrangements for patrons' parking and services are created. Most riverboat and land-based gaming communities, though, find that the most lucrative new business enterprises in casino towns are property speculation and parking lot management.

Ultimately, the best hedge against loss of business diversity is the gaming legislation itself. Although the Colorado gaming proposal was intended to favor development of small, locally owned casinos, at least in Black Hawk, Colorado, property speculation, consolidations, and competition have made it virtually impossible for smaller businesses and casino owners to compete against large, well-financed, external casino-hotel corporations. In Deadwood, South Dakota, the number of gaming devices in each casino was restricted to thirty, an effort that effectively reduced investment by large casino and entertainment companies.

Redevelopment Issues

Although the increase in absolute numbers of new gambling tourists and new gaming-related tax revenues may appeal to governments in both new and existing casino locales, researchers studying economic impacts have generally concluded that even in the best situations, there is a significant lag time in local redevelopment beyond casino-related investment. The lack of congruity between economic expectations and community outcomes begins with exaggerated claims in the campaigns promoting gambling development (Nickerson, 1995). The logic of gaming promotion, in fact, is for supporters to employ a "rhetoric of despair" to describe current conditions in communities seeking gaming, with casinos as the only solution that could provide the necessary windfall of profits, allegedly without substantial costs (Stokowski, 1996). Yet, a review of case studies about new riverboat and land-based gaming locales shows that gaming consistently fails to live up to the goals promised by supporters. Truitt (1996, p. 89), for example, concluded that "riverboat gambling in Illinois has not stimulated economic development and tourism to the degree that had been advertised and expected."

The disappointment of expectations for broader community development does not, apparently, depend on whether the community's gaming industry is new or established. Rubenstein (1984, p. 61) saw similar patterns in Atlantic City, noting that, "While the casinos have become successful, and jobs and revenue have been created, the revitalization of Atlantic City beyond the Boardwalk remains to be achieved." A 1989 article in a popular news magazine concurred, calling Atlantic City "an American monument to self-delusion" (Painton, 1989, p. 66). In the Colorado gaming towns, redevelopment beyond the casino district for the benefit of the community has also been slow to materialize. New casino resort complexes include plans for hotels, restaurants, and convention facilities, but noncasino hotels, restaurants, entertainments, and services, such as groceries, gas stations, and copy centers, are not in evidence and not planned, nearly seven years after gaming was introduced.

Economic Costs

Though there is general agreement that economic, social, political, and environmental costs may emerge with gaming development, most studies do a poor job of actually assessing these costs. In fact, Kindt (1994) calls gambling a "black hole of economics" because estimates of its economic benefits rarely take into account either the associated social costs or their potential economic values. He notes that social, economic, business, and governmental costs include problem gambling behaviors, increased social welfare provision, lost business productivity, insurance fraud, increased police and emergency services provision, bankruptcy, underage gambling, family crises, and a host of other problems, many of which are difficult to quantify. The problems are both theoretical and practical: terms such as "pathological gambling" are sometimes difficult to operationalize, while accounting difficulties ensue when costs must be tabulated across governmental entities that keep accounts in noncomparable forms (for example, data management procedures regarding social services provision often vary across agencies). Trends data may be difficult to summarize when data collection and processing change over time (as with crime statistics). Nevertheless, increases in social problems such as compulsive gambling carry potentially huge costs in lost work time, legal fees, and rehabilitation.

Beyond these difficulties is a philosophical problem: economic costs are often not included in analyses because those supporting the research are often advocates for specific types of growth policies, and costs do not contribute to growth. Stokowski's (1996) examination of the "growth machine politics" of community gaming development in Black Hawk and Central City showed that not only did different groups of gaming advocates (industry representatives and government leaders are two of these groups) favor policies that would protect their own special interests, but each group downplayed the community costs of their particular growth agenda. In such a political environment, key actors in the gaming development focus on ways to make the community a better place to do business rather than a better place to live. Casino industry spokespersons point out that it is not their role to look after community needs—they are operating a business, after all—but it is equally difficult to ascertain who is looking after the community needs when local and state governments become tacit partners in accommodating the industry to maintain their desired tax revenues. Using gaming tax monies to improve streets, fix sewers, and build sidewalks improves the appearance and functions of a place, but it is not an investment in training individuals for jobs, ensuring that all residents have reasonable housing, or otherwise raising human capital.

In many small communities, the huge revenues accruing to the community do not offset problems affecting individual or community quality of life. Traffic, noise, congestion, parking problems, and crowds of gambling tourists intrude on daily life. Housing becomes especially problematic, as Evart (1994, p. 44) observed in Biloxi, Mississippi: "low income housing is being purchased at exorbitant prices, renovated for middle income people, while, at the same time, low income people, fixed income people are put on the streets in search of alternative housing." So, although depressed areas may be improved with the new community services that accompany gaming development, the poorest members of a community often are adversely affected. Indeed, a person must have a basic level of income, education, and living standard before they can even take advantage of new opportunities offered by the gaming industry, as Labalme (1994) explained about some residents of Tunica, Mississippi: without a car, low-income residents could not get jobs in a casino because no buses ran between the poorer neighborhoods and the riverboat areas. Yet, home rents increased, so that people were ultimately worse off with the introduction of casinos than before. Similar problems of a "wealth gap" have been documented in the Colorado gaming towns where many elderly and poor were displaced (Stokowski, 1996) and in other riverboat gaming communities (Chadbourne, Walker, and Wolfe, 1997; Popkin, 1994).

Additionally, personal and collective costs of gambling are not often factored into estimates of gaming revenues. Because individuals must lose money in order for the industry, community, and state to profit with revenues, the most successful gaming locales are those where tourists, rather than local residents, come to gamble. This condition is achieved in Las Vegas and Atlantic City, but is problematic for some gaming communities that are not vacation destinations. For example, in their economic analysis of riverboat gambling in Illinois, Thompson and Gazel (1996, p. 10) found that "Casinos have drawn monetary resources away from depressed communities and away from individuals who are economically poor," rather than primarily drawing tourists to the new riverboat attractions.

Another difficulty in evaluating costs of gaming development is uncertainty about future opportunities or conditions. If a riverboat sails away because a better deal is offered in another state, or if promised development does not occur, real individuals and communities are affected. As Guskind (1991, p. 2206) noted, "when the party's over, some small river towns could find themselves owners of costly loan guarantees and vacant real estate." This is the current fate of Central City, Colorado, which has nearly $20 million in gaming development-induced community debt, but has had difficulty retaining a viable casino industry. The unkept promises for local development also have costs in community conflict and anger, as demonstrated by the recall elections and continual public political bickering in that town, even into 1998, nearly seven years after gaming began there.

TRENDS AND PROJECTIONS

The recent proliferation of casino gambling across rural and urban areas of the United States indicates that both the industry and governments remain convinced of the economic benefits of recreational gaming. Public acceptance of gaming has encouraged some analysts to predict that even broader dispersion of casinos will occur in the future, so that most Americans will eventually live within a 100-mile radius of some form of land-based, riverboat, or Native American casino development. The industry is most interested, though, in those projects that make money, so their efforts will probably focus on places near major metropolitan areas. The trend toward mega-casino-resort projects in Black Hawk, Colorado, near Denver, will make it a destination vacation spot; likewise, legislative approval for three major casinos in Detroit, Michigan, will make the gaming industry the largest employer in that state by 1999.

Smaller or rural locales, and places that do not yet have casinos, may find it more difficult to gain public support for casino development, unless state legislatures are exceedingly generous in their enticements (Shapiro, 1996). Competition from Native American casinos and from nearby states reduces the viability of the industry in some locales and also affects the potential for government gain from casinos. The rhetoric of despair that so characterized progaming campaigns in the early 1990s does not carry as much weight in the latter half of the decade, when people believe that economic conditions are improved. (Whether gambling truly does proliferate when the economy is weak, or whether it emerges as a development option when public commentary is used to persuade people that conditions are desperate, even if they are not, is a research question that has not been fully addressed.)

Case studies from a variety of land-based and riverboat gaming locales reveal patterns in the development and impacts of the new casino economies. Initially, the number of gamblers visiting the new casinos often exceeds a planner's initial projections. Only longitudinal research will determine whether this indicates a pent-up demand for gambling (the argument of the casino industry) or reflects simply another kind of entertainment option for consumers who have disposable income and time. The extent to which people are shifting their expenditures from other types of recreational activities to gambling is also not yet clear.

Although the influx of gambling tourists is good news for the industry, it often results in unexpected impacts for a community. On the macro level, local and state governments profit from an infusion of tax revenues, supporting programs that might otherwise be poorly funded. In Colorado, for example, nearly one-third of the state's gambling tax revenues are dedicated to supporting historic preservation projects; over $30 million was distributed by the state in the first four years of gaming (Stokowski, 1996). In Mississippi, twenty-nine riverboat casinos in seven counties have produced about $234 million in gaming tax revenues, with public education receiving about $48.2 million of that and social welfare programs receiving $12.9 million, while over $111 million goes back to the gaming counties, and the rest goes into the state treasury (Gordon, 1998). Deadwood, South Dakota, earmarks gaming tax revenues for historic preservation, while other states use the tax revenues for capital improvements, education, or discretionary spending (Chadbourne, Walker, and Wolfe, 1997). These benefits are in addition to new revenues, capital development, and public and social services enhanced by tax dollars gained on the local level.

The other side of the coin, though, is that individuals and communities are affected negatively when hordes of gamblers descend upon a community. Personal and collective costs are associated with the new developments, and if those developments are extensive, the costs are also very large. Citizens in every new land-based and riverboat casino locale have expressed frustration with the minor and major difficulties associated with living in a gaming community. These irritations ranged from construction period disturbances to traffic congestion, loss of community services and special places, difficulties finding parking in residential and commercial areas of the town, perceptions of increasing crime, and other forms of community upheaval. The excitement of the new development is not sustained when residents feel they have "lost" their town. In addition, many of the new casino communities were unprepared to handle the administrative difficulties associated with gaming development: record keeping, hiring decisions, budgeting, planning, meetings, and permitting processes needed to be professionalized nearly overnight—an impossible task for traditionally small or part-time local government staff.

The reliance, moreover, on gaming tax revenues to support public services makes the state a tacit partner in casino promotion, raising concerns about whether governments should encourage risk-taking behaviors by citizens or encourage personal loss as a basis for public policy. Analyzing the pattern of educational support in Illinois, Truitt (1996) voiced concern that monies designated for education were being reduced and replaced with gambling tax dollars. The practice of substituting gambling tax revenues for revenues based on more stable forms of state income is not new, and it has generally been condemned by analysts who are aware of the potential for collapse of the targeted social programs if gambling revenues decline.

The question of whether gambling provides new monies for a community or state, or simply redistributes monies from other sports, cultural, or entertainment activities, remains unanswered in most analyses of the economics of gaming. Specific, detailed data about spending patterns across different population subgroups and different economic sectors in a variety of casino locales are needed. This question becomes increasingly important as gambling opportunities, in the form of riverboats or land-based casinos, spread across the country. What seems clear at this point is that the industry is involved in a notable period of expansion and diversification. Whether the communities that adopt land-based or riverboat casinos are also becoming more diverse economically, more stable, and more civic-minded remains open to question.

REFERENCES

Arthur Andersen (1996, December). *Economic impacts of casino gaming in the United States.* Volume 1: *Macro study.* Prepared for the American Gaming Association. Las Vegas, NV: Arthur Andersen LLP.

Braunlich, C.G. (1996). Lessons from the Atlantic City casino experience. *Journal of Travel Research, 34*(3), 46-56.

Chadbourne, C., Walker, P., and Wolfe, M. (1997). *Gambling, economic development, and historic preservation.* Chicago, IL: American Planning Association.

Christiansen, E.M. (1994). 93 gross annual wager. *International Gaming and Wagering Business, 15*(8), 14-44.

Christiansen, E.M. (1997). 96 gross annual wager. *International Gaming and Wagering Business, 18*(8), 1-78.

Cummings, R.G., Schulze, W.D., and Mehr, A.F. (1978). Optimal municipal investment in boomtowns: An empirical analysis. *Journal of Environmental Economics and Management, 5*(3), 252-267.

Doocey, P. (1994). Did Iowa miss the boat? *International Gaming and Wagering Business, 15*(6), 1, 39, 40, 42, 44.

Dworin, P. (1994). North American gaming report. *International Gaming and Wagering Business, 15*(7), 1-80.

Eadington, W.R. (1996). The legalization of casinos: Policy objectives, regulatory alternatives, and cost/benefit considerations. *Journal of Travel Research, 34*(3), 3-8.

Evart, C. (1994, Summer). Troublesome environmental concerns: Some suggested solutions. In Advocacy, Witness and Justice Ministries Unit of the National Episcopal Church and the Diocese of Nevada (Ed.), *The social, economic and environmental consequences of casino gambling* (pp. 41-46). New York: The Episcopal Church Center.

Gordon, M. (1998, January 18). Revenues from gaming defy odds. *The Jackson Clarion-Ledger*, p. 1A.

Grinols, E.L. (1994). Bluff or winning hand? Riverboat gambling and regional employment and unemployment. *Illinois Business Review, 51*(1), 8-11.

Guskind, R. (1991). Casino round the bend. *National Journal, 23*(37), 2205-2209.

Harrah's Entertainment, Inc. (1996). *Survey of casino entertainment.* Memphis, TN: Author.

Harrison, K. (1992). Economic effects of commercial gaming in New Jersey. In W.R. Eadington and J.A. Cornelius (Eds.), *Gambling and commercial gaming: essays in business, economics, philosophy and science* (pp. 105-115). Reno, NV: Institute for the Study of Gambling and Commercial Gaming.

Heubusch, K. (1997). Taking chances on casinos. *American Demographics, 19*(5), 35-40.

Hevener, P. (1992). Has Deadwood overdeveloped? *International Gaming and Wagering Business, 13*(3), 1, 69.

Kallick-Kaufmann, M. (1979). The micro and macro dimensions of gambling in the United States. *The Journal of Social Issues, 35*(3), 7-26.

Kindt, J.W. (1994). The economic impacts of legalized gambling activities. *Drake Law Review, 43*(1), 51-95.

Labalme, J. (1994). The great riverboat gamble. *Southern Exposure: A Journal of Politics and Culture, 22*(2), 10-14.

Madden, M. (1992). *Economic and fiscal impacts associated with gaming: Deadwood, South Dakota.* Pierre, SD: South Dakota Commission on Gaming.

Mandel, M.J., Landler, M., Grover, R., De George, G., Weber, J., Rebello, K., and bureau reports (1994, March 14). The entertainment economy. America's growth engines: Theme parks, casinos, sports, interactive TV. *Business Week, 3362,* 58-64.

McGowan, R. (1994). *State lotteries and legalized gambling: Painless revenue or painful mirage.* Westport, CT: Praeger.

Nickerson, N.P. (1995). Tourism and gambling content analysis. *Annals of Tourism Research, 22*(1), 53-66.

Painton, P. (1989). Boardwalk of broken dreams. *Time, 134*(13), 64-69.

Popkin, J. (1994). A mixed blessing for "America's Ethiopia." *U.S. News and World Report, 116*(10), 52-53.

Ring, R. (1995). The new West's servant economy. *High Country News, 27*(7), 1, 8-14.

Rubenstein, J. (1984). Casino gambling in Atlantic City: Issues of development and redevelopment. *Annals of the American Academy of Political and Social Science, 474*(July), 61-71.

Schwarz, B. and Schwarz, C. (1996). Mississippi Monte Carlo. *The Atlantic Monthly, 277*(1), 67-82.

Shapiro, J.P. (1996, January 15). America's gambling fever. *U.S. News and World Report, 120*(12), 53-61.

Stokowski, P.A. (1993). Undesirable lag effects in tourist destination development: A Colorado case study. *Journal of Travel Research, 32*(2), 35-41.

Stokowski, P.A. (1996). *Riches and regrets: Betting on gambling in two Colorado mountain towns.* Niwot, CO: University Press of Colorado.

Suits, D.B. (1979). Economic background for gambling policy. *The Journal of Social Issues, 35*(3), 43-61.

Thompson, W.N. and Gazel, R.C. (1996*). The monetary impacts of riverboat casino gambling in Illinois.* Study prepared for the Illinois Better Government Association. Chicago, IL: Better Government Association.

Truitt, L.J. (1996). Casino gambling in Illinois: Riverboats, revenues, and economic development. *Journal of Travel Research, 34*(3), 89-96.

SECTION III:
SOCIAL IMPACTS

Chapter 9

Social Impacts of Casino Gaming: The Case of Las Vegas

Haemoon Oh

INTRODUCTION

The city of Las Vegas has been an emblem of rapid economic and social growth based upon the gaming industry. Since its inception as a casino town, circa 1940, Las Vegas has continued to change its social as well as economic profile every year by dint of increasing demands for casino entertainment. In recent years, for example, the visitor volume has risen nearly 340 percent, from 6.8 million in 1970 to 29.6 million in 1996. According to the U.S. Travel Industry Association's survey, 38 percent of all U.S. residents have been to Las Vegas in their lifetime (Las Vegas Convention and Visitors Authority, 1997). Accelerated by continuous growth in both room inventory (about 300 percent) and annual average occupancy rate (from 68 percent to 90 percent) during the same time period, the gaming industry contributed to the city's account more than $91 million of room tax revenue alone in 1996. This economic growth has also accompanied a dramatic increase in the residential population, which has almost tripled, from 125,787 in 1970 to 371,809 in 1995. In the first five years of the 1990s, an average of 346 people has moved into Las Vegas every week. This in-migration is phenomenal considering no people were living in Las Vegas at the dawn of this century. Yet, numerous ongoing casino projects suggest that the city will continue to experience enormous social as well as economic dynamics in years to come.

A number of researchers and organizations have recorded changes in the economic and social environments of Las Vegas.

Most notably, the Las Vegas Convention and Visitors Authority has published statistics on visitors periodically. Comprehensive statistics on both community economics and demography are collected by such organizations as Clark County Comprehensive Planning, the Nevada Development Authority, and the University of Nevada–Las Vegas Center for Business and Economic Research. The Nevada Gaming Control Board also collects and distributes monthly, quarterly, and annual gaming revenue information. The publications of these organizations have contributed to the public's understanding of the direct, as well as indirect, impacts the Las Vegas gaming industry has on the local economy and society.

Many previous publications, however, have highlighted mainly the economic impacts of the gaming industry, typically in a positive way, while neglecting the industry's social implications. Only recently have a few researchers attempted to address specific social and environmental issues tied to, or caused by, the gaming industry in Las Vegas (Chiricos, 1994; Hadjian, 1992; Hulse, 1986; Misrach, 1992; Nassir, 1994; Scriven, 1995). Moreover, even the few researchers who examined social issues showed diverging viewpoints and often reached contradictory conclusions due to methodological differences (e.g., Chiricos, 1994; Hadjian, 1992). Thus, the public has limited understanding of the social impacts of the Las Vegas gaming industry on local communities. Although the economic manifestation of the gaming industry has often dwarfed the significance of social and other issues related to gaming, this should not mean that social issues are not as important as economic aspects. In the long run, the importance of social issues may overshadow the economic benefits people obtain from the gaming industry in Las Vegas.

ASSESSING SOCIAL IMPACTS OF GAMING IN LAS VEGAS

Nature of the Problem

The task of assessing the social impacts of gaming in Las Vegas poses several conceptual difficulties. First of all, it is not easy to separate social impacts from economic impacts; a definitional overlap is unavoidable. Second, the target of social impacts needs to receive a structural clarification. Because Las Vegas began as a casino city, assessing the social impacts of gaming in Las Vegas is unlike cases in other casino cities where social changes in the local community are more visible and easily comparable between before and after the casino industry was introduced. A within-Las Vegas assessment of social impacts may lead to biased interpretations. In addition, the scope of Las Vegas gaming and its social impacts defy a clear boundary. The social impacts of Las Vegas gaming are not limited to local communities; they challenge all Americans' attitudes toward casino entertainment, and related debates still go well beyond America. Even in the Las Vegas area, five different cities (i.e., Boulder City, Henderson, Las Vegas, Mesquite, and North Las Vegas) are socially intertwined, constituting the "Mecca" of gambling. Another conceptual difficulty relates to the locus of social impacts. It is logical that social impacts be assessed at the societal and individual levels. Many social indexes can be studied to infer social impacts at the community, city, state, or country level. Equally important are the social implications or impacts an individual perceives. Assessments of an individual's perception of social impacts are difficult, particularly in a city where the gaming industry has attracted individuals to migrate from other areas.

Exploratory Methods

In this chapter, an attempt is made to assess the social impacts of Las Vegas gaming at a city level, based on selected "socially relevant" variables, and compares Las Vegas to four different U.S. cities over an identical time period. This exploratory approach is interesting because little research shows the social impacts of Las Vegas gaming at the city and individual levels. Ochrym (1990), for example, examined crime rates at the city level by comparing Atlantic City to other nontourist areas in an effort to assess the social impact of gaming in Atlantic City. Scriven (1995) also supported such comparative assessment methods.

Specific methods used for this chapter are as follows. Social impacts were inferred from such selected variables as demographics, traffic and transportation, crime, cost of living, health care environment, and government expenditures that were believed to affect individuals' lives in the city. The past two decades were of primary interest for three reasons. First, the 1980s and the 1990s represent the fastest growth and widest acceptance of the gaming industry in the United States. A second reason is that this period saw monopolistic casino operations in Las Vegas changed to a more competitive situation in the United States. Third, understanding the most recent trends is believed to help predict the near future. Four cities were chosen for comparisons with Las Vegas: Austin, Texas; Fresno, California; Raleigh, North Carolina; and Virginia Beach, Virginia. The selection of these cities was based on five criteria: (1) similar population growth rates, (2) cities in a medium size category, (3) geographic representation, (4) relative geographic independence, and (5) major economy based on industries other than gaming. According to World Almanac Books (1981; 1997), the population growth rate, for example, was 42.3 percent for Austin, 72.9 percent for Fresno, 46.8 percent for Raleigh, and 59.1 percent for Virginia Beach during the 1980-1992 period. Las Vegas recorded 79.5 percent for the same period. All these cities ranked within the top twelve for population growth during the period. Although other cities showed a strong population growth, they were not chosen because their geographic location made it difficult to assess social impacts separate from neighboring cities (e.g., Mesa, Arizona, as a satellite city of Phoenix). However, it was unavoidable that as the chosen cities expanded, they also tended to merge with neighboring cities. For example, Raleigh has expanded to merge with Durham over time, while Virginia Beach has become part of the Norfolk–Virginia Beach–Portsmouth zone in later census statistics. In 1992, the population density was 3,548 people per square mile in Las Vegas, 2,260 in Austin, 3,795 in Fresno, 2,503 in Raleigh, and 1,680 in Virginia Beach (World Almanac Books, 1981; 1997).

SOCIAL IMPACTS OF GAMING IN LAS VEGAS: A COMPARATIVE APPROACH

In this section, actual comparisons of the five cities including Las Vegas are conducted according to the methods explained previously. Because little related research has been reported in the literature, the comparisons are a fresh, exploratory attempt and are based

extensively on the U.S. Census statistics summarized in such peri-
odic publications as *Census of Population and Housing Census
Track* (U.S. Department of Commerce, 1990), *County and City
Data Book* (U.S. Department of Commerce, 1981; 1997), *The
World Almanac and Book of Facts* (World Almanac Books, 1981;
1997), and *Places Rated Almanac* (Boyer and Savageau, 1981;
1989; Savageau and Loftus, 1997). Note that because the census is
taken every tenth year, the most comprehensive statistics on all
compared cities and variables are based on the 1990 census data.
The most recent county and city data were in the 1994 publication.

Demographics

Based on several selected variables, the population profile of Las
Vegas shows no major difference when compared to that of the
other four cities in the 1980s. Table 9.1 summarizes the population
profiles of the four cities for a number of selected variables. As
illustrated in the table, Las Vegas shows quite similar population
trends as the other cities in regard to persons with different ethnic
origins. The white population in Las Vegas has decreased slightly
(-2.46 percent), as in Austin (-4.43 percent), Raleigh (-1.45
percent), and Virginia Beach (-5.82 percent). This decrease, however, was a small change when compared to that of Fresno (-11.84
percent). The black population of Las Vegas followed that of Fresno
and Raleigh, showing a slight decline (less than 2 percent) over the
ten-year period. This decrease was against a slight increase of
0.2 percent and 3.9 percent in Austin and Virginia Beach, respectively. The decrease in the white and black populations was com-
pensated by the corresponding increase in the Asian and Hispanic
populations. All five cities recorded an increase in the Asian and
Hispanic populations, with Fresno showing the largest increase. In
sum, Las Vegas has remained somewhat stable throughout the
changes in population composition during the 1980s.

Table 9.1 also compares the five cities on additional aspects of the
population. First, except for Fresno, where the Asian and Hispanic
populations have exhibited a strong growth, the number of single-
person households has risen 0.7 to 4.8 percent. Las Vegas has experienced the slowest growth. Second, as with Austin and Fresno, Las

TABLE 9.1. Comparisons of Population Characteristics[a]

Variable	1980					1990				
	Las Vegas	Austin	Fresno	Raleigh	Virginia Beach	Las Vegas	Austin	Fresno	Raleigh	Virginia Beach
White (%)	81.57	75.59	71.72	70.60	86.49	79.11	71.16	59.88	69.15	80.67
Black (%)	12.78	12.19	9.47	27.44	10.03	11.44	12.43	8.31	27.04	13.91
Asian (%)	2.03	1.05	2.81	1.05	2.51	3.60	3.04	12.53	2.42	4.33
Hispanic (%)[b]	7.77	18.75	23.60	0.92	1.97	12.50	22.95	29.88	1.39	3.09
One-person household (%)	25.50	29.50	26.30	27.40	15.30	26.20	34.10	24.10	32.20	17.10
Male/100 females	100.60	97.60	92.00	94.60	103.20	102.90	99.70	94.70	94.20	103.10
Median age	29.80	26.20	28.10	27.90	26.90	32.60	28.90	28.40	30.30	28.90
Persons 65 or older (%)	8.30	7.50	10.90	8.30	4.50	10.30	7.40	10.10	8.80	5.90
Bachelor's degree or higher (%)	11.50	30.60	16.50	33.00	22.40	13.40	34.40	19.10	40.60	25.10
Divorced (%)	10.30	7.30	7.20	5.40	4.10	12.10	8.90	12.00	7.20	5.70
Annual per capita income	8,135	7,309	6,967	7,804	7,704	14,737	14,521	11,824	16,896	15,242
Civilian labor force, females (%)	42.80	45.80	41.40	47.20	46.20	44.70	46.60	45.80	48.10	50.20
Persons below poverty level[c] (%)	10.50	15.80	15.70	12.20	8.90	11.50	17.90	24.00	11.80	5.90

Source: Adapted from World Almanac Books (1981; 1997).

[a] Entries expressed in percentage are scaled against the population.
[b] Persons of Hispanic origin may be of any race.
[c] Comparisons are between 1979 and 1989 rather than between 1980 and 1990.

Vegas has had a slight increase in the male-to female ratio. Raleigh and Virginia Beach have remained quite stable in this aspect. Note that, similar to Virginia Beach, Las Vegas has more males than females. Third, population aging, based on the median age, has been a general trend in all five cities. The population of Las Vegas has aged 2.8 years over the ten-year period, while that of the other cities has become, on average, 1.85 years older over the same time period. Interestingly, Las Vegas has the oldest population among the five cities, though the difference is not substantial. Fourth, Las Vegas tended to attract a larger number of people age sixty-five or older than the other cities. The city has shown, among the five cities, the fastest growth in the senior citizen population in the 1980s. Fifth, Las Vegas has the smallest proportion of population that has attained a bachelor's degree or higher, although the percentage has increased over time. Moreover, the growth rate of this educated population was slower in Las Vegas than in the other cities. Finally, the proportion of divorced people in Las Vegas was larger than in the other cities, although the growth rate was modest over time. In summary, Las Vegas, when compared to the other cities collectively, does not show any notable change ratio in the single-person household population, male-to-female ratio, sixty-five or older population, the proportion of the population having a bachelor's degree or higher, and the proportion of divorced people. However, in an absolute sense, Las Vegas's population tended to be more male-oriented, more aged, more divorce-ridden, and less educated than the other four cities. Examinations of these variables over a longer period of time may detect notable change ratios.

Table 9.1 includes three additional econodemographic variables for the five cities. First, the per capita income level has risen only modestly in Las Vegas (81 percent) over the ten-year period. Although this figure compared favorably to that in Fresno (70 percent), it was considerably lower than the growth rate in Austin (99 percent), Raleigh (117 percent), and Virginia Beach (98 percent). Second, the percent of female civilian labor force participation in Las Vegas was modest when compared to that in the other cities. All cities have shown increased rates of female labor force participation in the 1980s. Finally, the population proportion falling below the poverty level was not specific to Las Vegas. Austin and Fresno have recorded higher accelerated growth rates than Las Vegas, while Raleigh and Virginia Beach have exhibited a decline. Except for a relatively slow growth in the per capita income level, Las Vegas does not show city-specific trends in its female civilian labor force participation, nor in the population proportion below the poverty level.

Traffic and Transportation

Discussions and data presentations on traffic and transportation in this section are based on the work of Boyer and Savageau (1981; 1989) and Savageau and Loftus (1997). In line with the rapid growth of the city population, the amount of traffic has increased significantly in Las Vegas. In 1979, Las Vegas accommodated 179 flights (thirteen carriers) every day; this number increased to 375 flights each day (twenty-three carriers) in 1988. This more-than-double increase in air traffic compared similarly to that of Austin where forty-seven flights per day (five carriers) have increased to 105 flights (ten carriers) over the same time period. However, this increase was outweighed by the air traffic growth in Fresno and the Norfolk–Virginia Beach–Portsmouth (NVP) area. Fresno experienced a 435 percent increase, from twenty flights per day (two carriers) in 1979 to 107 flights (nine carriers) in 1988, while the NVP area hosted forty-two flights (five carriers) in 1979 and 125 flights in 1988. Only Raleigh-Durham has experienced decreased air traffic during the same period (fifty-three to sixteen flights per day).

The number of city buses also increased dramatically over time in all five cities. Las Vegas, for example, operated twenty-one city buses in 1979; this number increased nearly 470 percent to 119 buses in 1996. During the same time period, Austin experienced an increase of 313 percent, from 61 to 252 buses; Fresno, 55 percent, from 80 to 124 buses; the NVP area, 67 percent, from 138 to 231 buses; and Raleigh-Durham, 203 percent, from 35 to 106 buses.

The increase in the average daily commuting time in Las Vegas was modest during the 1988-1996 period. In 1988, a commuter spent approximately 41.6 minutes a day traveling between home and work. This commuting time rose to 44.1 minutes in 1996. By comparison, the daily average commuting time in Austin was 41.8 minutes in 1988 and 46.3 minutes in 1996. During the same time period, Fresno and Raleigh-Durham have also experienced a slight increase, from 40.5 to 41.2 and from 42.5 to 43.3 minutes, respectively. However, the NVP area recorded a slight decrease, from 47.1 to 45.6 minutes. It can be inferred from these figures that Las Vegas does not show city-specific traffic congestion, given the rapid population growth rate, as in the other cities.

Crime

According to the Federal Bureau of Investigation (FBI) Uniform Crime Reports, all five cities have recently shown a general decreasing trend in the rates of both violent crimes (such as murder, forcible rape, robbery, and aggravated assault) and property crimes (such as burglary, larceny-theft, and motor vehicle theft). Table 9.2 summarizes crime rates in the five cities over the three time periods. Specifically, Las Vegas reported a 41 percent decrease in murder rates between 1980 and 1996. Over the same time period, murder rates also decreased by about 45 percent in Austin. The murder rates in Fresno, Raleigh, and Virginia Beach remained virtually unchanged, although Virginia Beach was the only city showing a slightly increasing trend. Although Las Vegas showed the highest murder rate in 1980 and 1988, the rate decreased to below that of Fresno and Virginia Beach in 1996. Nonetheless, Las Vegas's murder rate is still much higher than that of Austin and Raleigh.

Table 9.2 also indicates that forcible rape has been reduced in Las Vegas by 7 percent between 1980 and 1996. Similarly, a 7 percent decrease has occurred in Fresno over the same time period. However, Austin, Raleigh, and Virginia Beach have experienced an increase in forcible rape incidents by 3 to 9 percent. Despite the continued decrease in reported rape cases, Las Vegas still shows the highest rate of forcible rape among the five cities over the last two decades.

In the case of robbery, only Las Vegas shows a decreasing trend over time. The city reduced robbery incidents by about 28 percent between 1980 and 1996. All the other cities recorded increased robbery, 25 to 84 percent for the same period. Note, however, that despite the decreasing trend, Las Vegas still shows a higher robbery rate than Austin, Raleigh, and Virginia Beach. Only Fresno's robbery rate exceeded that of Las Vegas in 1996.

The rate of aggravated assault followed the trend of robbery in all cities. Only Las Vegas reported a slight decrease (2 percent) over

TABLE 9.2. Comparisons of Crime Rates[a]

City	Murder	Rape	Robbery	Assault	Burglary	Theft	MV[b] Theft
Las Vegas	22.4[c]	67.6	530.2	404.3	3,368.2	4,769.8	820.1
	13.7[d]	66.7	386.2	348.7	2,178.0	3,866.0	629.0
	12.8[e]	62.9	382.0	396.8	1,512.0	3,648.0	864.0
Austin	11.8	53.1	134.7	187.6	2,042.6	4,169.8	388.2
	10.3	65.7	158.2	235.9	2,066.0	4,781.0	377.0
	6.5	54.9	191.1	282.3	1,612.0	5,025.0	590.0
Fresno	16.6	59.3	310.3	459.8	2,615.1	4,221.5	756.9
	12.9	58.4	253.1	452.5	2,333.0	4,344.0	525.0
	15.3	54.9	388.2	606.1	1,812.0	3,646.0	1,873.0
Raleigh	9.5	33.7	114.3	280.4	1,624.4	3,797.8	324.4
	9.0	30.9	119.4	243.9	1,454.0	3,385.0	269.0
	9.7	36.0	210.0	345.8	1,680.0	3,534.0	331.0
Virginia Beach	11.9	44.1	205.3	239.7	1,323.5	3,543.2	309.2
	9.6	41.7	175.5	217.2	1,189.0	3,488.0	259.0
	13.1	48.6	269.8	285.8	1,052.0	4,029.0	500.0

Sources: Adapted from Boyer and Savageau (1981; 1989); Savageau and Loftus (1997).

[a] All entries are scaled to 100,000 persons.
[b] Motor vehicle
[c] 1980 index
[d] 1988 index
[e] 1996 index

the 1980-1996 time period. The other four cities reported an increased rate of aggravated assault by 23 to 50 percent. Despite the decrease, Las Vegas still had a higher assault rate than Austin, Raleigh, and Virginia Beach in 1992. The assault rate in Las Vegas fell below only that of Fresno over time.

A 55 percent decrease in burglary incidents is reported for Las Vegas between 1980 and 1996. This decrease was much larger than that for Austin (21 percent), Fresno (31 percent), Raleigh (3 percent), and Virginia Beach (21 percent). This decreasing trend positioned Las Vegas as the second lowest, next to Virginia Beach, in the burglary rate of 1996.

Larceny-theft has been reduced significantly in Las Vegas. The city achieved a 24 percent reduction in the occurrence rate of larceny-theft between 1980 and 1996. Fresno and Raleigh also reduced larceny-theft by about 14 and 7 percent, respectively, over the same time period. However, Austin and Virginia Beach reported a 21 and 14 percent increase, respectively. These two cities' larceny-theft rate exceeded that of Las Vegas in 1996. Fresno had about the same rate as Las Vegas, but Raleigh showed a lower rate in 1996.

All cities have reported increased motor vehicle thefts in the past two decades. Las Vegas, for example, reported a 5 percent increase between 1980 and 1996. During the same period, there was an increase of 52 percent in Austin, 147 percent in Fresno, 2 percent in Raleigh, and 62 percent in Virginia Beach. In 1996, only Fresno's motor vehicle theft rate was higher than that of Las Vegas.

In sum, Las Vegas has shown a notable trend toward crime containment during the past two decades. Las Vegas compared favorably to the other cities for the change rates of murder, aggravated assault, burglary, and larceny-theft. For the change rates of forcible rape, robbery, and motor vehicle theft, Las Vegas did not show city-specific characteristics. Despite the generally decreasing trend in crime rates, Las Vegas still showed a higher rate of forcible rapes, robberies, aggravated assaults, and motor vehicle thefts in 1996 than most other cities. For burglary rates in 1996, Las Vegas compared favorably to most other cities, and the same year's larceny-theft rate did not show Las Vegas-specific characteristics. These figures must be interpreted carefully, though. Curran and Scarpitti (1991) argued that using FBI crime figures might be erroneous because the figures do not differentiate crime that occurred in the community and crime that occurred in the casinos. Chiricos (1994) also contends that crime rates should be adjusted for visitors, as well as the resident population. These arguments are consistent with Ochrym's (1990) conclusion that tourist destinations have higher mean crime rates than other areas and that the crime rates grow due to increased tourism, regardless of the presence of casinos.

Costs of Living

To compare the five cities for the recent costs of living, several variables were selected. They included the annual average household income, median housing price and mortgage payment, property tax, utility costs, food costs, and transportation costs. Table 9.3 summarizes the costs-of-living indexes. Except for household income, all variables were adjusted to the average of all U.S. metropolitan areas' costs of living, which was normalized to 100. That is, relative interpretations are necessary: if the index falls below 100, it means that the city's residents pay less than the national average on that item; if, however, the index exceeds 100, the city is a more expensive place to live than the national average.

The first column of Table 9.3 suggests that Las Vegas residents have earned an above-average household income in recent years. Although the city's 1988 average household income was below the national metropolitan average, the situation was reversed in 1996 because of a nearly 45 percent increase. Fresno also shows a similar trend, with a 54 percent increase during the same time period. The NVP area has exhibited a 38 percent increase, which exceeded the average growth rate (30 percent) of the national average, but its household income fell below the average in 1996. Austin recorded a relatively slow growth (11 percent), eventually falling below the national average in 1996. Although Raleigh-Durham's growth rate (25 percent) was smaller than the national average, its actual level of household income far exceeded this average. Comparisons of the annual household income indicate that Las Vegas is one of the fastest growing cities, with residents earning more than the national average.

The second column of Table 9.3 contains two different, but related indexes: (1) median housing prices in 1988 and (2) mortgage

TABLE 9.3. Comparisons of Costs of Living

City	Household Income	Median Housing Price/ Mortgage Payment	Property Tax	Utility	Food	Transport
Las Vegas	$42,675[a]	88[c]	53[a]	79[a]	89[a]	128[a]
	61,700[b]	122[d]	69[b]	79[b]	106[b]	120[b]
Austin	52,416	93	114	77	99	100
	58,000	115	136	77	95	102
Fresno	38,497	134	123	101	102	115
	59,300	99	71	97	108	102
Norfolk–Virginia	40,827	81	69	103	102	110
Beach–Portsmouth	56,400	108	103	101	103	103
Raleigh–Durham	49,990	111	98	99	100	109
	62,300	138	139	96	100	98
National Metropolitan	45,144	100	100	100	100	100
Average	58,900	100	100	100	100	100

Sources: Adapted from Boyer and Savageau (1981); Savageau and Loftus (1997).

[a] 1988 index
[b] 1996 index
[c] Median housing price in 1988
[d] Median mortgage payment in 1996

payments for a home in 1996. Las Vegas shows a pattern similar to that of Austin and the NVP area. That is, the 1988 median housing prices for these cities were lower than the national average, but their 1996 mortgage payments were higher than the national average. Fresno's 1988 median housing price far exceeded the national average, though its 1996 mortgage payment index was similar to the national average. Raleigh-Durham has recorded a higher median housing price in 1988 and higher mortgage payment index in 1996 than the national average. No city-specific characteristic was found for Las Vegas in terms of housing and mortgage payments.

Las Vegas has enjoyed a consistently low property tax. In both 1988 and 1996, the city's property tax payment was far below the national average and lower than any other city in comparison. Its growth rate (30 percent) against the national average was lower than that of the NVP area (50 percent) and Raleigh-Durham (42 percent), but higher than that of Austin (19 percent). In contrast, Fresno's property tax imposition showed a significant decrease (− 42 percent) against the national average over time.

Las Vegas residents paid the second-lowest utility bill in both 1988 and 1996, next to Austin. The two cities' utility costs were far below the national average, and this low payment has continued over time. The other three cities' utility costs were near the national average over time, and their indexes were in a declining trend.

In recent years, food costs have risen substantially in Las Vegas, going against the national average. Although Las Vegas residents paid relatively low prices for food in 1988, they were writing a food check larger than the national average in 1996. The other cities have shown little change in food costs over time, although Austin has observed a slightly decreasing index.

In sum, Las Vegas shows some city-specific costs-of-living characteristics. The city's annual average household income has risen beyond the national average, but its property tax and utility costs were relatively lower than both the national average and the costs in most of the other cities. Nevertheless, the city's food costs are rising faster than in the other cities. Note that because the presented figures do not reflect city-specific inflation in prices, caution must be given to interpreting the costs of living in each city.

Health Care Environment

The five cities were compared for health care facilities and costs. Specifically, focal variables were (1) the number of licensed practicing physicians (including general/family, medical, and surgical specialists) per 100,000 residents, (2) number of accredited general hospital beds per 100,000 persons, (3) number of accredited hospitals (without discriminating specialty areas), and (4) health care costs. Table 9.4 summarizes the results of comparisons.

The number of practicing physicians per 100,000 persons is relatively small in Las Vegas, though the number is on the rise. The city's physicians-to-residents ratio has increased about 50 percent between 1988 and 1996. This increase was the largest, as compared to that of Austin (24 percent), Fresno (20 percent), the NVP area (-28 percent), and Raleigh-Durham (25 percent). Note that the NVP area observed a significant decrease in the number of physicians in recent years.

TABLE 9.4. Comparisons of Health Care Environments

City	Number of Physicians[a]	Number of Hospital Beds[a]	Number of Hospitals	Health Care Costs[b]
Las Vegas	648[c]	1,946	8	146
	975[d]	2,461	12	111
Austin	955	1,719	10	109
	1,180	1,712	10	102
Fresno	774	1,693	12	113
	932	1,721	13	107
Norfolk-Virginia Beach-Portsmouth	1,743	5,220	19	93
	1,261	2,634	12	103
Raleigh-Durham	1,397	3,638	12	96
	1,753	3,917	10	98

Sources: Adapted from Boyer and Savageau (1989); Savageau and Loftus (1997); World Almanac Books (1997).

[a] Per 100,000 persons
[b] Scaled against the normalized national average of 100
[c] 1988 index
[d] 1996 index

The number of accredited hospital beds also shows a trend similar to that for the number of physicians. The beds-to-residents ratio has increased 25 percent in Las Vegas between 1988 and 1996, and this increase was the largest when compared to that of Austin (virtually no change), Fresno (2 percent), the NVP area (-50 percent), and Raleigh-Durham (8 percent). Note that the NVP area has experienced a significant reduction in the number of hospital beds in recent years. As also shown in the fourth column of Table 9.4, Las Vegas added four hospitals between 1988 and 1996. Fresno added only one new hospital during the same time period. Austin remained the same, while NVP and Raleigh-Durham reduced the number of hospitals in the same time period.

Health care costs in each city again were scaled against the average of all metropolitan areas' health care costs in the United States. That is, the national average was normalized to 100, as was the case with living costs in Table 9.3. The results show that Las Vegas residents share the largest burden for their health care. In both 1988 and 1996, health care costs in Las Vegas were higher than the national average, as well as the costs in the other four cities. However, the city's health care costs have declined over time toward the national average.

In summary, Las Vegas has a relatively small number of physicians, though the number has recently increased. The number of both hospitals and hospital beds shows the fastest growth rate in Las Vegas. On the other hand, the city's health care costs are the highest among the five cities, though they have been decreasing in recent years.

Government Expenditure

The city government's expenditure for public services can reflect the contribution of the city's industries. This indirect contribution, in turn, could be interpreted as indirect social impacts of the city's industries. Therefore, several selected finance items of each city were examined as a means to assess indirect social impacts of gaming in Las Vegas. Table 9.5 summarizes the results. Note that the source publication did not provide complete information on the selected variables in some cases. For this reason, only three variables with complete information for the years of investigation are discussed here.

TABLE 9.5. Comparisons of Government Expenditure[a]

Variable	Las Vegas	Austin	Fresno	Norfolk- V. Beach- Portsmouth	Raleigh- Durham
Public Welfare	NA 0.2	NA 0.3	NA NA	NA 2.0	NA 0.4
Health and Hospitals	NA 0.8	25.1 22.2	NA NA	2.2 2.4	0.2 0.1
Police Protection	29.6 17.5	10.8 9.0	15.9 21.3	6.9 5.7	15.5 11.6
Fire Protection	NA 11.4	NA 6.0	NA 10.3	NA 2.8	NA 7.7
Highways	8.2 18.6	8.6 9.3	18.0 9.2	8.6 11.2	11.3 11.2
Sewerage and Solid Waste Management (Sanitation)	6.0 6.5	10.0 10.1	13.8 16.4	7.3 4.8	13.3 22.7

Source: Adapted from World Almanac Books (1981; 1997).

[a] The first entries are for 1980 and the second for 1990. All entries are in percentages.

First, during the 1980s, Las Vegas has committed a relatively large percentage of the city's budget to police protection, though this allocation has decreased over time. Austin and the NVP area also have allocated a slightly reduced percentage of their budget for police protection over the same time period. Raleigh-Durham has reduced its budget allocation for police protection somewhat substantially between 1980 and 1990. Only Fresno has increased its budgetary spending for police protection.

Las Vegas's expenditure on highway maintenance has jumped between 1980 and 1990. For the same years, there was also a slight increase in Austin and the NVP area. Raleigh-Durham has remained about the same. Only Fresno has curtailed its spending on highways significantly over time.

Las Vegas has committed a relatively small percentage of its budget to sewerage and solid waste management in the 1980s, when compared to Austin, Fresno, and Raleigh-Durham. The city's spending for waste management has remained virtually unchanged over time. Austin also has spent about the same proportion of its budget for waste management over time. Fresno has raised its budgetary allocation. A more substantial increase has occurred in Raleigh-Durham. However, the NVP area has cut its spending on waste management.

Although Las Vegas does not show any city-specific trend in government spending on public services, the city has cut its budget allocation for police protection during the 1980s. Perhaps this sizable reduction was a reflection of decreasing crime rates in the city during the same time period. Despite the reduction, Las Vegas was still budgeting a higher percentage for police protection in 1990 than Austin, the NVP area, and Raleigh-Durham, where crime rates were rising in general. For highway maintenance, Las Vegas has allocated a similar percentage as did Austin, the NVP area, and Raleigh-Durham. Finally, Las Vegas has afforded a relatively smaller percentage of its budget for waste management and sanitation than Austin, Fresno, and Raleigh-Durham. It should be noted, however, that, although analyses of government expenditure have focused only on the city's spending patterns, the actual amount of spending for the same percentage among cities could differ depending upon the actual size of each city's budget amount. Additionally, the city's needs for spending on the specific area should be considered in further analyses.

CITY-SPECIFIC SOCIAL IMPACTS OF GAMING

Although analyses presented in the previous section focused on objective indicators that were comparable across different cities, Las Vegas still has its own industry-specific social implications. Examples include residents' attitudes toward gaming, pathological and compulsive gambling, and other related social issues, such as drug abuse, prostitution, suicide, and potential political corruption. These issues are not directly comparable between Las Vegas and other nongaming cities. Unfortunately, little research has been published on these issues in Las Vegas, making any attempt to draw a conclusion difficult.

Only a few researchers and research organizations have raised questions regarding Las Vegas-specific social issues tied to gaming. Scriven (1995), for example, discussed gaming-related social norms and philosophical issues of choosing gaming as the city's major industry. His discussion was rather phenomenological, using no empirical data, and it covered a number of social aspects, such as prostitution, crimes, and drug abuses, which were viewed to result from legalization of gambling in Las Vegas. Although highlighting Las Vegas's recent efforts at reducing crime rates and changing the city's image to a family destination, Scriven concluded that the negative social impacts of gaming in Las Vegas should be a matter of "reasonable control" rather than something unavoidable.

The Center for Survey Research (1984) conducted a telephone survey of 802 Las Vegas residents to study residents' attitudes toward gaming in Las Vegas. For the question of whether the local existence of gaming had a negative impact on their family life, approximately 87 percent of the respondents either "disagreed" or "strongly disagreed." In addition, 63 percent of the respondents believed that most Las Vegas residents do not gamble. However, about 70 percent of the respondents reported that they had gambled once or twice in the previous month and that they had spent only a small amount of money when gambling. Almost 79 percent of the respondents reported that they gambled for purposes of fun and recreation. The survey also showed that approximately 45 percent of the respondents held an image of Las Vegas as being typical of most other American towns.

Thompson and colleagues (1993) also showed that Las Vegas residents did not have negative attitudes toward the presence of gambling in the city unless the presence was in their "backyard." They reviewed a number of local cases in which residents strongly protested the opening of new casinos in residential neighborhoods. Their survey of 967 randomly selected recent home purchasers revealed that proximity to casinos "did not fare that badly" (p. 56) in home purchase decisions when compared with other negative attributes, such as gangs/crime, crime/drugs, flooding, air pollution, freeways, industry, major streets, proximity to nuclear waste route, and airport. About 37 percent of the respondents said proximity to casinos was a "very important" or "important" factor affecting their home purchase decision, whereas 38 percent reported that it was either "unimportant" or "very unimportant." In general, purchasers of more expensive homes and those with children in the household were more concerned about casino locations than others. They also concluded that gaming did not cause local residents' hostility if appropriate geographical controls were imposed.

Smith (1986) argued that Las Vegas residents do not hold negative attitudes toward gambling. According to him, perhaps Las Vegans view gambling as a routine part of their lives, not in the sense of their own participation in gambling, but because gambling is so much a part of their own immediate environment. Smith also observed the recent legalization of casino gambling in America and speculated that the stigma attached to gambling was declining nationwide, although the phenomenon occurred unevenly. Smith and Preston's (1984) study of 233 tourists to Las Vegas provided support for this view by showing that "play, leisure, and recreation" were the most frequently cited motives by the respondents.

Several additional studies on social issues in Las Vegas are found in the literature, although their topics are fragmentary. First, according to Frey, Reichert, and Russell's (1981) study of illegal prostitution in Las Vegas, local residents tended to view the behavior as tolerable due to unavoidable demands in such a tourist-oriented city as Las Vegas. The study found that prostitutes, procurers, business leaders, taxi drivers, bellhops, and even police agencies often formed a social network within a supportive task environment in Las Vegas's tourist-recreation industry. Thus, such negative social behaviors as prostitution were viewed to be a by-product of maintaining the city as a popular tourist, and possibly gaming, destination.

Second, Kearney, and colleagues (1996) found that the accessibility and family-oriented nature of many new casinos in Las Vegas might be responsible for increased gambling problems among high school students. Their study of 109 adolescents from a religious high school and 84 adolescents from a juvenile detention facility in Las Vegas found that 37 percent of the adolescents (mean age = 15.9 years) gambled regularly. Surprisingly, the two contrasting adolescent groups showed many similarities in gambling patterns and problems. Moreover, both groups reported that their parents generally approved of their gambling and were aware of their regular gambling activities. An implication of this study may be that residents' general tolerance of gaming, or their perception of gaming as fun and as a recreational activity, causes relaxed parental supervision of adolescent gaming.

Finally, a local newspaper recently reported a study of suicide that analyzed death certificates in cities over various time periods ("Study:

Gambling Linked to Suicide," 1997). According to the report, such gaming cities as Las Vegas, Atlantic City, and Reno have higher suicide rates by both residents and visitors than comparably sized cities without gaming. Las Vegas, which has the highest suicide rate in the nation, had 497 suicides in 1990—187 more than expected in a city of that size. Visitors' suicide rates were also the highest in Las Vegas. One out of every twenty-five visitor deaths was reportedly a suicide. High suicide rates in these major cities imply that gaming may be responsible for frequent suicides by both residents and visitors.

SUMMARY

This chapter has attempted to assess the social impacts of gaming in Las Vegas in comparison to four different cities on a number of selected social variables. The identified general demographic trend was not specific to Las Vegas. The city has reported a relatively significant reduction in violent and property crime rates in recent years, although the crime rates still are high in comparison to other cities. The city's average annual household income has been growing beyond the national average in recent years, demonstrating one socioeconomic impact of gaming. Costs of living have also been on the rise in Las Vegas. The relatively small number of physicians, coupled with somewhat high health care costs, provides quite an undesirable health care environment for local residents when compared to the other four cities. Although Las Vegas does not show any city-specific trend in government spending on general public services, the city had significantly reduced its budget for police protection during the 1980s. Finally, several reported studies suggest that Las Vegas has its own social problems potentially associated with gambling. These problems include intrusion of gaming into private residential areas, youth gambling, and suicides.

The overall results of the exploratory study in this chapter provide a tentative conclusion: Las Vegas still seems to have some city-specific social issues tied to gaming, but the study equally suggests that the city is becoming more socially desirable. Salient current social problems in Las Vegas, as compared to the other four cities, seem to be crimes, health care conditions, and some gaming-related problems such as youth gambling, prostitution, and suicides. Nevertheless, it is clear that crime rates will soon reduce to a "normal" level if the significantly decreasing trend in violent crime rates continues. Data also show that the health care environment of Las Vegas is improving, as more medical staff and facilities are becoming available and as health care costs are rapidly decreasing toward the national average. Other gaming-related social problems, however, require tighter controls than ever before. In short, the city of Las Vegas, when compared to most other growing cities, promises a brighter future by virtue of its continued effort to become a family-oriented vacation destination. As several researchers indicated, a well-controlled growth of gaming may be critical to maintaining the city as a socially, as well as economically, desirable living space.

The information provided in this chapter should be interpreted carefully because of some methodological limitations. First, all analysis results and interpretations are limited to the five selected cities. Convenient selection of the compared cities could cause selection bias. Inclusion of more diverse cities may improve generalizability of the findings, although the task would become increasingly complex. Second, the scope of investigation was limited by both a recent time frame and a set of selected variables. Future studies may extend this work by including a wider time frame as well as a larger number of variables. Third, although some variables, such as crimes, were adjusted to the population size of the city, other variables were not adjusted to their proper criteria to accomplish more objective comparisons among cities. For example, the number of recreational facilities could be adjusted to population or demand size imposed by both residents and visitors. Finally, this chapter focused on secondary data available for all the selected cities. Discussions on other social issues that are specific to Las Vegas gaming deserve further space in future studies. With respect to this limitation, more research is needed on perceived social impacts of gaming in Las Vegas.

REFERENCES

Boyer, R. and Savageau, D. (1981). *Places rated almanac: Your guide to finding the best places to live in America*. New York: Prentice Hall.

Boyer, R. and Savageau, D. (1989). *Places rated almanac: Your guide to finding the best places to live in America*. Chicago, IL: Rand McNally and Company.

Center for Survey Research, University of Nevada, Las Vegas (1984). *1985 Las Vegas Perspective*. Las Vegas, NV: Metropolitan Research Association.

Chiricos, T. (1994). Casinos and crime: An assessment of the evidence. Las Vegas, NV: University of Nevada, Las Vegas, Special Collections.

Curran, D. and Scarpitti, F. (1991). Crime in Atlantic City: Do casinos make a difference? *Deviant Behavior: An Interdisciplinary Journal, 12*(3), 431-449.

Frey, J.H., Reichert, L.D., and Russell, K.V. (1981). Prostitution, business and police: The maintenance of an illegal economy. *The Police Journal, 54*(2), 239-249.

Hadjian, C.M. (1992). Tourism and crime in Las Vegas: Content analysis of components of tourism and crime in Las Vegas from newspaper articles. Unpublished master's thesis, California State Polytechnic University, Pomona, California.

Hulse, J.W. (1986). *Forty years in the wilderness: Impressions of Nevada, 1940-1980*. Reno, NV: University of Nevada Press.

Kearney, C.A., Roblek, J.T., Thurman, J., and Thurnbough, P.D. (1996). Casino gambling in private school and adjudicated youngsters: A survey of practices and related variables. *Journal of Gambling Studies, 12*(3), 319-327.

Las Vegas Convention and Visitors Authority (1997). *Las Vegas visitor profile study*. Las Vegas, NV: Author.

Misrach, R. (1992). Las Vegas runs dry. *Audubon, 94*(4), 56-63.

Nassir, D.E. (1994). Nevada welfare assistance caseloads and gaming: A cautionary tale. *Nevada Historical Society Quarterly, 37*(2), 115-141.

Ochrym, R.G. (1990). Street crime, tourism and casinos: An empirical comparison. *Journal of Gambling Studies, 6*(1), 127-138.

Savageau, D. and Loftus, G. (1997). *Places rated almanac* (Fifth edition). Chicago, IL: Macmillan Publishing.

Scriven, M. (1995). The philosophical foundations of Las Vegas. *Journal of Gambling Studies, 11*(1), 61-75.

Smith, R.W. (1986). Legalized recreation as deviance. *Quarterly Journal of Ideology, 10*(1), 37-42.

Smith, R.W. and Preston, F.W. (1984). Vocabularies of motives for gambling behaviors. *Sociological Perspectives, 27*(3), 325-348.

Study: Gambling linked to suicide (1997, December 17). *The Des Moines Register,* p. 7A.

Thompson, W.N., Schwer, R.K., Hoyt, R., and Brosnan, D. (1993). Not in my backyard: Las Vegas residents protest casinos. *Journal of Gambling Studies, 9*(1), 47-62.

U.S. Department of Commerce (1981). *County and city data book 1981*. Ann Arbor, MI: Bureau of the Census.

U.S. Department of Commerce (1990). *Census of population and housing census track*. Washington, DC: Bureau of the Census.

U.S. Department of Commerce (1997). *County and city data book 1981*. Ann Arbor, MI: Bureau of the Census.

World Almanac Books. (1981). *The world almanac and book of facts*. Mahwah, NJ: Author.

World Almanac Books. (1997). *The world almanac and book of facts*. Mahwah, NJ: Author.

Chapter 10

Social Impacts of Atlantic City Casino Gaming

Denis P. Rudd

INTRODUCTION

When I was a little boy, I remember my father taking me to see Atlantic City with its merry-go-rounds and Ferris wheels and the smell of popcorn and peanuts, hot dogs with French's mustard, Indian corn soaked in butter, and, the most exotic of all treats, salt-water taffy. We circled the town on the never-ending Boardwalk. Even then my father noted the decline and deterioration of the infrastructure and the city itself. Dombrink and Thompson, in their book *The Last Resort* (1990), summarized Atlantic City in decline, the epitome of glamour aging. Its streets had deteriorated into a crowded, noisy, dirty, and cheerfully vulgar resort. The population of Atlantic City had decreased by 20 percent between 1960 and 1970. Available hotel rooms had dropped by 40 percent, real estate, local luxury tax collection, and the number of conventions and convention delegates had also declined during this time. Between 1960 and 1975, Atlantic City lost 4,500 jobs as unemployment and the welfare rolls grew.

DEMOGRAPHICS

As for the demographics of Atlantic City, the city is declining and probably will continue to decline. Upon close examination, it is revealed that the decline started long before the 1978 advent of casino gaming. Although the city's population declined 10.9 percent from 1970 to 1977, and a further 5 percent from 1980 to 1990, the population of Atlantic County increased by more than 25 percent during that same time period. The net increase in population in Atlantic County was a result of direct and indirect employment opportunities made available by the Atlantic City casinos. More than 75 percent of the casino employees live in Atlantic County (Marfels, 1996). Some drastic measures would be required to pull the city back into a position of respectability, even to a position in which it could compete with other New Jersey resort towns.

In 1978, I returned to Atlantic City to visit a friend and fellow professional, Mr. Tony Ray. Mr. Ray had been the general manager of a hotel owned by a religious group on the Atlantic City Boardwalk. With the approval of the New Jersey State Legislature, casino gaming was coming to Atlantic City, and Mr. Ray's hotel had been chosen as the first new star of the Boardwalk. Resorts had acquired an option on a fifty-five-acre parcel of land on the Boardwalk and the Chalfonte and Haddon Hall Hotels. The Chalfonte would ultimately be demolished and the Haddon Hall Hotel would be renovated into a 560-room complex. The Haddon Hall's exhibition hall would be rebuilt into a casino and theater (Morrison, 1994). This return visit to Atlantic City was a field trip for twenty-five college students from Florida majoring in hospitality and tourism. It provided an opportunity to view the city and the effects casino gaming was having upon it. The students were amazed by the casino, but depressed by the surrounding slum that was one block from the front door of the casino.

Atlantic City was not a thriving metropolis before casino gaming. Stansfield (1978, p. 5) reported, in "Atlantic City and the Resort Cycle: Background to the Legalization of Gambling," that Atlantic City followed "a typical resort life cycle of development, expansion, shift in socioeconomic base of patronage, and decline." Atlantic City had reached its height as an international seaside resort in the early 1900s. This resort capital of eastern United States did not shift from one kind of patronage to another, allowing part of its traditional patronage to slip away, resulting in a decline within the industry (Funnell, 1983). In the 1930s, the city had begun its last stage in the marketing-product life cycle. In the 1940s, vacationers looked for, and received, more choices in destinations in the northeastern United States, both in locations and forms of transportation. In the 1950s, 1960s, and 1970s, vacationers had an expanding choice of vacation destinations. Modes of transportation such as automobiles, buses, and planes provided the impetus for this expansion. As the tourist arrivals decreased, the resort-focused economy of Atlantic City declined. Residents within the city left for better jobs and lifestyles, leaving behind a population of poor, elderly, and minorities. By 1975, Atlantic City had become one of the country's most economically troubled cities. The loss of tourists and the lack of conventions gave it a seasonally adjusted employment rate of 20 percent (Braunlich, 1996). It was hoped by the legislatures and Atlantic City itself that casinos would bring Atlantic City back to its former position as a true resort town. Mr. Ray mentioned to me that the casino industry would be good for Atlantic City because it would produce jobs, revitalize the city's infrastructure, and provide additional new growth to the region. Although these hopes were realized, the total impact of casino gaming on Atlantic City did not reach the desired level.

CASINOS

The revitalized side of Atlantic City is a stretch of Boardwalk one block wide and ten blocks long. This is what tourists see as they get off the long, sleek, silver buses and enter the casinos with their velvet-covered tables and a cacophony of bell tones. Unfortunately, the rest of the city is a semighetto. No matter where you walk, you see boarded-up windows, cracked concrete, split asphalt, broken bottles, garbage, and refuse of all kinds. With the exception of numerous pawn shops, most storefronts are vacant.

On November 2, 1976, New Jersey passed an amendment to the state constitution that allowed Atlantic City to operate gaming casinos. The purpose was to use the licensing fees and taxes from the gaming operations to lower taxes and help defer the expense of the state's elderly and disabled population. In May 1978, Resorts International became the first casino to open in Atlantic City (Rudd and Marshall, 1996).

According to the Atlantic City Consolidated Plan for 1995 Executive Summary (1995), the city reported that 61 percent of the households have been identified as low income or very low income. Based on statistics, it is estimated that 34 percent of all households in Atlantic City are subject to a cost burden greater than 30 percent of their gross monthly income. Severe cost burdens exist when gross housing costs exceed 50 percent of gross income. Based on the information provided by the city, it is estimated that 21 percent of the households in Atlantic City face a severe cost burden. Although Atlantic City consists of over 7,600 acres, only about 2,500 of these acres, or roughly one-third of the city, is capable of being developed. The lack of available land and high land costs, combined with excessively high construction costs, have a direct impact on the availability of affordable housing in Atlantic City. When land costs in Atlantic City are compared to other areas, they are found to be significantly higher, and the cost of developing projects in Atlantic City is substantially higher. The construction costs associated with Atlantic City are directly affected by regulatory jurisdiction overlapping, labor costs, and environmental impact conditions (Atlantic City Consolidated Plan, 1995).

When casinos first came to Atlantic City, there were 2,100 small businesses. Today, that number is 1,100, and serious crimes have tripled from 4,689 to 14,914 per annum (Demaris, 1986). Casino proponents continually mention that Atlantic City casinos have created over 43,000 jobs in just one industry. What is left out is that it took over ten years to develop these jobs. In Shenk's review of *The Luck Business* by Goodman, he stated that although casinos were intended to revitalize the downtown area of Atlantic City, they actually:

> hastened its decline. Rather than acting like a sponge soaking up visitors' money, as in Las Vegas, Atlantic City casinos became more like rats gnawing away at the remnants of small businesses, restaurants, and hotels. (Shenk, 1995, p. 57)

According to Goodman, cities such as Atlantic City do not fall into the gambling trap because its citizens are clamoring for more opportunities to gamble. In fact, many statewide referendums to expand gambling since New Jersey's in 1976 have failed. The casino boosters are the industry itself, and its eager followers are politicians seeking quick fixes for deep economic and social woes, as well as ensuring their own survival. As Goodman's book points out, political leaders are actually creating more of a crisis and being seduced by the promise of tourism money and thousands of new jobs. Politicians act as cheerleaders for expanding gambling (Goodman, 1995). The states are directly involved in lottery advertising, providing the general public with the impression that gambling is harmless and fun, launching slogans such as "You can't win if you don't play" and "A dollar and a dream."

Joseph Rubenstein, in "Casino Gambling in Atlantic City," acknowledged the success of the casinos and their creation of jobs and revenue, but saw no revitalization of Atlantic City beyond the Boardwalk. "This outcome may be accounted for by pointing to rampant land speculation following the passage of the casino referendum, ineffective government intervention, and a historic urban planning pattern that emphasized Boardwalk and tourism-association infrastructure development" (Rubenstein, 1984, p. 61). With the casinos in place, now is the time to develop and enforce a comprehensive redevelopment strategy.

PATHOLOGICAL GAMBLING

In an article titled "The Diceman Cometh," Ronald Reno (1996) spoke about his belief that, one day, addiction to gaming could rival that of drug addiction among teenagers. More than 1 million adolescents may already be addicted to gaming, and more than 75 percent of U.S. teenagers have gambled at least once. He wrote about Joe Koslowski who had recently won a bowling tournament and had headed for Atlantic City with his friends, all of whom were sixteen years old. All of the teenagers were allowed into the casino even though the age limit was twenty-one. He parlayed his initial bowling winnings into $2,000. Joe quickly came to see that Atlantic City casinos were the future for him. He returned frequently; although his winning streak ended, his taste and his thrill for gaming did not. Unfortunately, once he was out of cash, he opened credit accounts under family, relatives', and friends' names. He used the cash advances from the credit cards for gambling. The whole scheme finally crashed after he had amassed over $20,000 of debt. Now, at the age of twenty and with no prior criminal record, Joe is serving time in a Pennsylvania prison for credit card fraud. Joe is just one of thousands of young people who fall victim every year to America's gaming obsession.

A survey conducted of Atlantic City high school students, by Edward Looney (1997), revealed that nearly 86 percent had gambled in the last year. Thirty-two percent of Atlantic City high school students gamble weekly, playing dice or cards. Sports betting is the most popular illegal gambling in high schools. The survey indicated that 20 percent of students had family disputes due to gambling, 10 percent obtained money illegally to finance this gambling, 8.4 percent were considered problem gamblers, and 3.5 percent met the criteria for being compulsive gamblers.

Michael Frank of Stockton State College conducted a three-year survey of college students to determine the frequency and preference of students gambling at casinos in Atlantic City:

> The data suggest that gambling by underage college students is common and indicated that age control at casino entrances is quite poor. An additional finding of differential memory for wins and losses suggested the need for an information processing analysis of memory for gambling outcomes. (Frank, 1990, p. 907)

The study indicated that students had a tendency to remember positive events (wins), not negative events (losses).

The Council on Compulsive Gambling of New Jersey, Inc., which operates a national toll-free hotline (1-800-Gambler), reports that callers under twenty-one years old telephoned the hot line 4,300 times in 1994; these accounted for 11 percent of the total calls (Looney, 1997). Ed Looney, the council's executive director, explained that many young people who call his office are at the end of their ropes. He described a call regarding a sixteen-year-old who had slit his wrists after losing, in one day, $6,000 he had earned from four years of newspaper deliveries. Table 10.1 depicts the incidence of underage persons gambling in each of the Atlantic City casinos from January through September 1996.

TABLE 10.1. Gambling Incidents: Juveniles/Suspected Underage Persons

Casinos	Prevented from Entering Casino	Escorted from Casino	Found Gambling	Taken into Custody	Consuming Alcohol
Resorts	0	3,111	27	20	0
Caesar's	2,874	8,566	53	52	0
Park Place	9,762	1,399	32	27	0
Sands	3,592	1,326	28	27	0
Marina	5,086	3,524	9	6	0
Grand	3,367	757	38	20	0
Claridge	678	351	6	7	1
Tropicana	16,090	281	34	34	0
Plaza	131	565	26	21	0
Castle	629	124	14	13	0
Showboat	361	4,973	62	64	0
Taj Mahal	0	7,073	40	39	1
TOTAL	42,570	31,050	369	330	2

Source: Looney (1997).

According to Mr. Looney, the Council on Compulsive Gambling of New Jersey, Inc., provides the state legislature, the federal government, and Atlantic City with information on pathological gaming of the general public, employees, and customers of the casinos in Atlantic City. The social costs of compulsive gambling are exorbitant. Criminal and civil courts in New Jersey are filled with cases that originated through compulsive gambling. Suits for divorce issues, nonpayment of debts, and bankruptcy are excessive because of compulsive gambling. A national study conducted by the SMR Research Corporation (1997) showed a correlation between gambling growth and the significant rise in personal bankruptcies. A 250-page research report by SMR Research Corporation indicated that the number of personal bankruptcies surpassed 1.35 million, an increase of 43 percent in the past three years. The study further noted that those counties where residents had access to more than one gaming facility were more likely to have significantly higher rates of personal bankruptcy.

A meta-analysis of 120 primary studies of gambling disorders was completed by Shaffer, Hall, and Bilt (1997) of the Harvard Medical School Division on Addictions. The results of this meta-analysis revealed a number of important findings. These findings can be summarized briefly as follows:

> During the past two decades, gambling disorders have evidenced an increasing rate among adults sampled from the general population. To date, prevalence research has not demonstrated an increase in the rate of gambling disorders among adolescents or adults sampled from treatment or prison populations during the past two decades. Gambling disorders are significantly more prevalent among young people than among the general adult population. Gambling disorders are significantly more prevalent among males than females within every population segment considered in this study. Individuals with concurrent psychiatric problems display much higher rates of disordered gambling than either adolescents or adults sampled from the general population. There was no significant regional variation in the rates of gambling disorders identified across regions of Canada and the United States. To date, the overall methodological quality of disordered gambling prevalence research has not improved during the past twenty years. Methodological study quality did not influence the magnitude of prevalence estimates. (p. 4)

CRIME

Another social cost of compulsive gambling is the expense of police in dealing with crime. Illegal gambling leads to loan sharking, hijacking, employee theft, and a number of white-collar crimes, such as misappropriation, theft, and embezzlement. The prison system in New Jersey houses approximately 25,000 inmates. Studies show that 20 to 30 percent may be compulsive gamblers. At a cost of $25,000 to house one inmate annually, the burden to taxpayers is enormous (Looney, 1997). Compulsive gambling is also costly for the families of these gamblers. Compulsive gambling often leads to the disintegration of the family unit. It produces undue strain on husband-wife relationships, as well as problems with family communication and function (Looney, 1997).

According to Ochrym:

> Only recently have researchers begun to study the "causes" of crime in tourist destinations, particularly in those areas which offer casino gaming. . . . Casino gaming is a catalyst for tourism and one of the social consequences of tourism is increased crime. (1990, p. 127)

Ochrym further noted that tourist destinations have higher average crime rates than urban centers without major tourist attractions. Policymakers should consider both tourism and street crime as consequences of the legalization of gaming. For communities deciding against gambling and offering an alternative tourist attraction, policymakers will still have to consider the effects of such action with regard to street crime. With the opening of casinos in Atlantic City, crime increased, but crime also increased with the opening of Disney World in Orlando, Florida, allowing programming backers to compare casinos to tourist attractions (Thompson, 1994).

Albanese (1985), in his article titled "The Effect of Casino Gambling on Crime," researched the crimes in Atlantic City for the period between 1978 and 1982. Murder, rape, robbery, aggravated assault, burglary, larceny, and motor vehicle theft were "indexed" because they serve as an indicator of serious crime in the United States. The study found that increases in the "index" crimes are best accounted for by the increase in average daily population of Atlantic City:

> suggesting that growth in the number of visitors to Atlantic City has surpassed increases in crime to the point that the personal risk of victimization is declining to some extent. Therefore, the increase in serious crime in Atlantic City has been more than offset by an increasing population there. The result has been a slight reduction in the likelihood of being victimized there. (Albanese, 1985, p. 43)

This study indicated that supporters of legislature for casino gaming should not fail to consider legislation due to fear of increase in serious crimes against persons and property:

> Based on this analysis of the Atlantic City experience the advent of casino gaming has no direct effect on serious crime. Such findings suggest that any city that undergoes a significant revitalization, whether it be casino hotels, theme parks, convention centers, or other successful development that is accompanied by large increases in the number of large visitors, hotels, and other commercial activities may experience increases in crime. (Albanese, 1985, p. 44)

Gambling, in all of its forms, is proving to be nearly irresistible to the new generation, many of whom predict a bleak economic outlook for the next millennium. Traditional forms of gambling that were held in Atlantic City before casinos arrived, such as Monte Carlo nights and church bingos, were generally able to satisfy the compulsive gambler; however, government promotion of gaming, including almost $350 million spent by states advertising their lotteries, has been more pernicious. It communicates to the young people the subtly destructive notion that the work ethic is passé. All that is needed is "a dollar and a dream," as New York State lottery advertisers put it. According to the 1995 New Jersey Casino Control Commission's report on juvenile arrests and evictions, 135,000 underage juveniles were stopped at the casino doors and 25,000 were evicted from the casino floors in one year (New Jersey Casino Control Commission, 1995). Many more gamble undetected by the casinos. Ironically, many states' lottery profits are tied directly to public education. In an interview by Ronald Reno, Howard Shaffer, Director of the Center for Addictive Studies at Harvard Medical School, said:

> by sending young people the message that they need to gamble to get ahead we are telling them not to study calculus, not to study science, and we shouldn't be surprised that America is now falling behind other cultures in terms of intellectual pursuits. (Reno, 1996, p. 2)

It is important to understand that gaming addiction is just as real, and its consequences just as tragic, as drug or alcohol abuse. The American Psychological Association and the American Medical Association recognize pathological or compulsive gambling as a diagnosable mental disorder. Experts on pathological gaming have shown that the prevalence of the disorder is linked closely to the accessibility and acceptability of gaming within society. As with alcoholism, just a small percentage of Americans are susceptible, but as more people try gambling in its various forms, more of those prone to the illness are exposed to it. The more legalized gambling a state makes available, the more the pathological behavior is triggered. Fast-paced gaming, which maximizes the number of wagering opportunities, such as casinos and video gaming machines, will maximize gambling addiction. Whether roulette, slots, or lottery, the odds always favor the house in a casino. The more one gambles against these odds, the more certain it is that one will lose. When pathological gambling strikes, it rarely affects just one person. Families lose their savings, college education funds, retirement funds, and homes. Pathological gamblers lose all the money they have, then they proceed to run up credit card debt. They sell or pawn possessions and plead or beg loans from family members and friends. More than half end up stealing money, often from their employers. The average Gamblers Anonymous member will have lost all of his or her money and accumulated debts ranging from $35,000 to $90,000 before seeking treatment. Many file for bankruptcy, and many of those addicted contemplate suicide. In a study done by Robert A. Yaffee (1990) on gambling addiction in Maryland, when asked whether they had an alcohol problem, 58 percent of the compulsive gambling patients who had participated in the study for the past five years replied in the affirmative. When asked whether they have had, or did have, a drug problem, 26.7 percent of them answered in the affirmative.

According to the Atlantic City Free Public Library Web site (1995), the city's crime rate has dropped by over 50 percent from its high in 1990. Table 10.2 indicates the increase in crime rate percentage from 1977 to 1990 for selected areas.

Friedman, Hakim, and Weinblatt indicated in their article "Casino Gaming as a 'Growth Pole' Strategy and Its Effect on Crime" that

TABLE 10.2. Increase in Crime Rate, 1977-1990*

Crime Category	Atlantic City	New Jersey	Miami	Florida	Nationally
Rape	156	50	62.3	32.4	62.0
Robbery	159	76	228.0	123.3	55.0
Aggravated Assault	316	77	156.9	61.6	97.0
Larceny	451	8	76.2	19.5	35.0
All Index Crime	230	9	96.6	30.2	15.1

Source: Florida Department of Law Enforcement (1994).

* All numbers expressed as percentages.

many regions are hesitant to utilize casino development as a tool for revitalization because they fear voter rejection on the basis of adverse impact from crime. He also indicated that casinos as a growth pole are justified from a purely economic standpoint; however, when the social cost-benefit analysis of crime is added in, it may be high enough to outweigh the economic gains that might be obtained from a casino. In addition, the redistribution of wealth due to casinos may not be desirable. He suggested that the cost of crime needs to be considered for the entire region, a subject often neglected in regional impact studies (Friedman, Hakim, and Weinblatt, 1989).

ANTIGAMING

In 1994, a variety of grassroots citizens groups came together to form the National Coalition Against Legalized Gaming (NCALG). The members of NCALG span the entire political spectrum from conservative to liberal. The coalition encompasses business, labor, and religious groups and is active in every state. NCALG does not preach the immorality of gambling; rather, it seeks to stop the expansion of legalized gambling on public policy grounds—that it harms individuals, families, businesses, and society in general. The NCALG impacts Atlantic City by attempting to reduce the number of new jurisdictions available for gaming. It also attempts to educate the surrounding states and populations as to the possible negative aspects associated with casinos. On August 3, 1996, President Clinton signed HR497, the National Gaming Impact and Policy Commissions Act, which sets up a nine-member federal panel to investigate all facets of gaming in America (Horn, 1997). This panel could have far-reaching effects on casino operations in Atlantic City and around the country. The panel appears to be biased toward the NCALG.

NEW JERSEY CASINO CONTROL ACT

In *The Business of Risk,* by Abt, Smith, and Christiansen, the authors note that Atlantic City casinos produce a substantial sum. However, revenues generated from gaming privilege taxes levied on Atlantic City casinos are a very small percentage of the state's total budget. In the view of the New Jersey Casino Control Act, the purpose of the casinos was to foster the development of a badly decayed resort and the urban setting within Atlantic City. Unfortunately, little development has occurred outside the casino/hotel complex in Atlantic City. All of the jobs and capital investment generated by gaming through the New Jersey Casino Control Act have so far failed to provide Atlantic City with the kind of economic rebirth casinos have given southern Nevada. The reasons for the failure of the New Jersey Casino Control Act appear to be complex and have less to do with the casinos, which are economically successful, than the inability of the governments of Atlantic City and the state of New Jersey to use casino revenue and casinos' economic contributions as an effective redevelopment tool for Atlantic City (Abt, Smith, and Christiansen, 1985).

Jennifer Vogel's book *Crapped Out* addressed one of the main problems—casinos were supposed to be the catalyst to rebuild Atlantic City. The laws that established casinos made them islands unto themselves; they were constructed to be self-contained cities. The purpose of the casino was to gamble. To keep the public gambling, everything had to be provided within the casino: drink, dining, exercise, sleep, entertainment, and shopping. Vogel saw the Atlantic City casinos as factories, in "a distant location, served by a highway designed primarily to obtain raw materials and ship out finished products. The raw materials coming down the Atlantic City Expressway are wallets and pocketbooks, which are cleaned of their paper and plastic and then sent back up the highway to be filled again for another trip," never seeing nor contributing to Atlantic City (Vogel, 1997, p. 22).

POLITICS

Robert Goodman (1995), in his book *The Luck Business*, explained that gambling cannot be an experiment. Once a gambling enterprise is begun, there arises an instant dependency on that gambling enterprise to provide jobs and revenue. Politicians would find it difficult to close a casino that supplies a large proportion of the jobs in the area, as well as substantial tax revenue. According to Goodman, casino operators in Atlantic City wield a large amount of political power because few politicians would risk closing down such a large job source. Many of the original regulations governing Atlantic City casinos have been relaxed as a result of the large political pull they carry. These regulations included restrictions on floor space and the prohibition of twenty-four-hour gambling. The amending of these regulations was caused by the industry and not the state's regulatory committees. The responsibility for the assumed loss rests with a December 1980 operating loss and an industry newsletter circulated within local papers pointing out that the cause of losses was overregulation. Relevant facts were ignored, and headlines and long paragraphs that reflected the industry's propaganda were included.

According to Abt, Smith, and Christiansen, several reasons explain the apparent loss of revenue reported by the casinos: the seasonal nature of Atlantic City as a tourist destination in the winter; the decision of several casino companies to finance their construction at rates above the highest level ever in the history of the United States; that three of the six casinos opened late in the year, incurring an exceptionally high start-up cost; and the industry's voluntary decision to refrain from using junkets rather than comply with the state junket agent's licensing requirement resulted in this paper loss. The result of the casinos media campaign was that the state agreed to relax its regulations. After the regulations were relaxed, the industry's profitability was magically restored (Abt, Smith, and Christiansen, 1985).

URBAN REDEVELOPMENT

The resurrection of Atlantic City by the inception of casino gambling twenty years ago was a slow process, and with increasing competition, there is growing uncertainty as to whether the city's future will be one of continued growth, stagnation, or a return to the decay and decline that made Atlantic City turn to gaming in the first place. The unique tool of urban development has pumped billions of dollars into New Jersey's economy, generating billions in new tax revenue and creating more jobs than the city had residents. However, the casino industry has not restored Atlantic City to its former position as playground of the world or the major hospitality center of the United States, as was anticipated in the Casino Control Act. Mayor James Whelan has repeatedly admitted that local government wasted more than a decade: "For the better part of fifteen years we've screwed up," he said, in part because of the corruption and incompetence in city hall and the open hostility between government and the casino industry (Heneghan, 1993, p. 44). He and other politicians are attempting to rectify this problem. After years of delay, the work has been completed on the new convention center, and a new corridor is being developed from this convention center to the Boardwalk. The airport is being upgraded and beautification of the approaches to the city have begun (Heneghan, 1993).

Atlantic City has identified three housing needs: affordable rental housing; an increase in the number of total homeowners and increasing homeownership opportunities for special groups; and an increase in the number of housing opportunities that are available and planned, with serving components attached to them. The Atlantic City Consolidated Plan for 1995 Executive Summary developed three strategies for meeting these needs. First, provide affordable housing, including retaining the existing neighborhoods and homes, rehabilitating private as well as public housing, increasing the supply of affordable housing by assisting first-time buyers, establishing lcasc/ purchase agreements, and reducing the overall cost of housing production. Second, provide support services and housing for the homeless, including adding to and expanding the present emergency shelter beds and constructing and increasing more transitional housing facilities. Third, provide for nonhomeless persons with special needs. This will include increased housing, special needs groups, and support services. Included in these programs are state policies that are geared toward reducing the number of households below the poverty level by educating and training these individuals and increasing the variety, type, and scope of employment opportunities available. The agencies responsible for this coordinated effort are the Department of Community Affairs (DCA), the Council on Affordable Housing (COAH), and the New Jersey Housing and Mortgage Finance Agency (NJHMFA). Locally, the agencies providing assistance are the Casino Reinvestment Development Authority (CRDA), the Atlantic County Improvement Authority (ACIA), and the Urban Redevelopment Agency (URA).

Under state regulations, casinos are required to reinvest a percentage of their profits into housing and economic development projects in Atlantic City. This reinvestment is channeled through CRDA. The estimated cost of the beautification and restoration projects was $7 billion (Heneghan, 1993). These projects will be completed around the turn of the century and were designed with the hopes that Atlantic City will emerge from this massive face-lift with a new position as a year-round destination for conventioneers and vacationing families. In addition to the restoration projects that the city is undertaking, the various casinos and corporations interested in casino development have proposals, plans, and designs for the refurbishment and expansion of existing casinos, as well as plans for completely new casinos. These refurbishment plans include more family-oriented game park designs and are geared toward the total resort concept. The casinos will no longer be day-tripper paradises. The gentrification of the city is taking place alongside these realized and anticipated refurbishment goals (Heneghan, 1993). According to Shea (1997), "the city has demolished one abandoned building every three days for the past seven years."

CONCLUSION

Undoubtedly, Atlantic City casinos and hotels have experienced unprecedented economic prosperity, and, given the proper market atmosphere, they will continue to thrive. Other venues can use their experiences as a guide in what to do or not to do. Casino gaming in

New Jersey has experienced success for over two decades as a gaming mecca, with a monopoly of the East Coast. The casinos have created thousands of moderate-income jobs in a year-round environment, catering to millions of tourists per year. The once dead Atlantic City community has benefited from over $5 billion in capital investment. The state of New Jersey has received substantial tax benefits as a result of casino/hotel revenues. These, in some part, have gone to support a large number of programs for the low-income, elderly, and disabled.

The casino/hotel industry in Atlantic City has provided the needed resources for the redevelopment of Atlantic City. Unfortunately, because of disputes between Atlantic City, Atlantic County, and the state of New Jersey, the failing infrastructure and the social degeneration of the community continued up until five years ago. Under the New Jersey Casino Control Act, 2 percent of the gross revenue from casino operations was to be provided to the state of New Jersey for redevelopment projects within Atlantic City. Under the act, these funds were earmarked for urban redevelopment. The state believed that it did not need to use these funds in Atlantic City, assuming that the total investment in Atlantic City by hotels and entertainment facilities would be sufficient to stimulate growth within the community. The infrastructure and the need for city housing would be accelerated by the development of the casino industry itself. Unfortunately, as a number of authors have pointed out (Pollock, 1987; Warker, 1989), this did not occur. This experiment failed because of rampant land speculation, ineffective government intervention, and urban planning focused on the casinos rather than the infrastructure. In 1984, under the Casino Reinvestment Redevelopment Authority, casinos paid 2.5 percent of their gross revenue as a tax for urban redevelopment. The fund was committed to developmental projects with an increased focus on infrastructure improvement and beautification. An apparent cleanup of the city was underway. Now a cooperative effort among the three is resulting in the allocation of needed revenues from the casino hotels to the Atlantic City community, as is indicated by the revitalization downtown and the creation of a new convention center.

Hakim and Buck, from Temple University, conducted a study regarding the effect casinos had on the Atlantic City area as related to crime: "controlling for wealth, unemployment, and size of police force and standardization by population, it was found that the post-casino years showed a markedly higher incidence of crime. Also, crime fell with distance, in minutes traveled from Atlantic City" (Hakim and Buck, 1989, p. 410).

In recent years, the city has instituted a number of unique programs, including bike patrols, community policing, and the effective use of special units. In addition, the city has initiated a program offering police officers who reside in Atlantic City an incentive bonus so that they will become active in their neighborhoods as citizens. This has resulted in an overall drop in the crime index for Atlantic City. The Atlantic City Free Public Library (1995) noted that substantial progress has been made in the construction of housing and government buildings and that a reinvestment of the viable casino revenue within the community is now in place. An Amtrak link between Atlantic City and Philadelphia and the expansion of casinos into general family entertainment are underway. Construction is complete on the convention center, and a new Atlantic City High School has opened its doors.

Atlantic City is on the road to recovery from social and economic chaos. If it continues to allocate its resources from the casinos/hotels toward the improvement of infrastructure and societal improvements, it will be the resort mecca of the Northeast once again.

REFERENCES

Abt, V., Smith, J.F., and Christiansen, E.M. (1985). *The business of risk.* Lawrence, KS: University Press of Kansas.

Albanese, J. (1985, June). The effect of casino gambling on crime. *Federal Probation, 49*(2), 39-44.

Atlantic City Consolidated Plan for 1995 Executive Summary (1995). *Citizen's summary* (On-line). Available: http://www.hud.gov/epes/nj/atlantnj.html.

Atlantic City Free Public Library. (1995). *Atlantic City History* (On-line). Available: http://library.atlantic.city.lib.nj.us.

Braunlich, C.G. (1996). Lessons from the Atlantic City casino experience. *Journal of Travel Research, 34*(3), 46-56.

Demaris, O. (1986, May 11). What has it done for Atlantic City? Why casino gaming is a bad bet. *Parade Magazine,* pp. 12-14.

Dombrink, J. and Thompson, W.N. (1990). *The last resort.* Reno, NV: University of Nevada Press.

Florida Department of Law Enforcement (1994, August 15). *The question of casinos in Florida: Increased crime—Is it worth it?* Jacksonville, FL: Author.

Frank, M.L. (1990, December). Underage gambling in Atlantic City casinos. *Psychological Reports, 67*(3), 907-912.

Friedman, J., Hakim, S., and Weinblatt, J. (1989). Casino gambling as a "growth pole" strategy and its effect on crime. *Journal of Regional Science, 29*(4), 615-623.

Funnell, C.E. (1983). *By the beautiful sea: The rise and high times of that great American resort, Atlantic City.* New Brunswick, NJ: Rutgers University Press.

Goodman, R. (1995). *The luck business.* New York: Simon and Schuster.

Hakim, S. and Buck, A.J. (1989). Do casinos enhance crime? *Journal of Criminal Justice, 17*(5), 409-416.

Heneghan, D. (1993, May 23). Fifteen years of gambling. *The North Jersey Herald and News,* pp. 44-46.

Horn, B.P. (1997, May). Is there a cure for America's gambling addiction? *USA Today* (On-line). Available: http://www.umi.com/pqdweb.

Looney, E. (1997, January). Legislative guide for responsible gaming in your state. Paper presented at the meeting of The National Council of Legislators from Gaming States, St. Petersburg, FL.

Marfels, C. (1996). The case for casino gaming. *Gaming Research and Review Journal, 33*(1), 5-11.

Morrison, R. (1994). *High stakes to high risk: The strange story of resorts international and the Taj Mahal.* Ashtabula, OH: Lake Erie Press.

New Jersey Casino Control Commission (1995). *Juvenile suspected underage report.* Atlantic City, NJ: Author.

Ochrym, R.G. (1990). Street crime, tourism and casinos: An empirical comparison. *Journal of Gambling Studies, 6*(2), 127-138.

Pollock, M. (1987). *Hostage to fortune: Atlantic City and casino gaming.* Princeton, NJ: New Jersey Center for Public Analysis and Issues.

Reno, R.A. (1996). The diceman cometh: Will gambling be a bad bet for your town? *Policy Review, 76,* 40-45.

Rubenstein, J. (1984, July). Casino gambling in Atlantic City: Issues of development and redevelopment. *The Annals of the American Academy of Political and Social Science, 474,* 61-71.

Rudd, D.P. and Marshall, L.H. (1996). *Introduction to casino and gaming operations.* Englewood Cliffs, NJ: Prentice Hall.

Shaffer, H., Hall, M.N., and Bilt, J.V. (1997). *Estimating the prevalence of disordered gambling behavior in the United States and Canada: A meta-analysis.* Cambridge, MA: Harvard Medical School Division on Addictions.

Shea, B. (1991, September 7). The new and improved Atlantic City. *Newsday,* p. D10.

Shenk, J.W. (1995, November). Political booknotes—The luck business: The devastating consequences and broken promises of America's gambling explosion by Robert Goodman. *The Washington Monthly, 27*(11), 57-59.

SMR Research Corporation. (1997). *Personal bankruptcy crisis*. Atlantic City, NJ: Author.

Stansfield, C. (1978). Atlantic City and the resort cycle: Background to the legalization of gambling. *The Annals of Tourism Research, 5*(2), 238-251.

Thompson, W.N. (1994). *Legalized gambling: A reference handbook*. Santa Barbara, CA: ABC-CLIO.

Vogel, J. (1997). *Crapped out: How gambling ruins the economy and destroys lives*. Monroe, ME: Common Courage Press.

Warker, K. (1989). Casino gambling in urban development: A case study of political economics of Atlantic City, New Jersey (Doctoral dissertation, University of Delaware, 1988). *Dissertation Abstract International, 50,* 05A.

Yaffee, R.A. (1990). *Final Report of Task Force on Gambling Addiction in Maryland.* (On-line) Available: http://www.nyu.edu/acf/socsci/Docs/task_force_6.html.

Chapter 11

Social Impacts of Native American Casino Gaming

Cathy H. C. Hsu

Gaming facilities on Native American reservations existed long before the Indian Gaming Regulatory Act (IGRA) was passed in 1988. However, since the passing of IGRA, casino facilities have flourished on native lands. Due to decades of high unemployment rates, poverty, lack of education, dismal business success, and alcoholism, more than half of the nation's Native American tribes have turned to gaming as the "new buffalo." The main objective of Native American gaming is for tribal governments to use casino revenues to create employment opportunities for tribal members, invest in tribal infrastructure, and address social programs on the reservations. When properly managed and regulated, Native American gaming can provide prosperity as promised, in employment, housing, education, and cultural preservation. However, Native American gaming has been a mixed blessing (Oleck, 1993). Although some tribes have reported success in economic development and saving taxpayers' money by removing Native Americans from the vicious cycle of welfare dependency (Pico, 1994), other tribes have experienced exploitation by non-native people, an increase in crime, tribal division, and culture stripping.

The purpose of this chapter is to provide an overview of the social impacts of Native American gaming. There are many anecdotal reports on both positive and negative impacts of tribal casinos. However, finding relevant, objective academic research has been a challenge. A comprehensive review of current literature was conducted and the results summarized.

TRIBAL DIVISION AND RESIDENTS' ATTITUDES

The most frequently reported tribal division occurred in the Mohawk reservations of Akwesasne, Kahnawake, and Kanesatale of Upstate New York. The Mohawks split into pro- and antigaming factions and a "Mohawk civil war" was triggered. Thousands of gunshots were exchanged and two men died during the Mohawk versus Mohawk clashes in 1990 (Attinger, 1990). Bitter power struggles also occurred among competing tribal councils. Life at Akwesasne was interrupted by a surge of violence. The violence was so personal and pervasive that few people in the United States have seen such unrest (Johansen, 1993).

The California Pomo Indians had a six-day gun battle among tribe members over control of a casino (Orwall, 1996). The debate in Minnesota was not violent, but just as significant. The 1,300-member Meskwaki tribe in Tama, Iowa, is engulfed in one of its most bitter political struggles ever. The decision-making process of the tribal council, on such issues as the use of casino profits and management and expansion of the casino, was questioned (Petroski, 1997). Across Native American tribes, some tribe leaders and members believed casino operations have enhanced their tribes' quality of life, but others expressed doubts about the survival of their tribes, even with the profits generated by casinos (Carter, 1992).

The use of gambling proceeds has also become a volatile issue that caused internal division within gaming tribes. Strong pressure to show instant results often exists, yet investments in the future via education and housing may not provide immediate dividends (Carter, 1992). Some tribes have neglected social concerns and investments in the future and distributed a major portion of the gaming revenue to members on a per capita basis. Opponents of the per capita distribution program indicated that the program may be encouraging unemployment and other personal and social problems. According to Deller and Chen (1997), evidence suggests that the dividend payments have reduced incentives to work. The per capita distribution program also faces the issue of who is eligible for the distribution (Thompson and Dever, 1994). Many Native Americans who left their tribe before the gaming era are seeking permission to return. However, when they were allowed to return but were ineligible for casino dividend payments, tension within the tribe rose and resentment from the newly returned members surfaced (Deller and Chen, 1997).

Native American reservations are sovereign nations; therefore, residents in adjacent nontribal communities are unable to affect decisions made by tribal governments. However, the lives of residents in those nearby communities are likely to be affected by tribal gaming decisions. Anti-Native American hostilities have been reborn in some areas (Deller and Chen, 1997). Carmichael, Peppard, and Boudreau (1996) evaluated residents' perception of tribal gaming's impact on their non-Native American communities near the Mashantucket Pequot reservation in Connecticut. Data were collected in 1992, 1993, and 1995. Residents perceived that the quality of life in their towns was significantly reduced since the opening of the Foxwoods casino in 1992. Crime and traffic were perceived as much worse in 1995 than in earlier years. The historic value of the towns was seen as adversely affected and the communities as less desirable to live in than in 1992. The majority of the respondents disagreed that benefits outweigh costs to the region or the town, and their disagreement grew stronger over time.

INITIAL STRUGGLE AND EXPLOITATION

Native American gaming experienced significant struggles during the 1980s before IGRA was passed. Tribes went into gaming without expertise or government assistance, which made the tribes vulnerable to exploitation. They are especially susceptible to Mafia infiltration due to the need for start-up funds to purchase gaming equipment. Few banks approved loans to tribes; because of their sovereign status, their land cannot be foreclosed (Segal, 1992). An anonymous witness, who was a dealer and manager at a Native American casino, testifying before the Senate Select Committee on Indian Affairs, claimed that at least twelve bingo halls were controlled by the mob and nearly half of all Indian casinos were tainted by it—directly through management and investment or indirectly through suppliers. The witness also admitted that he padded expenses and robbed a tribe of over $600,000 a year (Segal, 1992; Popkin, 1993).

According to federal affidavits released in July 1994, a Minnesota company with major casino interests in Michigan, Louisiana, and Mississippi has links to, and may be controlled by, an associate of the Genovese Mafia family in New York (Ison and Kilzer, 1994). However, just two years earlier, Minnesota's attorney general reported no evidence of organized crime in the state's Native American casino operations (Carter, 1992).

In the mid-1980s, ninety/ten profit splits between management companies and tribes were not uncommon throughout Wisconsin and Minnesota. Native Americans received a 10 percent share of the profit for making space for the machines. Part of the reason for the Mohawk's internal conflict was that profits from their bingo halls were going exclusively to hall owners and their non–Native American management team (Segal, 1992). After the passing of IGRA, a 40 percent share to management companies is the highest allowed. However, other forms of exploitation are just as threatening. Under the most common contracts with management firms, Native American tribes are to receive 60 percent of profits after expenses. If management had intended to take advantage of the tribe, padded expenses can mean the tribe may receive a negligible amount of money as "profit" (Segal, 1992). Preliminary findings of an audit of a Native American casino in Minnesota indicated that the management company collected $1 million more in management fees than the contracted amount (Markels, 1996).

Despite their initial struggles, the majority of the Native American casinos are honest and clean (Popkin, 1993). Many of them employ Las Vegas or Atlantic City professional management companies—several are publicly traded and have good reputations—to oversee daily operations. More and more tribes also have developed their own expertise in casino management and have taken over daily operations.

GAMING CONTRIBUTION

Numerous magazine and newspaper articles reported tremendous social contributions made by Native American casinos to dozens of tribes across the United States. Contributions made by Minnesota and Wisconsin tribes are reported most frequently. The sheer numbers of Native American casinos in those two states and the size of casinos in some reservations may be two reasons for the attention. However, that those tribes have put their casino profits into good use may be the most important reason.

For the Mille Lacs Ojibwe, gaming revenues have enabled the tribe to link generations through the study of its language and culture (Hill, 1993). All students are learning the Ojibwe language, which had started to fade even among its elders. A new written form was created and a CD-ROM produced, with elders telling ancestral tales ("Highly Effective Indians," 1996). Teachers use culturally sensitive readings to teach core subjects and incorporate cultural lessons into the curriculum (Schnaiberg, 1994). The Mille Lacs' casinos also were instrumental in building a comprehensive new health clinic in 1993 and enhancing medical insurance benefits for tribal members and local residents (Stephenson, 1996). In 1995, the tribe spent an estimated $11 million on purchasing land that once belonged to them.

Wisconsin's Oneida tribe has used the proceeds from its self-managed casino to subsidize its own Head Start program and to build its own grade and high schools, which include state-of-the-art computer facilities. The Oneidas have seen their members increased by one-third in the past fifteen years (Segal, 1992). The Oneidas have outgrown the twenty-year-old federal Indian Health Service facility and plan to replace it, funded by gaming profits. Casino profits are also funding a fifty-bed nursing home, social service programs, such as a support group for families with disabled children, and a program for prenatal care for high-risk women. Gaming revenues have made it possible for the tribe to attract highly qualified physicians (Stephenson, 1996).

Connecticut's Mashantucket Pequots built a $130-million museum to preserve their heritage and chronicle their history (Lueders, 1994). The Pequots also are trying to recapture their language and traditional dances (Hill, 1993). Disease and past massacres, unfortunately, left the tribe with fewer than 200 members, and only one remained living on the 213 acres of land. Gaming revenues have been used to hire archaeologists to help identify traditional lands; the tribe has purchased back 1,500 acres of its original land (Thompson and Dever, 1994a). In addition to paying for the full costs of high school and higher education, the tribe also provides job-training and placement services for its members. Moreover, the tribe has established a tribal court and has organized a state-of-the-art tribal police department and fire and emergency medical service departments (Brown, 1996).

For many other tribes, profits from casinos have been used for education (K-8 schools, high schools, college scholarships and stipends, teen drop-in centers, school buses, adult education classes, after-school tutoring, vocational education, books, computer laboratories, music rooms, Head Start programs, scholarships for American Indian studies); cultural events (ceremonial buildings, language classes, traditional dances, cultural museums, arts and craft centers); housing (new housing, housing repairs, senior centers); infrastructure (roads, water and sewer systems, community center facilities); health care (health insurance programs, medical centers, elderly care, drug dependency care, mental health care); community services (extra police officers, tribal courts, social service departments, recreation facilities, fire and ambulance services); and land purchases (Hill, 1993; Moore, 1993; Pico, 1994; Long, 1995; Connor, 1993; Magnuson, 1994; Minnesota Planning, 1992).

Contributions of Native American gaming also include the reduced need for social services in some tribes and adjacent communities. The number of Aid to Families with Dependent Children (AFDC) recipients decreased by 14 percent between 1987 and 1992 in the eight nonurban Minnesota counties with tribal gaming facilities, while the statewide number of recipients increased 17 percent during the same period (Minnesota Indian Gaming Association, 1992). In addition to the significant decrease in welfare program enrollment, tribal members have become more optimistic about the future and have regained a sense of pride. Due to the economic success of tribal gaming and tribes' newly established financial power, Native Americans also have become major players in the political arena at the local, state, and federal levels (Deller and Chen, 1997).

NOT ALL ROSY

Along with the many benefits generated by casinos are the costs associated with gaming. The current literature has addressed three major areas of problems related to Native American casinos: traffic and demand on infrastructure, crime, and pathological gambling. Traffic congestion is particularly a problem for casinos located within easy driving distance of major population centers. The Jackpot Junction casino in Minnesota, two hours from Minneapolis, opened in 1984 as a 12,000-square-foot high-stakes bingo hall. By 1991, it had become an 80,000-square-foot casino and entertainment complex. Development of this size puts pressure on local facilities and services, such as water, sewer, waste disposal, highway, medical, fire, police, and housing. Many employees have to commute long distances due to shortages of available housing for rent or purchase. This puts further demand on roads (Minnesota Planning, 1992).

The traffic concerns are even more significant in Connecticut, where the largest casino in the United States, Foxwoods, is located. Local roads that were not designed for high speed and volume carry 40,000 vehicles a day and many more on holidays. On one winding state road near Ledyard, accidents were five times higher than on the town's other highway. Demands to increase police forces to deal with traffic and accidents have also increased. The town of Ledyard estimated that the casino created $114,000 in extra police costs annually (Peppard, 1995).

The Wisconsin Policy Research Institute commissioned a series of studies on the impacts of gambling in Wisconsin. Results of the casinos and crime study indicated that since the inception of Native American casinos, there has been an additional 5,277 serious crimes a year, at a public cost of $16.7 million, with an additional 17,100 Part II arrests, costing the society $34.2 million each year to investigate, arrest, arraign, and imprison criminals (Thompson, Gazel, and Rickman, 1996b). Serious crimes include violent crimes such as murder, forcible rape, robbery, and aggravated assault and nonviolent crimes such as burglary and larceny. Part II crimes include nonaggravated assault, forgery, fraud, embezzlement, weapons offenses, possession of stolen property, prostitution, sex offenses other than rape, gambling violations, driving while intoxicated (DWI), disorderly conduct, drug violations (possession and sales), and liquor-law violations other than DWI.

The rates of major crimes in the fourteen counties with casinos, and in counties adjacent to at least two casino counties, were 6.7 percent higher than if there were no casinos. As for Part II arrests, casino and adjacent counties had arrest rates 12.2 percent higher than other counties. In the major crime category, rates of burglaries showed the highest association with casinos. In the Part II arrest category, possession of stolen property, DWI, and drug possession had more significant relationships with casinos (Thompson, Gazel, and Rickman, 1996b).

As more visitors come to Native American land, littering and pollution and other negative environmental impacts on reservations increase. Visitors may also bring substance abuse problems (Thompson and Dever, 1994b). Although alcohol abuse is still the number one problem facing Native Americans, they now also have access to cocaine and designer drugs (Lueders, 1994). Even among the highly successful Oneidas, unemployment is still high, and drug and alcohol problems persist (Segal, 1992). According to Zitzow's study (1996), a correlation existed between alcoholism, poverty, and unemployment rates on reservations and the potential for increased gambling problems.

Another study, commissioned by the Wisconsin Policy Research Institute, investigated the social costs of gambling in Wisconsin. Of the 1,000 randomly selected Wisconsin adults, 0.90 percent were serious problem gamblers and 0.38 percent were serious problem gamblers because of the presence of Native American casinos in the state. A survey of ninety-eight members of Gamblers Anonymous in Wisconsin showed that fifty-five of them were considered to be primarily casino gamblers, spending more than 90 percent of their gambling activities in casinos (Thompson, Gazel, and Rickman, 1996a).

A study in North Dakota revealed a statewide compulsive gambling rate of 6 percent; the national average ranges between 3.4 and 4.5 percent. The study also examined the rate of pathological gambling in the general populations of Fort Totten and Belcourt, the major communities on the two reservations with casinos, and in the populations of Turtle Mountain Chippewa and Devils Lake Sioux who gamble at reservation casinos. Results showed that the compulsive rate for the Fort Totten general population, Belcourt general population, Chippewa members at casino, and Sioux members at casino were 14 percent, 10 percent, 23 percent, and 29 percent, respectively. The study also identified another 19 and 30 percent of

Chippewa and Sioux members, respectively, as probable pathological gamblers (Cozzetto and Larocque, 1996).

Another study, commissioned by the North Dakota Department of Human Services, found that 14.5 percent of Native Americans in the sample were compulsive or probable pathological gamblers (Volberg and Silver, 1993). Studies conducted by the Indian Health Service in Minnesota on an Ojibwe reservation found significantly higher rates of pathological gambling in the Native American population than in the non-Native American population (Zitzow, 1996a, 1996b). Specifically, unemployment, increased alcohol use, and lack of social alternatives may predispose Native American adults to greater problematic and pathological gambling behaviors. Increased direct and vicarious exposure to gaming and gaming availability among Indians also may have caused Native American adolescents to display greater frequency of gambling involvement, earlier onset of gambling experiences, and a greater tendency to exhibit problematic gambling behaviors than did non-Native American adolescents.

CONTINUED DEBATE

Debate continues about the costs and benefits of Native American gaming within tribes, and about the legitimacy of gambling as a Native American enterprise. Are those economic and social benefits worth the battle between Native Americans and "outsiders" and among tribal members? Will the visibility of large amounts of money threaten the traditional values of nonmaterialism and sharing that mark Native American culture (Carter, 1992)? Are gaming revenues a disincentive for economic diversification? When a tribe's gaming compact expires, there is no guarantee that the state will renew it. Increased competition from other casinos and gaming facilities can also slow the flow of gaming dollars into tribal coffers. Will casinos continue to be a viable economic development opportunity?

Limited objective studies were found on the social impacts of gaming on Native American reservations or nearby communities. As indicated earlier, Minnesota, Wisconsin, and Connecticut received the most publicity regarding their success in using gaming revenues for social services. What about the other 100-plus tribes that offer casino gaming but have had no documentation on its economic or social costs or benefits? Is gaming really the "new buffalo"?

More research and documentation are needed to provide proper assessment of the real impacts of gaming. It is essential to investigate changes, for better or worse, in Native American lives. It also is crucial to understand the impacts of Native American gaming on surrounding non–Native American communities. Those communities usually do not have any direct input on gaming policies and operations on reservations; however, the quality of life in those communities could very much be changed because of those gaming operations. Existing research reports offer a glimpse of some issues; however, they represent only the tip of the iceberg. Longitudinal studies are needed to monitor the long-term effects of Native American gaming on culture, society, crime, and problem gambling. Research methodologies used also present difficulties in obtaining a systematic, holistic view of the impacts of gaming across the United States because different researchers used different methodologies and research instruments. As more studies are conducted in the area, methodology refinement is another area worth exploring.

REFERENCES

Attinger, J. (1990, May 14). Mohawks, money, and death. *Time,* p. 32.

Brown, G.M. (1996, Summer). In New England. *Forum for Applied Research and Public Policy, 11*(2), 111-113.

Carmichael, B.A., Peppard, D.M. Jr., and Boudreau, F.A. (1996). Megaresort on my doorstep: Local resident attitudes toward Foxwoods casino and casino gambling on nearby Indian reservation land. *Journal of Travel Research, 34*(3), 9-16.

Carter, I. (1992). Gambling with their lives: American Indians and the casinos. *CURA Reporter, 22*(2), 1-6.

Connor, M. (1993). Indian gaming: Prosperity, controversy. *International Gaming and Wagering Business, 14*(3), 1, 8-12, 45.

Cozzetto, D.A. and Larocque, B.W. (1996). Compulsive gambling in the Indian community: A North Dakota case study. *American Indian Culture and Research Journal, 20*(1), 73-86.

Deller, S.C. and Chen, S. (1997). The impact of Native American gaming on rural areas: The case of Wisconsin. In W.R. Eadington and J.A. Cornelius (Eds.), *Gambling: Public policies and the social sciences* (pp. 247-254). Reno, NV: Institute for the Study of Gambling and Commercial Gaming.

Highly effective Indians. (1996, April). *The Economist, 339*(7960), 26.

Hill, R. (1993, October). Indian gaming allows tribes to rediscover and protect their traditions. *Indian Gaming, 4*(11), 3, 17.

Ison, C. and Kilzer, L. (1994, July 29). Minnesota firm linked to Mafia, U.S. alleges gaming business ties investigated. *Minneapolis Star and Tribune*, p. 1A.

Johansen, B.E. (1993). Life and death in Mohawk country. Golden, CO: North American Press.

Long, P.T. (1995). Casino gaming in the United States: 1994 status and implications. *Tourism Management, 16*(3), 189-197.

Lueders, B. (1994, August). Buffaloed: Casino cowboys take Indians for a ride. *Progressive, 58*(8), 30-33.

Magnuson, J. (1994, February 16). Casino wars: Ethics and economics in Indian County. *Christian Century, 111*(5), 169-171.

Markels, A. (1996, August 14). American Indian tribe dismisses contract with Gaming World. *The Wall Street Journal* (Eastern Edition), p. B6.

Minnesota Indian Gaming Association (1992). *Economic benefits of tribal gaming in Minnesota.* Minneapolis, MN: Author.

Minnesota Planning (1992). *High stakes: Gambling in Minnesota.* St. Paul, MN: Author.

Moore, W.J. (1993). A winning hand. *National Journal, 25*(29), 1796-1800.

Oleck, J. (1993, June 10). Tribal warfare. *Restaurant Business, 92*(9), 56, 58, 62, 66.

Orwall, B. (1996, July 22). The federal legislator of Indian gaming is also part advocate. *The Wall Street Journal* (Eastern Edition), pp. A1, A5.

Peppard, D.M. Jr. (1995, Fall). In the shadow of Foxwoods: Some effects of casino development in southeastern Connecticut. *Economic Development Review, 13*(4), 44-46.

Petroski, W. (1997, December 14). Meskwaki Indians embroiled in bitter political struggle. *Des Moines Sunday Register*, pp. 1B, 5B.

Pico, A. (1994, December). The new Indian land wars. *Indian Gaming, 6*(1), 3, 22.

Popkin, J. (1993, August 23). Gaming with the mob? Wise guys have set their sights on the booming Indian casino business. *U.S. News and World Report*, pp. 30-32.

Schnaiberg, L. (1994). Indian tribes put their money on gaming to boost education. *Education Week, 14*(14), 1, 10-11.

Segal, D. (1992, March). Dance with sharks: Why the Indian gaming experiment's gone bust. *Washington Monthly, 24*(3), 26-30.

Stephenson, J. (1996). For some American Indians, casino profits are a good bet for improving health care. *Journal of the American Medical Association, 275*(23), 1783-1785.

Thompson, W.N. and Dever, D.R. (1994a, April). A sovereignty check on Indian gaming. *Indian Gaming, 5*(5), 5-7.

Thompson, W.N. and Dever, D.R. (1994b, May). A sovereignty check on Indian gaming (Part II): The downside of the sovereignty equation. *Indian Gaming, 5*(6), 8-9.

Thompson, W.N., Gazel, R., and Rickman, D. (1996a). The social costs of gambling in Wisconsin. *Wisconsin Policy Research Institute Report, 9*(6), 1-44.

Thompson, W.N., Gazel, R., and Rickman, D. (1996b). Casinos and crime in Wisconsin. *Wisconsin Policy Research Institute Report, 9*(9), 1-20.

Volberg, R.A. and Silver, E. (1993). *Gambling and Problem Gambling in North Dakota*. Albany, NY: Gemini Research.

Zitzow, D. (1996a). Comparative study of problematic gambling behaviors between American Indian and non-Indian adolescents within and near a Northern Plains reservation. *American Indian and Alaska Native Mental Health Research, 7*(2), 14-26.

Zitzow, D. (1996b). Comparative study of problematic gambling behaviors between American Indian and non-Indian adults in a Northern Plains reservation. *American Indian and Alaska Native Mental Health Research, 7*(2), 27-41.

Chapter 12

Social Impacts of Riverboat and Land-Based Non-Native American Casino Gaming

Patricia A. Stokowski

The American experience with gambling can be traced as far back as colonial-era lotteries, but more recent interest in legalized gambling emerged with the opening of casinos in Nevada in 1931. The expansion of casinos to Atlantic City in 1978, coupled with the introduction of a state-sponsored lottery in New Hampshire in 1964, signaled a new period of public tolerance for institutionalized gambling. By 1995, forty-eight states, excluding Utah and Hawaii, had some form or combination of legal betting operations (casinos, lotteries, pari-mutuel racing, bingo, card rooms, charity gambling).

The spread of legal casino gambling beyond Nevada and Atlantic City is a very recent phenomenon, however. Casinos emerged on Native American reservations following the 1988 Indian Gaming Regulatory Act, which attempted to formalize the rights of tribes to conduct and regulate reservation gambling. The first non-Native American casinos appeared in Deadwood, South Dakota, when that town adopted casino gaming as an economic-development and historic-preservation strategy. A similar approach was initiated in 1991 in Black Hawk, Central City, and Cripple Creek, three former mining towns in Colorado. At about the same time, efforts were underway in several midwestern states to institute riverboat gambling. Iowa opened the first riverboat casino in 1991, and other states along the Mississippi River, Gulf Coast, and other major waterways opened riverboats later. More recently, casinos have been proposed for major metropolitan areas, including New Orleans, Detroit, and Chicago.

233

Contemporary initiatives in support of casino gaming generally have three common themes. First, gambling is consistently promoted as an economic revitalization strategy for communities. Proponents assert that gaming industry development will add jobs, improve personal and community wealth, provide new revenue sources, and reduce local taxes. Second, gambling is rationalized as a new type of entertainment tourism intended to impose minimal social or cultural disruptions on a host community. Gambling tourism is expected to provide economic benefits without destroying attractive and valued elements of community life. Third, gaming development is seen as a way to finance some traditionally underfunded community programs, particularly education and historic preservation. The inclusion of these and other social benefits is intended to allay the fears of critics who are opposed to the spread of gambling activities.

ASSESSING SOCIAL IMPACTS

Evaluating the social impacts of gambling and gaming development is, at present, an inexact science. Public and academic interest in the topic has increased as casinos disperse more widely throughout society, but in many cases, research has been ad hoc, initiated by a relatively small corps of academic researchers and private organizations, often atheoretical, and conducted only after casinos have opened in a locale, ignoring preopening impacts. Research problems can also be traced to measurement difficulties: unlike most economic measures, some social indicators—"quality of life" and "community attachment" are examples—are difficult to summarize in numerical form, even if they may be very real in personal experience. The dual problems of history and scale also challenge those conducting impact analyses. Over what time period should changes be evaluated, and how widely are the effects distributed across populations?

Despite these difficulties, though, the literature on social consequences of gaming and gambling extends our understanding of two important research areas: (1) the social impacts of individual gambling behavior and (2) the social impacts associated with community gaming development. This chapter reviews literature about each topic, discusses indicators used by analysts to assess impacts, and compares data across gaming places. Throughout, the focus is on land-based and riverboat gaming settings in the United States outside Nevada, Atlantic City, and Native American locales.

SOCIAL IMPACTS OF GAMBLING AND GAMING DEVELOPMENT

Dietz (1987, p. 56) defines social impact assessment as "the identification, analysis, and evaluation of the social impacts resulting from a particular event. A social impact is a significant improvement or deterioration in people's well-being or a significant change in an aspect of community concern." The ideal approach to social impact assessment employs a time frame that includes introduction of the project through opening of the project and across post-opening periods, and the appraisal of both objective as well as subjective social changes. Many studies about the social impacts of gambling and gaming development tend to be much more limited in scope, however, with most researchers focusing on very narrow aspects of outcomes. Nevertheless, some consistencies in the forms and characteristics of social impacts do emerge when casino developments and locales are compared.

Residents' Attitudes About Community and Gambling

Studies of residents' attitudes toward gambling and gaming development, and their perceptions of potential or actual community change, make up a significant portion of the current research literature about gambling impacts. This research tends to focus on two topics: (1) the ability of residents to predict what will happen in their communities if gaming is developed and (2) the perceived benefits and costs different groups of residents believe they would receive from gambling.

Research about the attitudes of community residents toward gambling is often conducted in settings in which casinos are being discussed as a development option. Under this line of research, residents are asked to consider the potential community effects if proposed casinos are developed. Pizam and Pokela's (1985) evaluation of public attitudes toward development of two hotel/casino projects in Massachusetts showed that residents expressed consensus about the possible negative impacts of such a development (they believed it would negatively affect the image of the town and would introduce crime), but were uncertain about the potential positive impacts. In a study attempting to project the likely impacts of casino development in Decatur, Illinois, Wicks and Norman (1996) found most residents were opposed to the project, though there were differences in preference for tax revenue spending if casinos opened. African Americans favored spending gaming taxes on social services, while Anglo residents preferred spending gaming tax revenues on police and fire protection and tax reduction.

A second approach to studying residents' attitudes toward gambling or its effects is analysis of the attitudes of various community subgroups after gaming has been established and casinos are operating. For example, attitudes toward tourism and gambling and perceived changes in the community after the introduction of gaming were the focus of a study by Canedy and Zeiger (1991). Through surveys of residents and business entrepreneurs in Deadwood, South Dakota, they found that most respondents could identify a variety of social and economic impacts resulting from the development of gaming and that these impacts were felt to varying degrees, depending on a person's job and education level.

This same line of research is visible in a series of articles analyzing residents' attitudes toward gambling and community change after casinos opened in Colorado and South Dakota. Long, Clark, and Liston (1994) surveyed residents of Colorado's three gaming towns one year after casinos opened and residents of Deadwood, South Dakota, then in its third year of gaming, to determine community attitudes toward the new developments. Residents generally agreed that gambling was an appropriate development option for their communities, but were somewhat uncertain about two other issues: whether they had made the right choice by adopting gambling and whether they believed their town was a better place to live after adopting gambling. Using the same data set, Perdue, Long, and Kang (1995) found that although residents might appreciate the economic benefits gaming development can bring to a community, they do not always perceive a direct personal benefit.

Though a popular topic, research about residents' attitudes and perceptions exhibits several critical limitations. Residents are often asked to speculate and offer opinions about their own future participation in gambling or about the future of their community, with little consideration for either the knowledge level of different respondents or the likelihood of different development outcomes. Data are often gathered after casinos are approved and opened, but there are usually no comparative measures of people's attitudes prior to the introduction of casinos. Beyond documenting attitudes and opinions across community groups, little effort is made to theorize about why groups might differ in their views, and little research has been replicated over time to assess aggregated attitude levels as population composition changes. Finally, results are assumed to be evidence of causality, when no causality may have been implied in the original survey questions. For example, opinions about the acceptability of gambling as a form of entertainment are reinterpreted by analysts as evidence of increasing demand for gambling opportunities.

Traffic

One of the earliest and most visible impacts of casino gaming development is an increase in traffic volume moving through a community and casino area. Indeed, traffic and parking are reported by residents to be two of the most vexing problems associated with the opening of casinos in all gaming locales. Many casino openings are accompanied by rapid increases in traffic, especially in rural gaming communities accustomed to substantially lower residential and visitor traffic flows. In Colorado, for example, traffic volume on the main state highway leading into the gaming towns of Black Hawk and Central City rose nearly 400 percent from 1990, the year prior to opening of casinos, to 1995 (Stokowski, 1996a). The pattern is repeated in other gaming locales: over 10,000 cars a day are reported to travel secondary highways to the riverboat casinos in Tunica, Mississippi, far exceeding before-gambling periods (Labalme, 1994). Other riverboat and casino towns report staggering increases in traffic volumes when residents, casino employees, service vehicles, general tourists, and gambler shuttle buses compete for the same stretch of roadway (Chadbourne, Walker, and Wolfe, 1997).

Traffic increases have been so overwhelming in new gaming communities that state and local transportation departments, police forces, and emergency service providers are required to rapidly upgrade their services to accommodate the increases. Road-widening and improvement projects, highway maintenance, police patrols, and ambulance and search and rescue operations demand larger portions of city and state government budgets once gaming is established in a locale. Since many of the new riverboat and land-based casinos are located in rural areas, these services often have been provided only at a marginal level, and the costs of expanding police forces, purchasing ambulances, or building new office space are substantial. Many of the smaller gaming communities, such as Tunica, Mississippi, Deadwood, South Dakota, the Colorado gaming towns, and others, find themselves poorly equipped to handle huge traffic increases on rural roads, especially when casino-related alcohol problems are factored into the equation.

When casinos are located in central downtown areas, as they are in some riverboat venues, South Dakota, and Colorado, parking availability also becomes an issue. In the Colorado gaming towns, for example, the parking problem was so severe that a residential permit parking system had to be implemented with the start of gaming. Even with this approach, residents still found it difficult to park to conduct normal business in the commercial center. Jury duty, attendance at church services, scheduling weddings and funerals, visits to the post office or county courthouse, and other regular activities were adversely affected (Stokowski, 1996a).

In addition to changing the patterns of daily life, traffic increases associated with gaming development often result in demands by the casino industry to allow construction of more parking lots and garages adjacent to or near casinos. Industry representatives claim that convenient parking is central to casino operation, and in most cases, they have been successful in convincing city governments to allow convenient parking. For casinos in downtown areas, this may result in increased pressures on vacant properties or those used for purposes other than gaming. For example, a trailer park in Black Hawk, Colorado, was bought for casino parking, displacing about twenty elderly residents (Stokowski, 1996a). In riverboat casino locales, new parking facilities may orient visitors away from downtown shops, thus bolstering casino business but risking viability in the noncasino business district, as in Natchez, Mississippi, and Davenport, Iowa (Chadbourne, Walker, and Wolfe, 1997).

Residential Population

The opening of casinos often displaces some community residents, while simultaneously presenting opportunities for new residents to move into a community. Stubbles (1990) noted that as early as a year after gaming began in Deadwood, South Dakota, some families were moving out, causing a decline in school enrollments and in church and civic group attendance. Stokowski (1996a) observed similar phenomena in Central City and Black Hawk, Colorado, where about half of the residents in those small towns moved away after gaming was introduced. In comparing Colorado and South Dakota gaming communities, Long and colleagues (1994) reported that 29 to 44 percent of residents surveyed in each community said they would like to move away from their town now that it had adopted gambling.

Many reasons exist for residential out-migration after casinos arrive. Some residents move to seek an improved lifestyle after profiting from selling land or buildings to casino developers. Others move because they are evicted when the land on which they maintain temporary housing is sold for casino development. Still others are left without accommodations when buildings where they have rented apartments are sold to developers. Other residents move because they cannot afford the increase in rents that accompanies market pressure on nearby properties or because they do not wish to live in a gambling community.

As some residents migrate away from a community, though, others move in. Communities with a primarily imported labor force begin to feel pressures to improve available housing stock so that casino employees and their families may move closer to their work. New housing construction projects with single-family residences, apartments, and condominiums are encouraged. The effect on local social fabric in these gaming locales is an issue for future study.

Community Services

Two distinct stages produce the most visible impacts of gaming development on community services: (1) the early construction period (the time after legalization, but prior to the opening of casinos) and (2) the extended period after casinos have actually opened. In each period, pressures on local government, casinos, and voluntary membership agencies vary, so that community services which are problematic in one period may not be in the other.

The provision and quality of community services depends at least in part on the arrangements community leaders have made with the incoming industry. Most local governments adopting gambling initially attempt to collect impact and device fees as a tax on casino business operations. Such fees are significant for a community, providing new sources of revenue to fund improvements to public infrastructure, including road projects, water system development, and wastewater treatment. Rarely are these fees adequate for funding all the necessities related to community growth, but they do help mitigate what Cummings, Schulze, and Mehr (1978) have called "front end problems": communities in transition have needs for improved services even prior to the opening of the new development project, but they often do not have adequate financial resources to pay for those improvements.

Once gaming has been established and infrastructure improvements are underway, the revenues from casino impact fees are often applied to funding cultural and aesthetic amenities. These projects include such activities as providing recreation, supporting cultural and historic projects, and improving landscaping and streetscaping. Even if communities obtain new sources of dedicated and general tax revenues from casino gaming development, they also incur costs. Three generalizations can be made about this process: (1) more services often require larger government systems, and it takes money to administer more personnel, more programs, and larger budgets; (2) though some community services and amenities may be impacted by gaming development, they may not receive direct monetary support to offset these impacts; and (3) projected community improvements do not always materialize on the schedule desired by either local leadership or residents. These problems also are more dramatic if the local population is small, if casinos are spread across a city's business zone, and if local government practices are informal.

Although pro-casino development campaigns claim that all forms of tourism will be enhanced by the opening of casinos, available evidence does not support this assertion. For example, tourist visits to museums, operas, festivals, historic homes, and local shops and restaurants declined after gaming was introduced in many of the nondestination riverboat and land-based casino locales, including Central City, Colorado, and Vicksburg, Natchez, and Biloxi, Mississippi. In places where gaming tourists stay overnight, visitation to other attractions may increase, as seen in Deadwood, South Dakota, and Davenport, Iowa. Typically, though, traditional forms of tourism available in a community prior to gambling decline when gaming is introduced, unless that locale restricts casino-related services (such as restaurants or hotels built as a component of the casino project) while promoting other noncasino forms of local business development. However, comparisons across gaming communities suggest that community revitalization tends to lag behind casino and casino-related development (Stokowski, 1993).

Community Amenities: Special Places

Local amenities that provide a sense of place and a special quality of life often feature aspects of a community's history or natural and built environments. Many of the new land-based and riverboat casino locales are situated in communities with valued historic architecture and significant cultural traditions. In most land-based gaming communities, though, the challenge of transforming historic structures into casinos has been substantial. Contemporary building codes, the weight of slot machines, and anticipated visitor numbers all combined to produce situations in which only the facades of historic buildings were kept intact, while interiors were gutted and reconstructed for gaming. Redevelopment of this nature tends to be less likely when there is a limit on the number of gaming devices allowed in a casino (as in Deadwood, South Dakota, where the limit is thirty). Nevertheless, the fate of historic structures is a continuing concern in many communities, even those in which gaming tax moneys are dedicated to preservation causes.

Pressures on historic structures increase when there is strong political pressure by a gaming industry seeking expansion and a growth-oriented local leadership. For example, the riverboat gaming community of Davenport, Iowa, granted permission to a casino to demolish a block of nine historic buildings to accommodate casino parking expansion (Chadbourne, Walker, and Wolfe, 1997). Residents and community spokespersons reported that gaming development had a negative effect on local historic properties in Joliet, Illinois, Black Hawk, Colorado, Davenport, Iowa, Natchez, Mississippi, and Lawrenceburg, Iowa (Chadbourne, Walker, and Wolfe, 1997; Miller, 1995). In fact, the development of casinos in the Colorado and South Dakota towns caused so much structural disruption that the National Park Service placed the historic mining districts in those towns on its list of "most endangered historic landmarks" in 1992.

A recent example in Black Hawk, Colorado, illustrates the dilemmas of using gaming to facilitate historic preservation. Property along the main street in that town was sold to a developer wanting to build a casino several stories high on a plot of land that enveloped, on three sides, a designated historic home. Though the development company proposed to move the home and several other historic houses to a new, protected location (a proposal supported by the city government), preservation groups across Colorado opposed the move because it would destroy the historic integrity of the structure. In fact, the Colorado State Historical Society was successful in stopping the relocation with court action in fall 1997.

In addition to the physical transformation of the environment that accompanies all forms of gaming development, new construction and casino marketing practices often fail to uphold the authenticity of local histories. When casino-sponsored entertainment and events are introduced, they tend to be promoted and marketed as professional productions rather than as accurate representations of community history. Although local historic preservation boards are often successful in restricting features inappropriate to the local context (such as neon signs or building colors), these boards generally have little authority over either interior gaming hall design or casino marketing approaches (Jensen and Blevins, 1995). The result is that a community's important local places and stories are forsaken for casino-generated "historical illusions" (Stokowski, 1996a). New buildings may make casino towns look cleaner and more appealing, and new festivals and events may stimulate tourism, but the process of sanitization reduces the sense of community and contributes an impression that casino theme parks have been created.

Communities that designate a portion of gaming tax revenues for projects that improve local (and sometimes regional) amenities, such as historic preservation, do find that they have new financial resources to protect or restore some significant aspects of their heritage. In Colorado, for example, where 28 percent of the gaming tax revenues were dedicated to historic preservation projects, the State Historical Fund distributed about $35 million for preservation projects in the gaming communities and throughout the state between 1992 and 1996 (Westover and Collins, 1997; Hunter, 1995). Local and regional preservation projects also were supported by gaming taxes in Deadwood, South Dakota, and Natchez, Mississippi. In addition, in Davenport, Iowa, revenues have gone to upgrade a convention center, and in Shreveport, Louisiana, gaming revenues have been spent on a new science museum. The benefits of these improvements may be shared by residents as well as tourists.

However, even communities that receive substantial revenues from gaming industry growth express mixed opinions. Particularly in communities where the casinos are located on or near primary streets in the main downtown area, residents often feel a decline in quality of life. A planner in Central City, Colorado, noted that "The quality of life has deteriorated. It's hard to get to the post office; it's hard to find a place to buy a gallon of milk" (Matzko, 1994, p. 51). Although residents in many gaming towns enjoy the increased entertainment offerings and variety in restaurants that often accompany the new industry, they also express mixed feelings about whether their town has been able to maintain an agreeable quality of life (Long, Clark, and Liston, 1994). Since most of the research on this topic has been conducted relatively soon after casinos opened, further research is needed on the relationship between gaming and community quality of life.

Crime

Although much public concern about gambling focuses on the issue of crime, relatively few scholarly studies systematically analyze the impacts of gaming development on crime; most focus on Atlantic City. Studies of crime patterns in Atlanta City (Albanese, 1985), studies of regional "crime spillover" after introduction of casinos in Atlantic City (Friedman, Hakim, and Weinblatt, 1989), and studies on the effects of crime on real estate values (Buck, Hakim, and Spiegel, 1991) all concluded that absolute numbers of crimes increased after casinos were introduced in that locale. Curran and Scarpitti (1991) further demonstrated that Atlantic City crime was primarily casino based, not community based; they advised that researchers adjust their models to reflect the huge increases in tourist visits that accompany gaming development. Ochrym (1990), though, explained that crime tends to increase in tourism locales generally, and increases are not particular to the casino community itself.

Beyond the Atlantic City research, a review of literature uncovers very few studies about crime patterns in other gaming locales. Evaluating police crime reports in the riverboat gaming town of Biloxi, Mississippi, Giacopassi and Stitt (1993) found that larceny-theft and motor vehicle theft increased after gaming was introduced, as did several other economic (robbery, burglary, fraud) and public order (aggravated assault, disorderly conduct, drunkenness, trespassing, prostitution) crimes. The increases were not statistically significant, however. Evart (1994) hypothesized that gaming towns might expect increases in white-collar crime, such as fraud, as gambling spread to more locales across the country. She also observed that disorderly conduct and arrests for driving under the influence (DUI) have increased in the riverboat town of Davenport, Iowa, and prostitution, assaults, and robberies increased after riverboat casinos were opened in Biloxi and Gulfport, Mississippi.

An analysis of crime patterns in the Colorado gaming towns of Central City, Black Hawk, and Cripple Creek, Stokowski (1996b) found that, although crime increased after gaming was introduced, crime levels had not increased in proportion to the huge numbers of gamblers visiting the towns. She noted, though, that any increase in the actual numbers of criminal behaviors places new demands on local governments (for more police staffing and for court and jail facilities) and affects residential and visitor perceptions of safety. As a result, gaming communities need to be especially vigilant about controlling crime and managing public perceptions.

Public and Private Social Services

Crime, availability of community amenities and services, and public perceptions of social change, population, and traffic volumes are examples of community-level impacts of gaming development. When gaming is proposed as a development strategy for a locale, however, immediate public concern tends to coalesce around individual-level impacts of gambling. Whether easy access to casinos will stimulate pathological gambling behaviors, encourage child neglect, foster overspending by low-income patrons, push gamblers into financial ruin, or break apart families, the personal consequences of gambling capture substantial public attention. Unfortunately, the measurement and evaluation of these impacts is usually very difficult, given the wide variability in reporting procedures, requirements for confidentiality, and the need for data that can isolate the effects of an array of variables.

Efforts to scientifically analyze the impacts of gambling and gaming development on the need for, and provision of, governmental social services have been quite limited. Accounts are mostly anecdotal and often fail to take into consideration the institutional practices, history, and context of service provision in different locales. Available published reports provide mixed conclusions. Researchers studying gaming developments in New Jersey, South Dakota, and Colorado all have concluded that both payments made for Aid to Families with Dependent Children (AFDC) and numbers of food stamp recipients tend to decrease after gaming is introduced in a county (Madden, 1991; Kinnel, 1992; Long, 1996; Stokowski, 1996a). It is projected that Mississippi will also exhibit similar trends, as populations increase in casino counties to include a younger, more educated, better paid workforce; with economic gain, there is less demand for public social services (Logue, 1994). In each of these states, though, reduced AFDC payments and food stamp requests result from a complexity of factors, of which gambling is only one. Changes in federal and state eligibility requirements, reorganization of the administering agency, and revisions to management philosophies after a change in leadership all affect program participation.

There is great public sensitivity to the issue of whether children are adversely affected when casinos are introduced into an area. Concerns are raised about whether children are left to wait in cars while parents gamble, whether children are the actual beneficiaries of support payments made to parents, whether school enrollments are affected by incoming employees and their families, and whether suitable activities exist for children and youth in the affected community. Available data about the provision of child protection services in communities with casinos tend to be limited; what is available provides mixed conclusions. In Gilpin County, Colorado, for example, the demand for child protective services increased between 1991 (when casinos were introduced in Central City and Black Hawk) and 1995, but according to the director of the county social services agency, the increase was related to organizational restructuring and changes in the scope of services rather than to gaming development (Stokowski, 1996a).

The potential for gambling addiction is another issue of public concern, and although much of the care of problem gambling has traditionally been vested in private treatment centers, state-funded programs are now emerging. The costs of problem gambling are potentially vast and include personal indebtedness, withdrawal from family and work activities, physical and psychological disorders, participation in illegal activities, and institutional costs (Lesieur and Rosenthal, 1991). Volberg (1997), who has conducted a series of studies about problem and pathological gambling, concluded that rates of problem gambling tend to be higher in places where gambling has recently been introduced. With the opening of casinos around the United States, Gamblers Anonymous chapters are also opening in states with gambling, and anecdotal reports indicate that participation is rising.

Studies of compulsive gambling consistently find that the number of people who can be identified as problem gamblers, the number of individuals seeking counseling help, and the number of visits to treatment centers all increase after casinos are introduced in a locale (Volberg, 1997). However, the problem does not stop there. Goodman (1994) suggested that the newest forms of electronic gambling may be even more addictive than traditional gambling activities. Individual participation in gambling activities may also be bolstered by social considerations. Rosecrance (1986) suggested that past efforts to explain participation in gambling, based on economic considerations (winning money) or psychological tendencies (willingness to take and accept risks), have been limited by a failure to consider the social aspects of gambling. He noted (Rosecrance, 1986, p. 374) that, "For many regular casino participants . . . the rewards of social interaction outweigh the costs of participation." Such a conclusion suggests that problem gambling behaviors cannot be reduced without a deeper understanding of the social contexts in which they exist.

CONCLUSIONS

Past efforts to locate casinos where people were not (namely, Nevada) or make membership or wealth a requirement for entry, as in some European casinos, have been supplanted by recent trends to situate casinos in or near major metropolitan centers. The potential economic gains that may accrue from this form of development are compelling, especially for communities used to viewing their options as limited. The arguments assessing costs and benefits of gambling and gaming development are often played out in the media, an arena not always conducive to objective analysis. Stokowski (1996a) found, for example, that proponents in the Colorado gambling campaign employed a "rhetoric of despair" to focus on the alleged economic death of the interested communities (contrary to trends visible in available statistics) and the overwhelming potential economic benefits of gambling. These findings confirmed Nickerson's (1995) study of the South Dakota progambling campaign, which showed that gambling was portrayed in the media in a very positive vein and that a critical analysis of potential benefits and costs was lacking. The same pattern also was observed in news reports about commercial gambling published in a Philadelphia paper. Evaluating the findings of their content analysis, Abt and McDowell (1987, p. 196) concluded that "The stories appear to suggest that the public interest is synonymous with the interests of the legal gambling industry and the states."

These three analyses suggest that a pressing need exists for better public information about the real benefits and costs of gambling and gaming development, whether these are social, economic, political, or environmental in nature. Eadington (1995, p. 185) observed that, "More and more frequently, autonomous jurisdictions . . . may decide they should move immediately on legalization because other competing jurisdictions have already done so or will soon do so." However, such actions remove from public scrutiny and debate the very issues that should be considered before casino legalization is pursued by a community.

There is an increasing body of scholarly research about the social impacts of gambling and gaming development. The data show that, although economic benefits accrue to local, county, and state governments, and to the gaming industry, economic, social, political, and environmental costs also are a consequence of gaming development. Although these may not always be reducible to numbers or dollars, the impacts are real in individual and community experience and cannot be ignored by policymakers. These concerns seem to be reflected in public sentiment about the expansion of casino gambling: despite acceptability of individual participation in gambling, the public remains ambivalent regarding allowing casino development to spread beyond current locales.

Some authors blame the problems of gambling-stimulated community transformation on local residents, writing that "little or no planning occurs" after gaming is legalized (Dimanche and Liliedahl, 1995), but this assertion is incorrect. Gaming development is a particularly fast-paced form of tourism development; the biggest gains accrue to those who are quickly able to set up operations and hold position in emerging markets. Generally, rural or small communities have little past experience with large, well-financed, fast-moving development projects, so institutional structures are not in place to manage the pace or scale of change. Indeed, local participation is often quite high in those exciting times, but both leaders and citizens may be uncertain about what is needed and how quickly things must be done. For communities choosing gambling as a strategy for economic development, the challenge is to effectively plan and manage the growth process so benefits are realized and social costs are contained.

In approving gaming development, the expressed hope of most people is that the casino entertainment will provide personal pleasures for residents and tourists with a margin of economic well-being for a community. Data show, however, that in most cases, industry business goals and community goals are not congruent. Moreover, the institutional systems that exercise care and control over debilitating gambling-related social behaviors are not yet evident across most communities in the United States. As industry pressures increase to open more casinos, a need arises for more comprehensive longitudinal research about the social consequences of gambling and gaming development. Until then, we must rely on the efforts of independent and academic researchers, who have only limited resources to undertake the complex research required.

REFERENCES

Abt, V. and McDowell, D.J. (1987). Does the press cover gambling issues poorly? Evidence from a newspaper content analysis. *Sociology and Social Research, 71*(3), 193-197.

Albanese, J.S. (1985). The effect of casino gambling on crime. *Federal Probation, 49*(2), 39-44.

Buck, A.J., Hakim, S., and Spiegel, U. (1991). Casinos, crime, and real estate values: Do they relate? *Journal of Research in Crime and Delinquency, 28*(3), 288-303.

Canedy, L. and Zeiger, J. (1991). The social, economic, and environmental costs of tourism to a gaming community as perceived by its residents. *Journal of Travel Research, 30*(2), 45-49.

Chadbourne, C., Walker, P., and Wolfe, M. (1997). *Gambling, economic development, and historic preservation*. Chicago, IL: American Planning Association.

Cummings, R.G., Schulze, W.D., and Mehr, A.F. (1978). Optimal municipal investment in boomtowns: An empirical analysis. *Journal of Environmental Economics and Management, 5*(3), 252-267.

Curran, D. and Scarpitti, F. (1991). Crime in Atlantic City: Do casinos make a difference? *Deviant Behavior: An Interdisciplinary Journal, 12*(4), 431-449.

Dietz, T. (1987). Theory and method in social impact assessment. *Sociological Inquiry, 57*(1), 54-69.

Dimanche, F. and Liliedahl, E. (1995, June). The impacts of gambling and related tourism development on a Mississippi urban area: A case study. Paper presented at the 26th Annual Travel and Tourism Research Association Conference, Acapulco, Mexico.

Eadington, W.R. (1995). The emergence of casino gaming as a major factor in tourism markets. In R. Butler and D. Pearce (Eds.), *Change in tourism: People, places, processes* (pp. 159-186). London: Routledge.

Evart, C. (1994, Summer). Troublesome environmental concerns: Some suggested solutions. In The Advocacy, Witness and Justice Ministries Unit of the National Episcopal Church and the Diocese of Nevada (Ed.), *The social economic and environmental consequences of casino gambling* (pp. 41-46). New York: The Episcopal Church Center.

Friedman, J., Hakim, S., and Weinblatt, J. (1989). Casino gambling as a "growth pole" strategy and its effects on crime. *Journal of Regional Science, 29*(4), 615-623.

Giacopassi, D. and Stitt, B.G. (1993). Assessing the impact of casino gambling on crime in Mississippi. *American Journal of Criminal Justice, 18*(1), 117-131.

Goodman, R. (1994). *Legalized gambling as a strategy for economic development.* Northampton, MA: United States Gambling Study.

Hunter, C. (1995). Transforming history into economic development. *Historic Preservation Forum, 9*(4), 20-27.

Jensen, K. and Blevins, A. (1995). Gambling on the lure of historic preservation: Community transformation in Rocky Mountain mining towns. *Journal of the Community Development Society, 26*(1), 71-92.

Kinnel, L. (1992). *Research response: Effects of casino gambling on welfare costs.* Springfield, IL: Illinois General Assembly, Legislative Research Unit.

Labalme, J. (1994). The great riverboat gamble. *Southern Exposure: A Journal of Politics and Culture, 22*(2), 10-14.

Lesieur, H.R. and Rosenthal, R.J. (1991). Pathological gambling: A review of the literature. *Journal of Gambling Studies, 7*(1), 5-39.

Logue, B.J. (1994, August). *Impact of the gaming industry on population in Mississippi: What recent projections show.* Jackson, MS: Mississippi Institutions of Higher Learning, Center for Policy Research and Planning, Working Paper #9403.

Long, P.T. (1996). Early impacts of limited stakes casino gambling on rural community life. *Tourism Management, 17*(5), 341-353.

Long, P., Clark, J., and Liston, D. (1994). Win, lose, or draw? *Gambling with America's small towns.* Washington, DC: The Aspen Institute.

Madden, M.K. (1991). Gaming in South Dakota: A statistical description and analysis of its socioeconomic impacts. Vermillion, SD: University of South Dakota, Business Research Bureau.

Matzko, M. (1994, Summer). Environmental impact of casinos: The story of Central City, Colorado. In The Advocacy, Witness and Justice Ministries Unit of the National Episcopal Church and the Diocese of Nevada (Ed.), *The social, economic and environmental consequences of casino gambling* (pp. 47-52). New York: The Episcopal Church Center.

Miller, M.W. (1995). Gambling doesn't pay in historic. *Historic Preservation Forum, 9*(4), 40-47.

Nickerson, N.P. (1995). Tourism and gambling content analysis. *Annals of Tourism Research, 22*(1), 53-66.

Ochrym, R.G. (1990). Street crime, tourism and casinos: An empirical comparison. *Journal of Gambling Studies, 6*(2), 127-138.

Perdue, R.R., Long, P.T., and Kang, Y. (1995). Resident support for gambling as a development strategy. *Journal of Travel Research, 34*(2), 3-11.

Pizam, A. and Pokela, J. (1985). The perceived impacts of casino gambling on a community. *Annals of Tourism Research, 12*(2), 147-165.

Rosecrance, J. (1986). Why regular gamblers don't quit: A sociological perspective. *Sociological Perspectives, 29*(3), 357-378.

Stokowski, P.A. (1993). Undesirable lag effects in tourist destination development: A Colorado case study. *Journal of Travel Research, 32*(2), 35-41.

Stokowski, P.A. (1996a). *Riches and regrets: Betting on gambling in two Colorado mountain towns.* Niwot, CO: University Press of Colorado.

Stokowski, P.A. (1996b). Crime patterns and gaming development in rural Colorado. *Journal of Travel Research, 34*(3), 63-69.

Stubbles, R. (1990). The Deadwood tradition: Putting gambling before planning in South Dakota. *Small Town, 20*(3), 20-27.

Volberg, R.A. (1997). *Gambling and problem gambling in Colorado.* Report to the Colorado Department of Revenue. Roaring Spring, PA: Gemini Research.

Westover, T.N. and Collins, C.O. (1997, September). Historic preservation and gambling in Colorado. Paper presented at the Rocky Mountain Regional Meeting of the Association of American Geographers, Bozeman, MT.

Wicks, B.E. and Norman, K.A. (1996). Urban riverboat casino planning: Including the African American perspective. *Journal of Travel Research, 34*(3), 17-23.

Index

Page numbers followed by the letter "i" indicate illustrations; those followed by the letter "t" indicate tables.

ABSCAM, 35
Aggravated assault
    in Atlantic City, 209, 212t
    five city comparison, 185, 186t, 187
    on Native American tribal lands, 227
Aid to Families with Dependent Children (AFDC)
    decrease in payments, 245
    recipients
        Atlantic City, 129
        Foxwoods Resorts casino, 142
        Oregon Native American gaming, 149
Airline travel, impact on Atlantic City, 115, 203
Alcohol abuse, gambling and, 211, 238
American Medical Association, gambling addiction, 211
American Psychological Association, gambling addiction, 211
Amusement parks, wages paid in, 146, 146t
Area Redevelopment Administration Act (1961), 44
Asians, as Las Vegas market population, 110
Atlantic City, *xiii*, 5, 25, 38
    casino legalization drive, 117-119
    casino's opening day, 30-31
    crime in, 204, 209-210, 211, 212t, 218, 243-244

Atlantic City (*continued*)
    decline in business diversity, 204
    decline of, 115-117, 201
    demographics of, 201-202
    establishment of, 113
    establishment of casino gambling, 117, 130
    infrastructure development, 132
    length of stay in, 119, 120t, 120-121
"Atlantic City and the Resort Cycle: Background to the Legalization of Gambling," 202
Atlantic City Casino Association, 34-35
Atlantic City Consolidated Plan for 1995 Executive Summary, 204, 215
Atlantic City Expressway Bill, 26
Atlantic City Free Public Library Web site, and crime rate, 211, 218
Atlantic City Housing Authority and Urban Redevelopment Agency, 131-132
    casino impact study, 118
    conventions decline, 117
Atlantic City: 125 Years of Ocean Madness, 114
Atlantic City Press, 30
Atlantic Community College, 29, 31, 32
Atlantic County, NJ, 25, 37-38
Atlantic County Improvement Authority (ACIA), 216

Austin, TX
  cost of living, 188, 189t, 190
  crime in, 185, 186t, 187
  demographics of, 181, 182, 183
  government expenditures, 193,
    193t, 194
  health care environment, 191-192,
    191t
  population density, 180
  traffic/transportation of, 184

"Baby boomers," market for
    gambling, 102
Bank Secrecy Act (1970), 20
Bankruptcies, gambling and, 207-208
Basic Magnesium Plant, Henderson,
    5, 7
Bible, Allen, Nevada Attorney
    General, 9
Biloxi, Mississippi riverboats, 75, 76
Bingo, 46, 48, 49. See also Class II
    gaming
Bingo Halls, Native American, 223
"Black Book," of Nevada Gaming
    Control Board, 11, 20
Black Hawk, CO
  business diversity in, 165-166
  casinos, 82, 83, 85
    development, 233, 242
    profitability, 160
  city budget, 160
  economic costs, 167-168
  out-migration, 239
  traffic congestion, 237, 238
Blue Ribbon Panel, NJ gambling
    statute development, 28, 33
Boulder (Hoover) Dam, 5, 6-7
Bureau of Indian Affairs (BIA),
    economic development,
    136-137
Burglary
  in Atlantic City, 209, 212t
  five city comparison, 186t, 187

Burglary (continued)
  on Native American tribal lands,
    227, 228
Business diversity, decrease in,
    164-165, 204
Business of Risk, The, 213, 214

Caesar's Palace, 11, 15
California v. Cabazon Band of
    Mission Indians (1987), 48
Californians, as Las Vegas market
    population, 110
Cape May County, NJ, 25, 37-38
Casino Association of New Jersey,
    report of, 120, 127-128
Casino-banked games, 50
Casino Career Institute (CCI),
    Atlantic Community College,
    29, 31, 33
Casino Control Act (1977), Atlantic
    City, 130, 213-214, 215, 217
Casino development model, 107-108
Casino employee migration, 164
Casino gaming
  growth of, 159-160, 159t, 233
  referendum, NJ, 27, 28
  three arguments for, 234
"Casino Gambling in Atlantic City,"
    205
"Casino Gaming as a 'Growth Pole'
    Strategy and Its Effect on
    Crime," 211-212
Casino locations in the United States
    (map), xiv
Casino Redevelopment Authority, 36
Casino regulations, 65t
Casino Reinvestment Development
    Authority (CRDA), 131-132,
    216, 217
Casino Revenue Fund, NJ, 129-130
Casino revenues, 155
  Atlantic City, 119, 120t, 121, 122i
  Las Vegas, 17, 95t, 105t, 106

Casinos
  entertainment economy, 155 156,
    248
  older in Las Vegas, 109
Center for Business and Economic
    Research (UNLV), Las
    Vegas, 178
Center for Survey Research, 195
Central City, CO
  business diversity in, 165
  casinos
    decline in revenues, 160
    development, 233
    economic costs, 167-168, 169
    infrastructure development,
      162-163
    out-migration, 239
Chalfonte-Haddon Hall hotel,
    Atlantic City, 113, 202
Charity gaming, 46
Chicago, riverboat casinos docking,
    75
Children, impact of casinos on,
    245-246
Chippewa tribe, St. Croix, 142
Clark County (Las Vegas),
    employment, 97
Clark County Comprehensive
    Planning, Las Vegas, 178
Class I, II, III gaming, 49-50
Class III Native American gaming,
    136
Colorado, land-based/non-Native
    American casinos, 82-85
  tax rates, 84i
Colorado Limited Gaming Act
    (1991), regulations, 83
Colorado State Historical Society,
    casino development and, 242
Commission on the Review of the
    National Policy Toward
    Gambling (1976), 3
Committee to Rebuild Atlantic City
    (CRAC), 27, 29, 30, 36, 39,
    118, 119-121, 123, 131

Community residents, attitudes
    toward gambling/gaming,
    235-237
Community services, casinos impact
    on, 239-241
Compact, between tribe and state,
    50, 51-52
Compulsive and Problem Gaming
    Fund, LA, 86
Compulsive gambling
  and casinos, 246
  crime and, 208
  in Las Vegas, 94, 109, 110
  mental disorder of, 211
  North Dakota rate, 228
  social costs of, 207, 208-209
Construction employment, Las
    Vegas, 98
Construction projects, Oregon Native
    American gaming, 149
Conventions, Las Vegas, 96t
Corporate taxes, Atlantic City, 125
Cost of living
  Atlantic city, 204
  five city comparison, 188, 189t, 190
Council on Compulsive Gambling of
    New Jersey, Inc., 206, 207
County and City Data Book, 181
Cow Creek Band, 147
Cow Creek Casino, Oregon Native
    American gaming, 148, 149
Crapped Out, 213-214
Crime
  in Atlantic city, 204, 209-210, 211,
    212t, 217-218, 243-244
  Colorado gaming towns, 244
  five city comparison, 185, 186t,
    187-188
  illegal gambling and, 208
  in Las Vegas, 94, 109, 179-180,
    185, 186t, 187-188
  on Native American tribal lands,
    227-228
  threat of on Native American land,
    58

"Crime spillover," 243
Cripple Creek, Colorado casinos, 82, 83, 85, 233
Currency Transaction Report (CTR), 20
Customer disputes, 21

Deadwood, SD
    business diversity in, 165
    casinos, 81, 82, 160, 233
    historic preservation, 160, 171, 242
    out-migration, 239
    traffic congestion, 237, 238-239
Democratic National Convention (1964), Atlantic City, 115-116
Demographics
    Atlantic city, 201-202
    five city comparison, 181-183
    Las Vegas, 181, 182t, 183-184
Desert Inn, 9, 11
Detroit, Michigan casino site, 88
"Diceman Cometh, The," 205
Disabled, New Jersey aid to, 129-130
Dividend payments, Native Americans, 221-222
Divorces, Las Vegas economic boom, 7
"Dockside" casinos
    Mississippi, 75
    Missouri, 78
Drug abuse, gambling and, 211, 238

Eating and drinking places, wages paid in, 146, 146t, 148
Economic benefits, indirect, Atlantic City, 127-130
Economic costs, gambling industry, 171-172
Economic Development Fund, Native Americans, 152

Economic Research Associates (ERA), casino impact study, 118-121, 123
"Economic, Resource, and Fiscal Impacts of Visitors on Washoe County, Nevada," 139
ECONorthwest, 148
Education Assistance Act of 1975, Native Americans, 137
Educational opportunities, Native American gaming, 56
"Effect of Casino Gambling on Crime, The," 209
Elderly, New Jersey aid to, 129-130
El Rancho Vegas, 7, 8
Employment
    Atlantic City, 119, 120t, 121, 123, 127-128, 204, 217
    Black Hawk, 163
    Central City, 163
    Deadwood, SD, 163
    Foxwoods Resorts Casino, 135
    land based-gaming industry, 163-164
    Las Vegas, 97-99
    Minnesota Native American gaming, 145, 146
    Native American casinos, 135, 138-139, 141-142
    Oregon Native American gaming, 149
    riverboat casinos, 163-164
    St. Croix Casino, 143
Entertainment
    gambling role in, 155
    industries, wages paid in, 146, 146t, 148
    in Las Vegas, 101, 106
    tourism, casino gambling, 234, 248
Environmental impact
    Las Vegas, 178
    on Native American tribal lands, 228

Equal Employment Opportunity
(EEO), and NJ casino
licensing, 28
European gaming, in Atlantic City, 36
Exploitation, Native American
gaming, 57-58

Family resorts, 16
Farley, Frank, 26
Federal Bureau of Investigation
(FBI) Uniform Crime
Reports, 185
Federal government, aid to Native
Americans, 45, 137, 138
Field of Dreams, 151
Flamingo Hotel, 8
Florida Seminole Nation, 46
"Forgotten people," 138
Fort Randall Casino, 140
Foxwoods Resorts Casino, 135, 136,
141-142
Fresno, CA
cost of living, 188, 189t, 190
crime in, 185, 186t, 187
demographics of, 181, 182, 183
government expenditures, 193,
193t, 194
health care environment, 191-192,
191t
population density, 180
traffic/transportation of, 184-185
"Front end problem," 162, 240

Gamblers Anonymous, 211, 228, 246
Gamblers, demographic profile of, 156
Gambling
addiction, concern over, 246
as a demand product, 101
economic benefits debate,
156-158, 172
government promotion of, 210
high school students, 196
Native American debate, 229-230

Gambling (*continued*)
Native American division over,
59, 60, 222-223
pre-Casino Atlantic City, 114, 118
public economic impacts, 161-169
and substance abuse, 211
Gambling disorders, meta-analysis
of studies of, 208
Gambling/gaming
community social impact of, 234
individual social impact of, 234
traffic congestion, 237, 238
Gambling/gaming industry
economic costs of, 167-169
growth of, 158-161, 159t,
169-170, 180
projections for, 169-172
Gaming, classes of, 49-51
Gaming Control Act (Nevada State
Bill 208), 5-6
Gaming Control Board (Las Vegas),
3, 4, 12, 13, 18, 20
establishment of, 10-11
operation of, 19
Gaming Policy Committee, 6
Gaming-related crime, Las Vegas,
94, 109
Gaming revenue, Native American
portion of, 136
Garden State Parkway Bill, 26
Gary, Indiana riverboats, 100
Government expenditures, five city
comparison, 192, 193-194,
193t,
Government revenues
Atlantic City, 119, 120t, 123, 125,
162
gambling impact on, 161-163
Native American gaming, 139, 140,
143, 144, 146, 148-149, 162
"Growth machine politics," 167

Harrah's Entertainment Inc., survey
of, 155
Harrah's Jazz Company, 86

Harvard Medical School Division
    on Addictions, gambling,
    208, 210
Health care environment, five city
    comparison, 191-192, 191t
Health, Native Americans, 44
Hefner, Hugh, 31, 36
High school students, problem
    gambling in, 196, 206
Hilton Corporation, 37
Hispanics, as Las Vegas market
    population, 110
Historic preservation
    casino development and, 241-243
    gambling revenue, 160, 170-171,
        243
Historical mining towns, 81
Ho-Chunk tribe, 139
Hotels
    Atlantic City, conversion of, 116
    construction, Atlantic City, 119,
        120t, 125
    Las Vegas, occupancy rates/rooms,
        17, 95, 95t
Housing, redevelopment, 131-132,
    215-216
Hughes, Howard, 11, 15

Illegal gambling, crime and, 208
Illegal prostitution, Las Vegas
    residents' attitude toward,
    196
Illinois
    riverboat casinos in, 73-75
    Riverboat Gambling Act (1990),
        regulations, 73
In-migration, Las Vegas, 177
Income tax, Native American
    casinos, 140
Indian Education Act (1972), 45
Indian Financing Act (1974), 45, 137
Indian Gaming Regulatory Act of
    1988 (IGRA), *xiii,* 48-54,
    221, 224, 233

Indian Health Service, 229
Indian Religious Freedom Act, 45
Indian Self-Determination and
    Educational Assistance
    Act (1975), 45
Indiana, riverboat casinos in, 79-81
Indiana Riverboat Gambling Act
    (1996), regulations, 79
Infrastructure
    CDRA, 132, 203
    concerns, Las Vegas, 111
    demands on Native American,
        226-227
    development of, 162-163
    tribal lands, 138, 226
Internal divisiveness, 59-60
International Association of Gaming
    Attorneys (IAGA), 14
Interstate highway system, impact on
    Atlantic City, 114-115, 203
Iowa
    land-based/non-Native American
        casinos, 87
    riverboat casinos in, 64, 71-73
Iowa Excursion Boat Gambling Law
    (1989), 71
    revisions 1996, regulations, 72
Iowa Racing and Gaming
    Commission, 71

Johnson, Lyndon, 44, 45
Joliet, Illinois riverboats, 103

Kefauver, Estes, 10

Labor shortage, Native American
    gaming, 143, 151
Lake Michigan, Indiana riverboats,
    79, 80, 81
"Land rush," 164-165
Land-based/non-Native American
    casinos
    business diversity, 165-166

Land-based/non-Native American
        casinos (*continued*)
    casino development, 233, 242
    Colorado tax rates, 84i
    economic cost, 167-169
    locations, 70i, 81-88
    state regulations, 65t
    taxes, fees, and distribution, 68t-69t
    traffic congestion, 167-168
Larceny-theft
    in Atlantic City, 209, 212t
    five city comparison, 186t, 187
    on Native American tribal lands,
        227
Last Resort, The, 201
Las Vegas, *xiii,* 5, 93-94
    cost of living, 179-180, 188, 189t,
        190
    crime in, 179-180, 185, 186t,
        187-188
    demographics of, 181, 182t,
        183-184
    economic benefits vs. social
        problems, 94
    gaming induced social issues,
        194-197
    government expenditures,
        179-180, 192, 193t, 193-194
    health care environment, 179-180
    mobster connection impact, 14
    population density, 180
    reorientation of, 160
    residents attitudes toward gaming,
        195-196
    response to competition, 104-106,
        105t
    social change in, 177
    traffic/transportation, 110-111,
        179-180, 184-185
Las Vegas Convention and Visitors
        Authority (LVCVA), 16
Las Vegas Strip, 94
    origin of term, 7
Ledyard, CT, 41, 53
Licensing process, 18-19

Lifeline Credit, 129
"Limited-stake gaming," 81
Locals-oriented casinos, 109-110
Lodging places, wages paid in,
        146, 146t
Los Angeles-Las Vegas,
        transportation, 111
Lotteries
    government-sponsored, 46
    Wisconsin, 54
Louisiana
    land-based/non-Native American
        casinos, 85-87
    riverboat casinos in, 77-78
Louisana Economic Development
        and Gaming Control Act
        (1989), 77, 85
Luck Business, The, 204, 214

Mafia, in gambling industry, 223-224
Making of the President, 1964, The,
        115-116
Marlborough-Blenheim hotel,
        Atlantic City, 113
Marshall v. Sawyer (1962/1966),
        11, 20
Mashantucket Pequot tribe, 54, 56
    casino profits, 225-226
    gaming casino of, 135, 139, 141
    hostility toward, 223
Mashantucket Pequot casino, 41
Mashantucket Pequot v. Connecticut,
        53
McAfee, Guy, 7
Medicare taxes
    Minnesota Native American
        gaming, 146
    Oregon Native American gaming,
        148
Megaresorts, 15
Meskwaki Nation, Iowa, 59
MGM Grand, 12, 16, 94
Michigan, land-based/non-Native
        American casinos, 87-88

Michigan Gaming Control and
    Revenue Act (1997), 87
Mille Lacs Ojibwe, casino profits,
    225
Minnesota Indian Gaming
    Association, 145
Minnesota Mille Lacs tribe, 56
Minnesota, Native American
    gaming, 144, 145t
Minnesota Office of Tourism, 147
Mirage, 15
Miss America Pageant, 25, 26
Mississippi, riverboat casinos in, 75-78
Mississippi Gaming Control Act
    (1972), regulations, 76
Mississippi River
    Illinois riverboats, 74
    Iowa riverboats, 71
    Louisana riverboat casinos, 77
    Mississippi riverboat casinos, 76
Missouri, riverboat casinos in, 78-79
Missouri River
    Iowa riverboats, 72
    Missouri riverboats, 78
"Mohawk civil war," 222
Montana, gaming operations, 88
Motion picture theaters, wages paid
    in, 146, 146t, 148
Motor vehicle theft
    in Atlantic City, 209
    five city comparison, 186t, 187
Municipal Limited Gaming Impact
    Fund, 85
Murder
    in Atlantic City, 209
    five city comparison, 185, 186t
    on Native American tribal lands,
    227
Mystic Lake casino, 136, 145t

National Coalition Against Legalized
    Gaming (NCALG), 212-213
National Gaming Impact and Policy
    Commission Act (1996), 213

National Indian Gaming
    Commission, 48
National Park Service, historic
    landmarks, 242
Native American casinos/gaming,
    41, 42t
    advantages of, 55-57
    competition and, 151-152
    disadvantages of, 57
    regulation, 47
    revenues, xx, 41, 51
    rural benefits of, 136
Native Americans
    hostility toward, 223
    population, 43
    substance abuse, 228
    use of casino profits, 225-226
Native Americans for a Clean
    Environment, 56
Native land repurchase, 56-57
Native nation trust lands, 43, 138,
    152
Nellis Air Force Base, 5, 7
Nevada Development Authority, Las
    Vegas, 178
Nevada Gaming Commission (NGC),
    3, 5, 12, 13, 18-19
Nevada, legalization of gambling, 4
Nevada State Bill 208 (Gaming
    Control Act), 5-6
"New buffalo," 221, 230
"New federalism," 137
New Jersey
    casino gambling referendum, 27, 28
    reinvestment income, 132
New Jersey Casino Control
    Commission, 33
New Jersey Division of Gaming
    Enforcement (DGE), 29, 34
New Jersey Housing and Mortgage
    Finance Agency, 216
NIMBY (not in my backyard), Las
    Vegas, 5-6
*1990 Census of Population and
    Housing Census,* 142, 181

Nonbanking games, 49
Nongaming enterprise investment,
    Native American gaming,
    55-56
Northeast, economic decline in, 135

Ohio River, Indiana riverboats,
    79, 80, 18
Oneida Casino, WI, 56
Oneida tribe, casino profits, 225
Oregon Native American gaming,
    147-150
Out-migration, casino induced, 239
Outside managment, Native American
    gaming operations, 51

Pathological gambling
    economic cost, 167
    Native American, 226-227, 228-229
    problem of, 205-208, 211, 246
Patoka Lake, Indiana riverboats,
    79, 80, 81
Patron claims, 21
Payment in lieu of taxes (PILT)
    Minnesota Native American
        gaming, 146
    Oregon Native American gaming,
        148-149
    St. Croix Casino, 144
Perskie, Steven, 29, 33
Pharmaceutical Assistance to the
    Aged and Disabled Program,
    New Jersey, 129
Places Rated Almanac, 181
Playboy casino, 31, 32, 36-37
Pomo Indians, division over casino,
    222
Population density, five city
    comparison, 180
Population increase, Las Vegas, 99
Posados de Puerto Rico Assoc.
        v. Tourism Co. (1986), 18
Potawatomi Nation, WI, 56

Poverty rate
    Native Americans, 43, 136-137
    St. Croix Chippewa tribe, 142
"Privileged" business, gaming as, 17
Property tax revenue
    Atlantic City, 119, 120t, 123, 125
    St. Croix Casino, 143
Public education, gambling revenue,
    171

Race-wire business, 8
Railroads, impact on Atlantic City,
    113
Raleigh, NC
    cost of living, 188, 189t, 190
    crime in, 185, 186t, 187
    demographics of, 181, 182, 183
    government expenditures, 193,
        193t, 194
    health care environment, 191,
        191t, 192
    population density, 180
    traffic/transportation of, 184-185
Rape
    in Atlantic City, 209, 212t
    five city comparison, 185, 186t
    on Native American tribal lands,
        227
Real estate values
    Foxwoods Resorts Casino, 142
    post-casino Atlantic City, 125,
        126i, 127
    pre-casino Atlantic City, 117
Redevelopment
    Atlantic City, 130-131, 166,
        215-216
    disappointment with, 166-167
Red Lake Band v. Swimmer (1980),
    48
Reservations, land area, 43
Residents, employment in Atlantic
    City casinos, 28, 127
Resorts, Atlantic City, 113-114, 201,
    202-203

Resorts International, Atlantic City, 29, 31, 203
Revenue source, casino gambling, 234
Revitalization strategy, casino gambling, 234
"Rhetoric of despair," 166, 247
Riverboat casinos, *xiii*, 64
    business diversity and, 165
    development of, 233
    economic costs, 168, 169
    locations, 64-81, 70i
    redevelopment impact of, 166
    state regulations, 65t
    taxes, fees, and distribution, 66t-67t
    traffic congestion, 237
Riverboat gambling
    impact of, 159, 162
    profitability of, 160
Rivergate Convention Center, New Orleans, 86
Rock Island, Illinois riverboat, 74
Rural communities, Native American gaming, 136, 150-151

Saginaw Chippewa tribe, 55
Salaries. *See* Wages
Sault St. Marie tribe, 55
"Second chance," job seekers, Las Vegas, 98
Seminole Tribe of Florida v. Butterworth (1981/1982), 46
Senate Select Committee on Indian Affairs, Bingo halls, 223
Shakopee Sioux, 136, 145t
Siegel, "Bugsy," 8
Slot machines
    California, 52
    Connecticut, 53
Social advantages, Native American gaming, 55
Social impact
    five city comparison, 179-194
    Las Vegas, 197-198

Social impact assessment, definition of, 235
Social security taxes
    Minnesota Native American gaming, 146
    Oregon Native American gaming, 148
South Carolina, gaming operations, 88
South Dakota, land-based/non-Native American casinos, 81-82, 160, 162, 165, 171, 233, 238-239
South Dakota Limited Card Game and Slot Machines (1991), regulations, 82
Sovereignty, threat to and Native American gaming, 58-59
Sports betting, 206
St. Croix Casino, 142-144
St. Louis, riverboat casinos docking, 75, 78
Stardust Casino Hotel, 10, 14
State Gaming Control Board (SGCB). *See* Gaming Control Board
State v. Rosenthal (1977), 13, 14
Statistical information, Las Vegas, 178
Suicide rates, gambling and, 196-197
Summer homes, Atlantic City, 114

Table games, 53
Tax equity issues, Native American gaming, 150
Tax policy, Las Vegas, 99
Tax revenues. *See also* Government revenues; Property tax revenue
    Atlantic City, 119, 120t, 123, 125
    Mashantucket Pequot tribe, 139
    Minnesota Native American gaming, 146
    Native American casinos, 139, 140
Touche Ross, 120, 128
Tourism, 149-150
    correlation with crime, 209
    Ho-Chunk tribe, 139
    Las Vegas, 97

Tourism (*continued*)
  Minnesota Native American
    gaming, 147
Traffic and transportation
  five city comparison, 184-185
  gambling/gaming, 237-239
  Las Vegas, 110-111, 184, 185
  Native Americans tribal lands,
    226-227
Traymore hotel, Atlantic City,
    113, 117
Tribal lands, economic development
    of, 136-138
Tropicana, 10, 14
Trump, Donald, 31, 38
Trust lands, Native Americans,
    43, 138, 152
Tunica (MS)
  economic costs, 168
  unemployment in, 164

Underage gambling, 21, 196,
    205-206, 207t
Unemployment
  Minnesota Native American
    gaming, 145-146
  Native Americans, 44
  Oregon Native American gaming,
    149
  post-Casino Atlantic City, 128
  pre-Casino Atlantic City, 117, 201
  St. Croix Chippewa tribe, 142
  Tunica, MS, 164
Uniqua Indians, 147
United States Travel Industry
    Association, visitor survey,
    177
Urban Redevelopment Agency
    (URA), 216

Vacations, in Las Vegas, 103
Video gaming terminals, 160-161

Vietnam Veterans Memorial,
    reinvestment income, 132
Virginia Beach
  cost of living, 188, 189t, 190
  crime in, 185, 186t, 187
  demographics of, 181, 182, 183
  government expenditures, 193,
    193t, 194
  health care environment, 191-192,
    191t
  population density, 180
  traffic/transportation of, 184
Visitors
  ages of in Las Vegas, 102-103
  Las Vegas spending patterns, 108t
Visitor volume
  Atlantic City, 119, 120-121, 120t
  Las Vegas, 96t, 97, 105t, 106t, 177
  Native American casinos, 139
  Oregon Native American gaming,
    150
  St. Croix Casino, 144

Wagering, total expenditures, 155
Wages
  Atlantic City casinos, 119, 120t,
    122i, 123, 124i
  Foxwoods Resorts Casino, 141-142
  Minnesota Native American
    gaming, 146, 146t
  Oregon Native American gaming,
    148
  St. Croix Casino, 143
Waste disposal, on Native American
    land, 56
"Wealth gap," 168
Welfare, decline in, 129, 141, 147,
    149, 221, 226, 245
West Lake, Iowa riverboat, 73
White, Theodore, 115-116
Wisconsin Policy Research Institute,
    227, 228
Women's Chamber of Commerce,
    Atlantic City, 117

Word of mouth advertising,
        gambling, 102
*Word Almanac and Book of Facts,
        The,* 181
Workfare programs, Las Vegas, 99
Work permits, gaming employees, 21

Order Your Own Copy of This Important Book for Your Personal Library!

LEGALIZED CASINO GAMING IN THE UNITED STATES
The Economic and Social Impact

_____ in hardbound at $49.95 (ISBN: 0-7890-0640-5)

COST OF BOOKS_____

OUTSIDE USA/CANADA/
MEXICO: ADD 20%_____

POSTAGE & HANDLING_____
*(US: $3.00 for first book & $1.25
for each additional book)
Outside US: $4.75 for first book
& $1.75 for each additional book)*

SUBTOTAL_____

IN CANADA: ADD 7% GST_____

STATE TAX_____
*(NY, OH & MN residents, please
add appropriate local sales tax)*

FINAL TOTAL_____
*(If paying in Canadian funds,
convert using the current
exchange rate. UNESCO
coupons welcome.)*

☐ **BILL ME LATER:** ($5 service charge will be added)
(Bill-me option is good on US/Canada/Mexico orders only;
not good to jobbers, wholesalers, or subscription agencies.)

☐ Check here if billing address is different from
shipping address and attach purchase order and
billing address information.

Signature_____

☐ **PAYMENT ENCLOSED: $**_____

☐ **PLEASE CHARGE TO MY CREDIT CARD.**

☐ Visa ☐ MasterCard ☐ AmEx ☐ Discover
☐ Diner's Club

Account #_____

Exp. Date_____

Signature_____

Prices in US dollars and subject to change without notice.

NAME_____

INSTITUTION_____

ADDRESS_____

CITY_____

STATE/ZIP_____

COUNTRY_____ COUNTY (NY residents only)_____

TEL_____ FAX_____

E-MAIL_____

May we use your e-mail address for confirmations and other types of information? ☐ Yes ☐ No

Order From Your Local Bookstore or Directly From
The Haworth Press, Inc.
10 Alice Street, Binghamton, New York 13904-1580 • USA
TELEPHONE: 1-800-HAWORTH (1-800-429-6784) / Outside US/Canada: (607) 722-5857
FAX: 1-800-895-0582 / Outside US/Canada: (607) 772-6362
E-mail: getinfo@haworthpressinc.com
PLEASE PHOTOCOPY THIS FORM FOR YOUR PERSONAL USE.

BOF96